DECOLONIZING FEMINISMS

Piya Chatterjee, Series Editor

Tea and Solidarity

Tamil Women and Work
in Postwar Sri Lanka

Mythri Jegathesan

UNIVERSITY OF WASHINGTON
Seattle

Tea and Solidarity was made possible in part by a grant from the Office of the Provost at Santa Clara University.

23 22 21 20 19   5 4 3 2 1

Photographs are by the author unless otherwise noted.

UNIVERSITY OF WASHINGTON PRESS
www.washington.edu/uwpress

LIBRARY OF CONGRESS CATALOGING-IN-PUBLICATION DATA
Names: Jegathesan, Mythri, author.
Title: Tea and solidarity : Tamil women and work in postwar Sri Lanka / Mythri Jegathesan.
Description: Seattle : University of Washington Press, [2019] | Series: Decolonizing feminisms | Includes bibliographical references and index. |
Identifiers: LCCN 2018046960 (print) | LCCN 2018051383 (ebook) |
   ISBN 9780295745664 (ebook) | ISBN 9780295745657 (hardcover : alk. paper) |
   ISBN 9780295745671 (pbk. : alk. paper)
Subjects: LCSH: Women plantation workers—Sri Lanka—Social conditions. |
   Women, Tamil—Employment—Sri Lanka. | Women, Tamil—Sri Lanka—
   Social conditions. | Feminism—Sri Lanka. | Sri Lanka—Social conditions—
   21st century.
Classification: LCC HD6073.P4692 (ebook) | LCC HD6073.P4692 S725 2019 (print) |
   DDC 331.4089/9481105493—dc23
LC record available at https://lccn.loc.gov/2018046960

Cover illustration by Hanusha Somasunderam
Cover design by Katrina Noble

To the workers and families on Sri Lanka's tea plantations
and my Amma and Appa

Contents

Preface

May 19, 2009. Delmon's Hospital. Wellawatte, Colombo. I was waiting to see my great uncle who had suffered from a stroke the month before. As I sat with my aunt in the lobby, the Sinhala teledrama playing on the government-run television channel, Swarnavahini, cut abruptly for breaking news. Doctors, nurses, patients, and visitors momentarily forgot their social hierarchies and crowded together below the mounted television, their eyes fixed on the moving image. The initial recording, released by Sri Lankan security forces, lasted approximately fifteen seconds but had been looped to give the appearance of continual footage.

The screen filled with the image of a man's corpse. Its eyes were wide open, its body bloated, stiff, and stained with blood, looking as surprised as all of us watching. A blue handkerchief covered what appeared to be a severe trauma to the front of its head and separated the brown-skinned body from the color swatch of green lagoon-like grass, which was later confirmed to be Nanthikadal Lagoon in Sri Lanka's northeast Mullaitivu district. In the island's North and East, Sri Lankan security forces and the Liberation Tigers of Tamil Eelam (LTTE) had been fighting intensely since the 2002 ceasefire agreement (CFA) between both parties. The 2002 CFA had temporarily halted fighting between both parties that formally began in 1983, but in December 2005 it officially broke down and fighting had resumed. On the television screen, soldiers milling around the body were smiling, talking quickly, and taking out their cell phones to capture images of the corpse's pruned flesh and bloodstained fatigues. In the commotion, one solider checked for a pulse by grabbing the right inner wrist of the lifeless body, which had already been laid down on its back with the hands touching each other on a white sheeted carrier for the dead. Another soldier brushed away a fly, which had landed on the corpse's chin.

The corpse was that of Velupillai Prabhakaran, leader of the LTTE. Rising to power in the 1970s, the LTTE fought the Sri Lankan government for nearly three decades, aiming to establish a separate state for Sri Lankan Tamils living in the island's North and East. Prabhakaran's death had made official the end of Sri Lanka's twenty-six-year civil war. Hours after the government of Sri Lanka's military victory, then-president Mahinda Rajapaksa gave a speech to members of Parliament: "We have removed the word minorities from our vocabulary. No longer are the Tamils, Muslims, Burghers, Malays and any other minorities. There are only two people in this country. One is the people that love this country. The other comprises the small groups that have no love for the land of their birth. Those who do not love the country are now a lesser group."[1]

Celebrations of military victory fueled Sinhala nationalist euphoria in the weeks to follow, but as I carried out my anthropological research in Sri Lanka's Hill Country in the immediate aftermath of the war I observed that minorities were anxious about their futures in the country. When would the state of emergency, constant surveillance, and militarization of civil society cease? Would demands for patriotism deny expressions of cultural difference, struggles for equal rights, and spaces for political dissent? Is the love of one's country or the art of politics, for that matter, so simple? What is the fate of minorities whose obligation to and love of their home are complicated and entangled in histories of oppression, trauma, and loss?

• • •

August 31, 2013. Kāthai Muthusamy has died in Colombo.[2] Kāthai was a sixty-eight-year-old woman from Adawaththa Estate, Lunugala, in Badulla, located in southeastern Uva Province. She had died from complications of cancer in a government hospital. In 1994 Sri Lankan security forces arrested Kāthai under the 1979 Prevention of Terrorism Act and charged her with providing passage and shelter to LTTE cadres traveling from the eastern coastal town of Batticaloa through her resident tea plantation town.

Kāthai was incarcerated for three and half years after the end of the war and for a total of nineteen years until she died in prison. While the end of the war created new possibilities for former LTTE leaders, Hill Country Tamil women plantation workers such as Kāthai were not explicitly included as beneficiaries of such newfound social and political recognition. In the years immediately following the military's defeat of the LTTE, former president Mahinda Rajapaksa led a largely majoritarian government and state in nationalist victory, focusing on large-scale plans for economic and militarized development in the North and East. But the government failed to effectively deal with the aftermath of the violence that Sri Lanka's residents and displaced had experienced across ethnic, religious, and class lines. Judged against the unresolved disappearances in the North and East, war crime allegations, and urgent constitutional reforms, Kāthai's death was deemed relatively insignificant in Sri Lanka's postwar political imaginary. As a Hill Country Tamil woman, she was a fragment and an anomaly—a loss with few stakes and little recognition among those invested in Sri Lanka's national postwar plans for reconciliation, political reform, and transitional justice.

This anthropological study focuses on the social and legal peripheries within which Hill Country Tamil women workers, such as Kāthai, reside and struggle for dignity and equity in the postwar Sri Lanka. Kāthai's detainment and death were deliberately unfinished afterthoughts of the transformation of Hill Country Tamils' lives on the tea plantations and in Sri Lankan politics and daily life. The tea industry's desires to accumulate profit at the expense of cheap labor and the sociopolitical landscape of a minority community working to create a secure sense of belonging under unjust conditions keeps this limbo intact. This ethnography explores this ongoing work as a praxis of desire and solidarity that Hill Country Tamil plantation workers and their families take on in their daily lives.

In *Living a Feminist Life* Sara Ahmed asks, "If we become feminists because of the inequality and injustice in the world, because of what the world is not, then what kind of world are we building?"[3] As a child and young adult I did not know Sri Lanka without knowing its violence, traumas, and injustices. Born and raised in the United States, I learned about my own Sri Lankan Tamil heritage through fragmented moments of reflecting on losses and fears, which remain unresolved in my parents' birthplace. Some moments—like the assassinations of politicians and suicide bombings—were distant news stories; others hit closer to home. In the 1980s, I watched my father and mother mourn from afar the LTTE's killing of my uncle. I watched as they received airmail that told of months with no electricity and cousins taking their school exams in camps for the internally displaced. My knowledge was unstable. It was filled with redefinitions, questions, and recantations, and these doubts often left me in a state of not knowing what information to trust. I had a feeling that my knowledge held more distortions than truths, but it was all I had during my childhood.

Because of this history, my love of, and obligations to, Sri Lanka have always been complicated. During my fieldwork in 2008–9, these obligations, manifested as they did for many others, as anticipatory anxiety and blunt horror. In the five months leading up to the war's end, those living outside the immediate war zones in the North and East knew that both Sri Lankan security forces and Tamil militants were committing atrocities against innocent civilians. These occurred often without witnesses, and in April 2009 the United Nations estimated that since January, nearly 6,500 civilians had been killed and 14,000 injured in the war zones where Sri Lankan security forces and the LTTE were continuing their fight.[4] Outside the war zones, the certainty of distant but continuous violence created everyday embodiments of emergency. When the war ended in May, Sri Lankans living inside the country continued to anticipate the worst, which they had sadly come to know all too well.

Two weeks after the war ended I was in Colombo for a meeting of Sri Lankan intellectuals and concerned citizens who had gathered to discuss the postwar state of affairs. Over the course of our discussion the sun had set and it had become dark. From outside the undisclosed space in which we were talking, a flash of yellow moved across the room. The lights were coming from a white van, which had become a familiar indicator of disappearances and abductions in Sri Lanka over the last thirty years. It pulled up directly in front of the window and came to a stop. Our conversation halted abruptly. When the van began to reverse and drive away, we burst into nervous laughter, purging ourselves of the anxiety that had grabbed hold of us. The conversation about postwar conditions resumed. The moment had passed, but like doubt, irritating our confirmations, we knew it would return. Although defeat of the LTTE and the end of a civil war had been declared, dissenting critics and Sri Lankan minorities remained at risk.

Given the conditions, I gravitated toward particular types of knowledge about Sri Lanka, namely those that emerged from the stories Sri Lankans themselves told me. One narrative came from my great uncle, who told me his story when I stayed with him and his family in June 2006 while conducting preliminary fieldwork in Colombo. In the late 1990s, Tamil paramilitaries shot him and his politician colleague in her home in Jaffna town. In shock, he did not process the feeling of the bullet entering his body. He ran outside to his bicycle to get help for his colleague, who later died from her injuries. Outside the house, a bystander stopped him and pointed out that he had been shot. He looked down at his own leg, saw the blood pouring from the wound, and fell unconscious on the road. In the weeks following the incident and his colleague's murder, he lay in bed recuperating, and the men who had shot him and their leaders sent him multiple death threats ordering him to resign from his public servant post. Eight years later, as we sat talking over tea, he told me in English with a smile:

> They threatened me to resign, so I did. I did not want to, you know. But as I lay in bed, she [pointing to his wife, my grandmother's younger sister, who was smiling and listening in the kitchen] and this one [pointing to their only daughter, who was also cooking] were going mad. So now I am happy to translate immigration papers in a shop here [in Colombo]. I have to listen to them. I am responsible *to them*, right? I tell you, I am not afraid of the person who might kidnap or detain you when you go out to do this research every day when you stay with us here. I am afraid of what *your mother* will do to me if you are hurt while in my care.

We both laughed at his remark at the time, but I believe him still, even nearly ten years after the end of war. In moments of loss and uncertainty about the future, these responsibilities—those that connect us—and the desires to care for someone or something—a home, an income, or the struggle for dignity—are some of the strongest determinants of human action. Our records of loss and insecurity continually create new forms of knowing the world and our place in it. Under these conditions of vulnerability, we can say that what we strive to know best is that which is in our care. These stories—the ones that bring out the bonds of care—are what move this ethnographic account of dignity, work, and life on Sri Lanka's tea plantations.

Acknowledgments

This book would not have been possible without the workers and families on Kirkwall and those individuals who consider the tea plantations across Sri Lanka's Hill Country their home. Since 2008 they opened their homes, took the time to speak with me outside work, shared their meals and tea, and allowed me to observe and record their lives. This book does not do justice to their humanity. It is a mere slice of the fullness with which they live and work, and I am indebted to them for trusting me. Any and all errors are mine alone.

I thank the individuals at University of Washington Press whose diligence helped bring this book to light. To Larin McLaughlin and Piya Chatterjee, thank you for your encouragement and vision from the beginning; to Mike Baccam, Julie Van Pelt, Michael Campbell, Laurel Hecker, and Nicholas Taylor, thank you for your care and assistance; to the two anonymous reviewers, thank you for your generous and useful comments. I also thank Puja Boyd, who directed me to this necessary series.

Several individuals, organizations, and communities in Sri Lanka have been integral to the writing of this book. Since 2009 my friendships in Hatton have continued to be my ground, and this work would not exist without them. To late Andrew, your generosity and love of tea led me to Kirkwall; no words can describe my gratitude and how much you are missed. To late Aunty Rita and to Shayamalie, Kanna, and their families, thank you for opening your homes and lives to me. Your care and understanding have allowed me to stay focused and extend this research beyond what I thought possible. To Mr. Dhanaraj and his family and to Paul, Sinna Rani, and Periya Rani, thank you for bringing me into your homes for meals, festivals, and celebrations. To my research assistant,

Sasikala, thank you for dedicating time to my research as a working mother. To Rebina Akka, thank you for your warmth and assurance; I cherish the time I can spend with your family in your home. I thank the Centre for Social Concern for sponsoring my research in Hatton— Fr. Beni, Fr. Leonard, Fr. Prem, John, Yogitha, Shastha, Priya, Rani, and Mr. Nagalingam. I appreciate all of you for allowing me into your community with warmth and intention; your presence in Hatton embodies this book's call for Malaiyaka Thamilar dignity. To Hanusha Somasunderam, whose artwork is featured throughout this book (including on its cover), I am grateful for our meetings as well as your vision and call for Sri Lanka and the world to recognize the lives of Tamil women working on the hills.

In Kandy I thank the staff of Satyodaya, whose support was instrumental to the initial stages of my research—particularly Amara Akka, Harsha Wanninayake, Noeline Akka, and the late Fr. Paul Caspersz. I thank the Working Women's Front—K. Yogeswary, Ambika, Deepa, Mageswary, Aruljothi, Krishanthani, Geeshani, Thamil, and the women members—who allowed me to record their work. To the staff of the Institute of Social Development—Nanthakumar, Karthik, Chinta, Mohan, Sathya, Shathik, and Pasani—this book would not be possible without your work and voice in the Hill Country. I am grateful for the time we spend together in solidarity. I am especially indebted to Periyasamy Muthulingam for challenging me to think about what Hill Country Tamils deserve and desire. Thank you for teaching me about the sacrifices and complexities of implementing long-lasting social change and for informing my thinking with your life of activism and social justice. To his family of strong women—Saumy, Vindy, and Yoga—thank you for giving me a second home in Kandy during my research.

In Sri Lanka I thank my family for their care since I began returning to the country yearly in 2005. It is not easy having a stubborn anthropologist live with you during a civil war, and I am indebted to you for keeping me safe. In Colombo I thank those individuals whose thinking and approaches have been integral to this work: Kumari Jayawardena, Selvy Thiruchandran, Balasingham Skanthakumar, Asha Abeyasekera, Ahilan Kadirgamar, Harini Amarasuriya, Malathi de Alwis, and the late Vijay Nagaraj. I thank the staff at the following organizations for allowing me to use their resources during research: the American Institute of

Lankan Studies—including Deepthi, Mr. Weerasooriya, Vagisha Gunas-ekera, and the late Ira Unamboowe—the Centre for Poverty Analysis, Women's Education and Research Centre, Social Scientists' Association, Law and Society Trust, International Centre for Ethnic Studies, Marga Institute, the Department of National Archives in Colombo, and Saskia Fernando Gallery.

In addition to those in Sri Lanka, I am grateful to have co-thinkers in my life who inspire and support me. The empire of academia breaks many individuals, and I am fortunate to have people in my life who inspire my own commitment to mentoring and who challenge me to think about making our fields more ethical and robust.

I thank Valentine Daniel for encouraging me to think about the Hill Country Tamils and for his support over the last fifteen years and for encouraging me to choose humanity over indifference in co-thinking with me. To his late wife Pegi, thank you for opening your home to me as a graduate student and for your warmth and kindness. You continue to be missed.

I thank David Scott, Pegi Vail, Elizabeth Povinelli, Paul Kockelman, and Paige West for their research, teaching, and mentorship. To my Columbia family with whom this all began—Adriana Garriga-Lopez, Nima Paidipaty, Siva Arumugam, Ravi Sriramachandran, Gajendran Ayy-athurai, Thushara Hewage, Antina von Schnitzler, Amanda Gilliam, Marie Varghese, Kaori Hatsumi, Nadia Guessous, Yogesh Chandrani, Jon Carter, Christina Sarnito Carter, Sayo Ferro, and Scott Freeman—thank you for thinking with me. To my former colleagues at Georgetown and William & Mary—Brad Weiss, Denise Brennan, Susan Terrio, and Gwen-dolyn Mikell—thank you for your mentorship.

Research for this book was made possible through awards and fellow-ships from the National Science Foundation, Green Harbor Financial, the American Association for University Women, the American Insti-tute of Sri Lankan Studies, and Santa Clara University's Miller Center for Social Entrepreneurship, Bannan Institute, and Offices of the Provost and Dean. I also thank the University of Hawai'i, the National Univer-sity of Singapore, the Chicago Tamil Forum, UC Davis's Global Tea Institute, Stanford University's Geballe Series, San Jose State Univer-sity, UC San Diego, and the World Tea Expo for hosting lectures, panels, and workshops for which I developed the chapters of this ethnography.

I thank my friends in South Asian studies and anthropology whose scholarship and thinking informed my own. In Sri Lankan studies, I thank Mark Whitaker, Dennis McGilvray, John Rogers, Jonathan Spencer, Michelle Gamburd, Jeanne Maracek, Cynthia Caron, Neil de Votta, Sandya Hewamanne, Caitrin Lynch, Vidyamali Samarasinghe, the late Isabelle Clark-Decès, Kamala Visweswaran, Nimanthi Rajasingham, Siddharthan Maunaguru, Ponni Arasu, Vivian Choi, Neena Mahadev, Dominic Esler, Alessandra Radicati, Nethra Samarawickrema, Nadia Augustyniak, and Alexios Tsigkas. In South Asian studies and anthropology, I am grateful to think alongside the following individuals: Maura Finkelstein, Karen Rignall, Andrew Willford, Sarah Besky, V. Geetha, Svati Shah, Inderpal Grewal, Sareeta Amrute, Amrapali Maitra, Jelena Radović Fanta, Lalaie Ameeriar, and Jeremy Walton. I especially thank Christina Davis, Sasikumar Balasundaram, and Daniel Bass for their support and for thinking with me about the Hill Country and Tamil language. Dan, I am fortunate to have you as my fieldwork *anna*—thank you for your encouragement. I also thank Sharika Thiranagama for our friendship and assuring me that this research was important in times when I was unsure. To her children and to Thomas, thank you for opening your home to me and making me pause and laugh over the years. This book would not have been possible without the support of my department, colleagues, and students at SCU. I especially thank the members of the Bannan Gender Justice Faculty Collaborative and Culture, Power, Difference reading group for their feedback on earlier drafts and also my research assistants, William Pollard and Maya Kaneko, for their dedication and passion.

To my friends, in movement—Hesham, Tania, Baller, Jeanne, Jeanine, Jill and Elisabeth—thank you for keeping me grounded; to my 6:00 a.m. crew, twice a week, your presence is home. Marcy, Heather, and Danielle, you have been brilliant since we were twelve; thank you for your friendship and love. Andy, Gautam, and Indhika, every time I see you, I cry tears of laughter, and being in your lives—and a Chitty to Maya, Juna, Penny, and Loki—is a gift. Jeri, thank you for finding function in dysfunction and for being the ledge of optimism that keeps me sane. To Z, thank you for your pancakes, warmth, and love. Lanka Solidarity, thank you for giving me purpose in June 2009 when our worlds felt broken and uncertain. Vivek, Kitana, and Sugi, my oldest friend, if I could build a place to be with all three of you along with kneading kittens, *sambol* and bananas, fudge, and mutton biryani, I would be complete. I am grateful to think, rage, and laugh alongside you.

To Vondel and Aja, we didn't choose to share our lives together, but the warmth you bring me and in which I bury my head is everything. To my siblings—Meera, Mithila, Chai, and Jeff—thank you for your love and support, even when I am a buzzing bee, and to Lena, Jun, and Aran, thank you for making me a Chitty. Lastly, to my Amma and Appa, thank you for raising me to stand tall even though I am short, for staying by my side when I push you away, and for teaching me to work hard and be kind. Your investments, love, and the values they generate in me are at the heart of this book on work and aspiration.

Abbreviations

CA	Collective Agreement
CBO	community-based organization
CILC	Ceylon Indian Labour Congress
CNC	Ceylon National Congress
CWC	Ceylon Workers' Congress
DPF	Democratic People's Front
DWC	Democratic Workers' Congress
EFC	Employers' Federation of Ceylon
EPF	Employees' Provident Fund
ETF	Employees' Trust Fund
EWHCS	Estate Worker Housing Cooperative Society
FBR	Family Background Report
HSZ	High Security Zone
ILO	International Labour Organization
ISD	Institute for Social Development
LTTE	Liberation Tigers of Tamil Eelam
MDGS	Millennium Development Goals
NBRO	National Building Research Organization
NIC	National Identity Card
NPA	National Plan of Action
NUW	National Union of Workers
PAC	Planters' Association of Ceylon
PHDT	Plantation Human Development Trust
PTA	Prevention of Terrorism Act No. 48 of 1979
RPC	regional plantation company
SAARC	South Asian Association for Regional Cooperation

SLBFE	Sri Lanka Bureau of Foreign Employment
TNA	Tamil National Alliance
TPA	Tamil Progressive Alliance
UNDP	United Nations Development Programme
WWF	Working Women's Front

Note on Transliteration

This book uses both the standard system of transliteration and diacritic forms and phonetic spellings of non-English words pronounced in spoken form. For example, in the Tamil word for one's natal home, *ūr*, the long *ū* is pronounced as "oo" as in the English word "pool" or "mule." I retained the spellings of Sinhala and Tamil words transliterated from Tamil and English primary and secondary sources to preserve how each language was transliterated and written and to highlight how respective authors desired the languages to be spoken. Any kinship, spoken form, or colloquial terms in this book arose in the context of my research and do not speak for more general usage of these terms in Sri Lankan society or in communities in and beyond Sri Lanka.

Abbreviated Transliteration Guide to Tamil Consonants

c in *vayacu*	as in the English word "*s*oul"
cc in *paccam*	as in the English word "*k*ite"
d in *durai*	as in the English word "fa*th*er"
k in *kanakupillai* (second *k*)	as in the English word "*g*arish"
ll in *pillai*	as in the English word "pi*ll*ing"
nk in *catanku* or *kankāni*	as in the English word "ru*ng*"
tt in *tōttam*	as in the English word "ro*tt*ing"

Tea and Solidarity

Introduction

Unbecoming Labor

IT WAS A BRIGHT BUT COOL MORNING AS I WALKED DOWN THE side of the main road toward Kirkwall tea estate division.[1] Part of a larger tea plantation in Sri Lanka's South-Central Hill Country, Kirkwall was home to 480 Hill Country Tamils, 124 of whom were registered as full-time workers when I began ethnographic research in 2008. From the opposite direction, a three-wheeler approached and then slowed to a stop beside me. Inside sat Sadha and her older brother, Kanageswaran. The call had finally come from a Tamil broker living on a nearby estate the day before. Sadha was on her way to Colombo. She would take a public bus from Hatton, the hill station closest to Kirkwall, and travel to Maradana, a suburb of Colombo. There she would be a domestic worker for a Sinhala family—a husband, wife, and nine-year-old boy. As we talked on the road, the young three-wheeler driver pulled out his phone and began fiddling with it but kept the engine running.

"Did you bring the photos?" Sadha asked.[2]

"Yes," I replied as I reached into my bag. A few days earlier, I had taken portrait-style photographs of Sadha dressed in her sister-in-law's wedding sari. Kāmāci, her mother and a recent widow, had asked me to take her photograph and have it printed so that they could use it in their search for a groom. At the time she was twenty-six years old and, according to Kāmāci, getting too old. "I have them," I said. "I made two copies. Take one with you."

"No," she told me. "Leave them with Amma at home.[3] She is the one who needs them." She held one photograph in her hand as her elder

3

brother peered over her shoulder to have a look. "*Sha*, see how beautiful I look, Akka," smiling as she looked at her own image.[4] I agreed.

I asked Sadha what she would do in Colombo. She told me she would cook, clean, and care for the couple's child after he got home from school. Her eyes were bright and brimming with tears, but she smiled and told me she would be okay. Kanageswaran would make sure she got on the right bus and would tell the driver and ticket agent where to let her off when they reached Maradana. He would then give a call to her employers, and they would pick her up from the bus stop. She told me to see Kāmāci who was at home and to show her the photos. From her purse, which sat on top of a large double-lined plastic bag that held her clothes and belongings, she took out a crumbled piece of paper on which a landline telephone number was written. "This is the *durai*'s call number, Akka. Take it down so that we can talk after I arrive," she said.

Cre-Ā Tamil-English Dictionary defines *durai* as the "word used (formerly) to refer to a European" or "one who behaves in a lordly way."[5] It is fitting that "formerly" is in parentheses. In my research I heard the word almost daily—mostly in reference to plantation managers, whose positions were once filled by white British men and later by Sri Lankan men trained to manage tea, rubber, and coconut operations within Sri Lanka's 150-year-old plantation industry.

I pulled out my phone and entered the number into my contact list, quickly noting the entry "Sadha Durai." She told me not to call the number until she rang my cell later that evening, because she did not know if it would be okay for her to receive calls on her employer's line. The driver clutched his gears and looked up impatiently. Kanageswaran told us they had to go to catch the bus so that Sadha would not get into Colombo too late. We clasped hands and said goodbye. She squeezed my hand and smiled briefly. The three-wheeler continued down the road.

I walked up to Kirkwall on the narrower paved path, which cut between two manicured fields of brightly green tea bushes. As I approached, I heard the bell of the Māriamman Hindu temple ringing.[6] Two estate overseers (*kankānis*) were waiting anxiously at the top of the hill. One of them was Siva, Sadha's maternal uncle. As I approached, he smiled and asked if I was here to see Kāmāci, his older sister. "Yes. What is happening?" I asked. While walking, I had seen women working in the fields above the main road, but as I got closer I noticed that Siva and his colleague were not dressed for work. Instead of their usual khaki vests, blue shorts, knee-length socks, and hiking boots, today they wore bright white sarongs and crisply ironed dress shirts.

"A minister is coming," Siva told me. "A small ceremony will take place. He promised to give us roofing sheets for the hole in the temple's ceiling. Afterward he will speak."

"What time is he coming?" I asked.

"Now. His assistant will call anytime." He held up his cell phone, checked his watch, and then looked over the hill, down at the main road.

In two months Sri Lanka would hold its first island-wide parliamentary elections since the civil war ended less than a month earlier. Local candidates were making their rounds to speak to Hill Country Tamils living and working on regional plantation company (RPC)–run tea estates in and around the hill stations of Hatton, Dickoya, and Maskeliya in Central Province, where I had been conducting field research since 2008.

I asked him which minister was coming, and he told me the candidate's name. I had seen this minister's ballot number and the English acronym for his political party's name and union alongside the ballot numbers and acronyms of competing candidates and their parties. The numbers and letters had been chalked in white on the surfaces of the eroding cliffs below the hills of tea bushes; they had been chalked on the stretches of paved cement on the main road below Kirkwall and pasted on campaign posters and signs in and around town and on neighboring estates. I asked Siva if he could let me know when the minister arrived. He told me to keep watch with Kāmāci from her line and wait for the temple bell to ring.

"You will know when the minister arrives," he said.

I walked past the estate temple, which was on the far side of an open quadrangle of "lines" where the workers on Kirkwall lived with their families. *Lines* is an English word that when spoken becomes "layam" in Tamil; it is short for *line rooms*, the colonial twelve-by-seven-foot barrack-style housing structures that Tamil plantation wage laborers were given to live in as a resident labor force during the British period and which still serve as housing for many Hill Country Tamils on the plantations.[7] I made my way up the smaller, makeshift stone steps that led to Kāmāci's line. In the sun-dried brush beyond the stone steps, a pile of trash was burning and a few chickens were pecking around but keeping their distance. After nearly two weeks of steady rain and cold weather, the sun was strong and the sky was a bright blue that morning. Taking advantage of the warmer and dry conditions, many residents had washed their clothes earlier and placed them to dry on top of taller green bushes and over the wooden fence that partially lined the stone steps.

At the top of the steps Kāmāci was sitting down. She was sobbing loudly, her chest folded over her thighs, her head in her hands. As I approached, her crying stopped and she looked up. "Did you see Sadha? She just left," she told me. "I know, I saw her," I said softly. I sat down next to her and stared at the ground. She resumed crying.

Letchumi—a retired woman living in the adjacent line who had worked together with Kāmāci as a plucker in Kirkwall's fields for over twenty years—stood opposite us on the veranda of her own line room. She smiled at me and squatted down on her stoop so that she was level with us and folded her arms across her knees. In a stern but gentle voice Letchumi told Kāmāci not to cry and nervously tapped her fingers on her elbows. But she herself had tears in her eyes and on her cheeks as she looked distantly away over Kāmāci's body toward Siva and his fellow *kankāni* who were still looking at the main road. A few more men in white sarongs and dress shirts had joined them.

I told them that Sadha had given me her employer's number and relayed her instructions to call. I moved over to sit next to Letchumi on the veranda so that I could have a better view of the road and the group of men waiting. Eventually Kāmāci stopped crying, wiped her face with the edge of her sari, and joined us. After a minute of watching, she asked me if I had eaten breakfast, similar to the way my own mother would ask me if and what I had eaten when she herself had not prepared my meal. Throughout my fieldwork this was usually one of the first questions older women would ask me and a common gesture of concern and care women would make toward younger individuals in their circles of kith and kin. I replied yes, and then she asked what I had eaten. "Roti," I told her.[8] Letchumi prepared some betel leaf (*vettilai*), areca nut (*pākku*), dried tobacco leaves (*pōyilai*), and limestone paste (*sunām*) and handed it to Kāmāci to chew.[9] They chewed together as we sat in silence, watching Siva and the other men on the hill.

I.1.   The view from Letchumi's line room verandah on Kirkwall division in
June 2009

The minister never came that day. In August 2014, when I returned
to Kirkwall, the temple was closed for repairs and a black tarp was
covering its roof. That year, Siva assured me that it would reopen in a few
months. When I returned to Kirkwall in 2015, 2016, and 2017, each time
I found a closed temple.

Sensing that the minister would not come that morning, Kāmāci and
I went back to her line room home. She prepared mid-morning cups of
tea for her grandchildren and me, and we sat in the kitchen area of her
room. She was worried about Sadha being in Colombo by herself. She
felt her only daughter was too young to work alone in the capital, even
though she had once been a domestic worker there when she was twelve.
I mentioned Sadha's history of Colombo labor in an effort to reassure
her, but Kāmāci insisted that back then it was different. She knew the
family that Sadha had gone to when she was younger because another
woman from the estate had gone to work there before and had returned
to get married. Additionally, when Sadha had worked in Colombo in

her youth, Kāmāci had trusted relations working close by and they would check in on her from time to time to make sure she was safe.

Now, she told me, beyond a first cousin who was a shop worker in Colombo, she would not know anybody else there. "An unmarried girl [komari pillai] like her should stay at home, work, and get married," she said. "I could have gone in her place, but if I went, who would take care of my son's children while everyone works?"

Sadha and her family made the decision to have her return to domestic work in Colombo because Kanageswaran had recently become ill and taken leave from his full-time estate job. Causing additional financial strain, her one-year-old niece—Kanageswaran's daughter, Abirāmi—had been having seizures for the past seven months and had to be taken to multiple doctor's visits and neurological scans at the nearby local hospital, the closest government base hospital (a one-hour trip by bus), and more follow-up scans at Kandy Children's Hospital, over two and a half hours away from Kirkwall. His wife, a full-time employee on Kirkwall, had taken multiple days of unpaid leave to accompany her daughter (whom she was still breastfeeding at the time) and husband to their medical visits.

The desired outcome of Sadha being a domestic worker was the promise of an Rs.[10] 8,000 monthly salary, which in June 2009 amounted to approximately $69.68. That salary would be significantly more than the monthly net income Sadha would be able to earn in one month's work on the estate as a full-time plucker. With the loans that her family had taken out of her wages to survive, her monthly salary had been around Rs. 1,300 to 1,500 (between eleven and thirteen US dollars in 2009) for the past three months. Given the difference, her family would be able to use that salary to survive and possibly lower the debt they had accrued. To prepare for her transition, Sadha changed her registration status from full-time to casual worker on Kirkwall. This way she would be assured work on the plantation upon her return, which, like many domestic workers from the plantations, was to be expected.

While Sadha was in Maradana, I called her weekly. The telephone number she gave me belonged not to her male employer as she had thought, but to his wife, who spoke perfect English and was working full-time in a financial office in Colombo. The first time I called, Kanageswaran told me to ask for Sadha by her formal name. It was a name that

I had not heard before but had seen written down once on her National Identity Card (NIC) when she had pulled it out at a security checkpoint on the road while we traveled together by bus in April that year.

A little over three weeks after she left, Sadha called to tell me that she would return to Kirkwall with her cousin the following Sunday. The young child she was caring for—only nine years old but, according to Sadha, big for his age—had started to treat her disrespectfully and had hit her. She was also lonely and missed her family. She would take the one-month salary she earned plus the round-trip transportation costs to and from Colombo she had been promised and return home to work full-time on the estate.

When she got back, Sadha showered her extended family with gifts—candy, toys, and pens for the children, and clothing for her mother, uncle, brother, sister-in-law, and aunts. She showed me a faded scar on her lower forearm where the boy had scratched her. She told me that while her employers were more or less kind people, she could not bear to stay and was happy to be home. Life was different in Colombo. There, after finishing all her domestic work, she could watch television and rest in her own room. She was given a bed to sleep on, considerably more than other employers had given her when she had been a domestic before and had to sleep on a mat in the hallway outside the kitchen.

The day after she got home, I chatted with her as she brusquely swept the front sitting room of their home while her nieces and the little boy from the neighboring line room were running and playing around us. In the commotion, her five-year-old niece spilled her tea and dropped and smashed the biscuits Sadha had given her. Irritated, Sadha quickly grabbed a towel to mop it up, swept up the crumbs, and yelled at the children to stop running and to sit quietly while they ate and drank.

"I tell you, Akka, I was better off in Colombo without all of them making a mess!" She turned to them and yelled, "If you continue to play the fool, I'll go back!" Hesitation filled the eyes of her niece for a split second until she saw the humor in Sadha's eyes. She then giggled and ran out of the room behind her older sister. Sadha and I laughed, and she continued to sweep the room.

While Sadha was in Colombo, I attended a meeting in Hatton town convened by the Christian Workers' Fellowship (CWF), an Anglican, socialist trade union registered in 1958 and one of several unions that represent Sri Lanka's tea plantation workers. Twenty-three people were in attendance—sixteen men and seven women. On the meeting's agenda was a debate about the daily wage for plantation workers being negotiated through the collective wage agreement (or Collective Agreement, CA) contract between the twenty-three RPCs and three representing trade unions. Incited by failed negotiations, the CWF and other unions had begun to organize local-level public meetings to discuss possible interventions in the larger bargaining process.

One woman in attendance was Rani, a Hill Country Tamil, Catholic, and former plucker who had become an NGO worker and community organizer after giving birth to her first of two children. She was listening to the others speak and waited patiently in the back of the room. Male trade unionists were dominating the forum, arguing about undignified uniforms, corrupt field officers, and doctored wage rolls. In the first available moment of silence, Rani raised her hand, stood up, and spoke in Tamil with exasperation: "In five to ten years from now, there will be no more laborers working on these plantations! All the youth will be in Colombo, in schools, or abroad. There is no honor in estate work. Children living on the estates do not want to live like their parents live. They want respect! They want dignity!"

The frustration that Rani articulated that day is what Sri Lanka's RPCs, trade unionists, NGO workers, and politicians still struggle to resolve in 2018, nine years after that CWF meeting. Hill Country Tamils on Sri Lanka's tea plantations are not able to live with dignity on the plantation wage and within the current system. More important, Hill Country Tamils on Sri Lanka's tea plantations *do not want* to live on this wage. Their desires to move, be seen, and live beyond an unlivable wage are shifting the social dynamics and agro-economic future of Sri Lanka's tea plantation industry.

Tea and Solidarity examines minority Hill Country Tamil workers' desires for dignity as they work and live on and beyond Sri Lanka's tea plantations. Drawing from ethnographic research I conducted in Sri Lanka between 2008 and 2017, I map the desires of workers and their families onto the plantation's imperial, residential, and industrial landscapes and within the wider frame of Sri Lanka's postwar calls for political reform and economic development. Hill Country Tamils are a marginalized and often-invisible minority whose manual labor and collective heritage of dispossession as "coolies" in colonial Ceylon are central to the country's global recognition, economic growth, and history as a postcolonial nation. While ethno-linguistic and religious minorities in Sri Lanka justifiably remain dissatisfied with the current mechanisms for political representation and transitional justice after twenty-six years of civil war, Sri Lanka's Hill Country Tamil plantation workers, statistically, experience the lowest levels of educational achievement and socioeconomic mobility on the island. Despite gradual improvements to their life and working conditions through industrial and political change, they are stigmatized in larger Sri Lankan civil society, and a history of exclusionary national politics and the ongoing structural violence of caste discrimination, landlessness, and labor precarity continues to negatively affect their lives.

Sri Lanka's past and present politics of exclusion is central to the unfolding story of Ceylon tea. Hill Country Tamil women in particular bear the brunt of systemic structural inequalities that date back to the arrival of their laboring ancestors from South India's Tamil Nadu: today, the labor and gender expectations held for them inform not only their social relations and employment practices within the industry but also the persistent realities of land and labor dispossession that they and their families experience. In this book, I explore how Hill Country Tamil women and their families strive to create a sense of home in a country that was built and sustained through their labor. The unfolding of their desires challenges us to think beyond former representations of plantation life and gendered work and commit to a future of tea production in Sri Lanka grounded in a praxis of solidarity with those desires. Using archival and ethnographic evidence, I trace how women workers want to be seen and the structural constraints they face as they move, work, and live in the face of everyday, systemic forms of marginalization. Key features of tea plantation life, when examined from a feminist and humanistic perspective, make clear the complicated relationship between the value of women's work, political forms of recognition, and sustainable mechanisms to ensure the rights of minorities. This book argues that women workers' desires for dignity and better futures have the potential to productively disrupt and positively transform the story of Ceylon tea and the industry's ethical future.

Sri Lanka's "Coolies"

The current context of Hill Country Tamils' marginalization in Sri Lanka traces back to the English word *coolie*. This term precedes the emergence of colonial Ceylon's coffee, tea, and rubber plantation industries. Like its origins, an explanation of this word's multiple meanings must precede the historical and political contours of Hill Country Tamil tea plantation residents' contemporary experiences. According to historical and anthropological scholarship, a coolie was a person strategically imagined and locatable at intersections of labor, race, gender, class, and rank under imperial rule. The coolie was a member of the "lowest level of the industrial labour market,"[11] a "beast" to be "tamed" in the project of colonial order,[12] and a racialized labor commodity;[13] geographically, the coolie was dispersed and moving across European and Asian empires as early as 1581 and first noted in the archive ambiguously, and later with more precision, as menial, subhuman labor.[14] In "The Making of a Coolie," Jan Breman and Valentine Daniel trace the origins of the English word *coolie* to both Tamil (*kūli*, or "payment for menial labor") and Gujarati (*Kuli*, or "person of the Kuli tribe" associated with plundering and thievery), claiming that through the English word, "the distinct humanity of the individual was, in a single move, appropriated and eliminated; the person collapsed into the payment."[15] Breman and Daniel further characterize this collapse and movement as "unsettling": "coolies are unsettling; they are unsettled themselves and unsettle others."[16] This last feature—the capacity of coolies to destabilize and create discomfort among those who considered them as such, even when enduring sustained oppression and instability—is of most importance to this book.

Integral to these former concepts of *coolie* is movement—the physical move from homeland to industrial landscape, the capitalist move from person to payment, the calculated move from labor to commodity, and the oppressive move from human to subhuman. These moves did not completely rupture or break from the historical, social, or labor practices that Ceylon's plantation workers had experienced prior to their migrations. Coming from districts across South India, the majority of Tamils who migrated to British Ceylon as laborers between 1832 and 1839 were members of subordinated castes who, well before British colonial rule, were experiencing caste-based oppression in the form of agrestic enslavement and servitude, indentured labor, and socioeconomic marginalization.[17] While the Indian Slavery Act of 1843 abolished select economic practices of slavery in India, transactional coolie labor practices under British colonial rule reflect what Indrani Chatterjee calls "abolition by denial"; planters, through a series of legislative actions, agro-industrial labor practices, and economic and security-based agreements with the government of Ceylon, were able to exercise control over the laborers who had migrated.[18]

Historians and anthropologists of Asia and Africa have well documented the calculated blurring of lines among slavery, indentured, and coolie labor in the life and work practices of global plantation industries during the early nineteenth century.[19] In Ceylon, Patrick Peebles notes that although termed "free labor," Tamil coolies working on the tea plantations were anything but free; relationships of debt, kinship, and hierarchical labor sustained their wages and created a bonded residential worker community and industrial system that relied on and maintained workers' permanent residence in Ceylon rather than India.[20] Daniel Bass, building on John Kelly's work on the racial categorization of Indian coolies in Fiji, aptly points out that beyond socioeconomic hierarchies informed by caste and ethnicity, Ceylon's plantation coolies were a racialized labor force and colonial elites saw them as members of "a lesser race."[21] The intersections of race, caste, and class discrimination did not emerge with the plantation industry in Ceylon but had earlier foundations in India and were reworked in an industrializing colonial polity with new sets of caste and class interests as native Ceylonese elites looked up to the immanent horizon of decolonization and independence. To say that the status of coolie is an economic and labor category truly distinct from slavery and indentured labor is misleading. Rather, the category of the coolie falls within what Rupa Viswanath calls the "trope of gentle slavery," within which colonial and postcolonial Sri Lankan politics thrived and which built and sustained the Sri Lankan nation-state and current plantation industry.[22]

In 1992, the same year that Breman and Daniel published "The Making of a Coolie," Mauritian poet Khal Torabully called for writers and historians in Afro-Caribbean and Indian Ocean studies to contribute to the "Coolitude" movement. Finding kinship with Négritude and the decolonization movements of African francophone intellectuals like Aimé Césaire, Coolitude seeks to revise essentialist framings of trans-cultural migration of Indian-Origin laborers during colonial rule and to reclaim the word *coolie*, in order to deconstruct stereotypical narratives of India's dispersed indentured laborers. Since the early 1990s, Coolitude has continued to define the contemporary experiences of those who claim their ancestors as coolies within India's global diaspora.[23] In Sri Lanka, however, gestures to Coolitude exist only within artistic engagements grounded in feminist perspectives. In 2013 activist, researcher, and actor Ponni Arasu debuted *Karuppi* (The dark woman), a one-woman play in Tamil that brings together the diverse experiences of Tamil-speaking women migrant workers from the nineteenth century to present day to highlight their experiences at the intersections of racialized and gendered violence; more notable is that the play later incorporated English and Cre-ole to extend to the histories and current experiences of indentured and migrant women workers beyond Sri Lanka and India.[24] In the same year, Sri Lankan Tamil feminist writer and scholar Sumathy Sivamohan debuted *Ingiruthu* (Here and now), a film that depicts the histories, lives, and struggles of Hill Country Tamils from their arrival to the present day; notably this work features Hill Country Tamil actors and was shot around and on the tea plantations themselves, giving its audience an accurately sensorial but fictional portrayal of plantation life. From 2015 to 2017, his-torians Crispin Bates and Andrea Major organized "Becoming Coolies" a collaborative research project aimed to produce a digital, multimedia archived collection of narratives that detail the migration and life histo-ries of Indian diasporic families and their ancestors and challenge the "reproduction of conventional colonial and nationalist tropes of inden-tured victimhood, exploitation and abuse."[25]

Sri Lanka, however, has been mostly absent from these broader dia-logues of decoloniality and reclamation; with the exception of Valentine Daniel's ethnohistorical poem "The Coolie,"[26] which speaks to the struc-tural violence and "bardic heritage"[27] of Hill Country Tamils, the major-ity of coolie records—poetry, song, and essays about Hill Country Tamils' past—are primarily in Tamil; in English, the word *coolie* remains a dark but accepted token of Sri Lanka's historical connections to and investments in inhumane labor forms and relations.

Tea and Solidarity seeks to acknowledge the discomfort and transitions that Sri Lanka faces as Hill Country Tamils call for a distinct disentanglement from their present-day circumstances of oppression and marginality. While the word has a wider currency in Caribbean and Indian diasporic communities, when spoken the term remains derogatory and stigmatizing among Hill Country Tamils in Sri Lanka. Writing of the word and its historical use in British Ceylon in Tamil, M. Nithiyanandan, a Hill Country Tamil expatriate and writer, argues that the word itself was foreign to the people to whom it applied and that the British imposed the word on the working communities on Ceylon's plantations.[28] After seeing the works of Arasu and Sivamohan in 2014, I was moved to include the word in the title in solidarity with emergent global movements of reclamation. But when I asked members of the Hill Country Tamil community about doing so, they told me that it was a painful word that had nonetheless concretized as integral to the nation's economic development and growth. Despite *coolie* being a staple word in Sri Lanka's colonial archives until it was mostly replaced in the 1920s by "Indian immigrant labourer," contemporary Sri Lankans and members of Sri Lanka's diaspora have yet to fully acknowledge the deep pain and actualized forms of social and economic violence that this word does when executed in its original, foreign form.[29]

Despite its declared foreign imposition, *coolie* has become more than familiar in Sri Lanka and inextricably part of the country's past and present. It is intimately known and heard across all communities, continues to breathe within the archive, and is embedded in present linguistic, scientific, and industrial forms of knowledge and ideologies about agro-industrial plantation labor. It has come to justify the most marketable socioeconomic labor practices for maximum profit on plantations across the Indian Ocean world, and it infuses locally felt hierarchies of social relations among Hill Country Tamils. It frames what the tea industry's economic and nominal survival means for the Sri Lankan nation, and how the state sees its postcolonial past and postwar future. Lastly, and most important, this word signifies why today's Hill Country Tamils on Sri Lanka's tea plantations, as descendants of Ceylon's Tamil-speaking coolies, desire to be recognized with dignity as equal citizens in a post-colonial, postwar Sri Lanka.

On Naming and Claiming

Like the word *coolie*, names for communities also have politically charged histories and deployments. To name a community is to make it known to a wider world. Once termed coolies in the colonial archive, Hill Country Tamils have assumed several names: Plantation Tamil, Estate Tamil, Indian Tamil, Indian-Origin Tamil (IOT), and Up-Country Tamil (or in Tamil, *Malaiyaka* ["of the hills"] Tamil). Some of these names, such as Estate Tamil and Plantation Tamil, have now been deemed inappropriate for contemporary usage within the community; nevertheless, they gained traction in the colonial record, political alliances, and earlier scholarship.[30] Other English terms, such as Indian Tamil, Indian-Origin Tamil, and Up-Country Tamil, originated in Ceylon's official census language and today have currency in emerging legislation, political-cum-union rhetoric, and anthropological scholarship.[31]

The politics of naming this community is contingent on the postwar reconfigurations of Sri Lanka's political representatives and calls for transitional justice. Following the 2015 presidential election of Maithripala Sirisena and parliamentary victory of the Tamil Progressive Alliance (TPA), which claims to represent Sri Lanka's non–Sri Lankan Tamil communities, a March 2016 *Report of the Experts Committee on Constitutional Reforms* for the TPA suggested the name Indian-Origin Malaiyaka Thamilar (IOMT). The report claimed that this name aligned well with proposals for non-territorial councils for IOMTs in the postwar context: "An identity that in whole or part has a direct reference to a territory in Sri Lanka is considered necessary. Constitutional recognition of this identity as a distinct national entity with a shared sense of history and belonging in Sri Lanka will be a necessary step in according due dignity for the community and in affirming Sri Lanka as a pluralistic society. After discussing various possibilities, we propose 'Indian-Origin Malaiyaka Thamilar' as the long form of identification of the Hill-Country Tamil community."[32]

This book uses Hill Country Tamil to refer to communities of Tamil speakers who self-identify their place of origin and residence (or either of the two) on Sri Lanka's tea plantations. Apart from honoring the reasons stated by the committee above, my decision is twofold. First, the communities with whom I primarily worked were residing or had resided on tea plantations for most of their lives. When I asked them how they wanted to be referred to in my research, they told me, in Tamil, "Malaiyaka Thamilar," which I translated into English as Hill Country Tamil. Second, this book focuses on how gender and labor relations as well as investments map onto the residential-industrial landscapes of Sri Lanka's tea plantations. These spaces include the hills, which Hill Country Tamil residents maintain and imagine as contributing to their often-conflicted but ever-present sense of home and place in Sri Lanka. Many individuals with whom I spoke work in hill station towns, Colombo, and abroad, but their places of origin, in both labor and life, are on the hills. The term Hill Country Tamil honors their self-identified senses of home, the presence of their laboring ancestors on these industrial-residential sites, and their calls for a future that recognizes them as a diverse and dignified Tamil-speaking minority in a multilingual, multiethnic Sri Lanka. On a technical note, the plantation comprises smaller estates, which then comprise divisions. In everyday parlance, the Tamil term for plantation, *peruntōttam*, is rarely used, but it is more common in political, legal, and industrial discourse. In its place, estate, or *tōttam*, is more often heard. In this ethnography I will shift between using plantation and estate depending on the context of my research.

Inherited Dispossession

Sri Lanka's tea industry took form in early nineteenth-century Ceylon under British rule. The island of Ceylon underwent a massive and extended process of industrialization following its entry into the British Empire in 1796 after periods of mercantile-led and non-unitary colonial rule under the Portuguese (1505–1658) and the Dutch (1658–1796).[33] These far-reaching industrial schemes resulted in the creation of internal transportation systems and a number of export economies for colonial profit. To fulfill the tasks of building both roads and railroads and cultivating coffee, British planters employed overseers, recruited primarily among Tamil-speaking migrant laborers from South Indian villages. Akin to historical accounts of migrant workers across the British Empire in former colonies such as Fiji, Mauritius, Guyana, South Africa, and Trinidad, Tamil-speaking laborers endured many hardships during and after their arrival in the 1820s, including deplorable working and living conditions. Among other forms of casual and formal labor, they worked on the coffee estates until a leaf virus destroyed Ceylon's coffee economy around 1869.[34] In addition to producing rubber, the British began to commercially produce tea, which had been planted earlier but in small numbers and experimentally, and it became a successful crop in the 1880s. Given the demand, planters were able to use the labor force that had emerged in an already resident community of Tamil laborers.

Sri Lanka's Hill Country Tamils constitute a linguistic and ethnic community distinct from other Tamil-speaking communities on the island, such as Sri Lankan Tamils who claim their origin in the island's North and East; Colombo Tamils; and other ethnic and religious minorities such as Muslims, Colombo Chetties, Burghers, the indigenous Vedda community, and Sinhala speakers. They live in various rural and urban concentrations throughout the country, with nearly one million claiming residence on Sri Lanka's RPC-run estates.[35] What makes this community distinct is their place within Sri Lanka's shared coolie heritage and its ties to colonial and postcolonial forms of industrial production, nation building, and land and labor dispossession. Though legally given franchise in 1831, the community was not fully accepted into an elite-driven Ceylon polity due to caste-, class-, and ethnic-based discrimination. This culminated when the first independent government of Ceylon disenfranchised the Hill Country Tamils through the Ceylon Citizenship Act No. 18 of 1948 and Indian and Pakistani Residents Act No. 3 of 1949, and in 1956 the government enacted the Sinhala Only Act, which removed Tamil and English from the national language register. In 1964 India and Sri Lanka implemented the Sirimavo-Shastri Pact, an eighteen-year repatriation scheme under which stateless Indian-Origin persons could apply for quota-based citizenship in either India or Sri Lanka. During this period, many Hill Country Tamils left the country for India, a mother nation that, as they would find upon their return, wanted them as citizens as much as Sri Lanka wanted them as their own.[36] The repatriation scheme officially ended with the escalation of ethnic violence and onset of civil war in 1982, but the miscalculated, politically diplomatic arrangement continued to create further physical and emotional fractures within an already vulnerable political and laborer minority.[37]

From the 1950s through the 1990s, Sinhala and Tamil nationalist and militant movements were on the rise in the North, East, and South, and the escalating civil and ethnic violence also affected the Hill Country Tamils living on the plantations in the South-Central provinces. Apart from the Ceylon Drāvida Munnētra Kalagam (CDMK),[38] few Tamil militant groups in the North and East included Hill Country Tamils in their claims for self-determination and their vision for an all-Tamil "homeland" (Eelam).[39] In an attempt to weaken these movements, the government enacted the Prevention of Terrorism Act No. 48 of 1979 (PTA), which gave Sri Lankan security forces the right to search, seize, and arrest any individual if there was any suspicion of unlawful activity. Under the PTA, Hill Country Tamil plantation residents such as Kāthai Muthusamy were arrested, detained, and imprisoned without trial.

The prolonged state of emergency also required that individuals in Sri Lanka carry appropriate forms of identification for routine checkpoints on the road and unexpected cordon and search operations of areas with high concentrations of Tamils.[40] For stateless Hill Country Tamils, emergency rule not only restricted their physical mobility and work opportunities but also instilled in them a perpetual fear of detainment without reason. Beyond these extralegal forms of discrimination, the anti-Tamil riots in 1958, 1977, 1981, and 1983 resulted in several hundred casualties among Hill Country Tamils and many more internally displaced from their plantation homes.[41] During this same period, the plantation sector went through a series of infrastructural changes. In 1972, land reform acts nationalized the plantations, handing over management of the tea and rubber fields to the Sri Lankan state. During this period, faith- and community-based NGOs formed to provide relief to workers and plantation residents in response to the escalation of human rights violations, such as famine and rapid increases in poverty in the sector, two more factors that led Hill Country Tamils on the plantations to migrate to the North and East.[42] In 1991, Sri Lanka reprivatized the plantations under a series of liberalization policies that swept over the industry, and work and living conditions on the plantations again significantly deteriorated.[43] During these transitions, the Sri Lankan government, RPCs, and industrial stakeholders did not evenly give Hill Country Tamils the opportunity to exercise land and housing rights equally afforded to non-plantation residing citizens of Sri Lanka's wider civil society.[44]

With the welfare of plantation residents in the hands of the twenty-three RPCs and two state-run plantations, Hill Country Tamil political and union representatives formulate many of their grievances around basic needs, quality of life, and, most important, the plantation daily wage. With politically motivated unionists and the industry dictating wage increases that do not accommodate the rising cost of living, plantation workers continue to experience economic, legal, and civic forms of marginality. Although the rate of poverty in the estate sector dropped between 2006 and 2015, it still surpasses that of the rural and urban sectors.[45] Despite reinstatement of Hill Country Tamils' citizenship rights through the Grant of Citizenship to Persons of Indian Origin Act No. 35 of 2003, many Hill Country Tamils struggled to obtain their citizenship documents well after the law was enacted. For instance, in a survey conducted before the February 2009 Central Provincial Council elections, an estimated 71,520 Hill Country Tamil residents in Nuwara Eliya district did not have NICs and therefore could not vote.[46]

Social indicators of deficiency across health care, literacy, and higher education are most prominent among Hill Country Tamil women, who constitute more than half of the plantation workforce but suffer the greatest marginalization due to patriarchal forms of domination, unequal labor practices, and, in some cases, physical violence. RPCs and industrial stakeholders have begun to introduce new models of production through outgrowing and revenue-sharing wage programs to combat low labor output and productivity since 2005, but implementation has been uneven, and in-sector studies conducted between 2007 and 2017 have noted ongoing structural challenges that stem from the hierarchical nature of production and company profit.[47]

Additionally, owing to postwar preoccupations with development and reconciliation in the North and East, concerns about the welfare of Hill Country Tamils have been marginalized in the Sri Lankan Tamil and Sinhala nationalist agendas and pushed to the background of Sri Lanka's political landscape.[48] Since 2009, new rifts among former union-cum-party opposition alliances and even within majoritarian government alliances have emerged. After 2010, two former opposition party-cum-trade unions—the major party, National Union of Workers (NUW), and the smaller party, Democratic Peoples' Congress—switched allegiances and joined the United People's Freedom Alliance government, executing a politics of patronage seen again in the August 2014 Uva Provincial Council elections, where leading candidates were appointed as deputy ministers just days before the vote. Before the January 2015 election of United National Party (UNP) candidate, president Maitripala Sirisena, NUW joined forces with the Democratic People's Front and Up-Country People's Front to form the TPA in alliance with the UNP, and not with then-president Mahinda Rajapaksa.

Unbecoming Labor

These political struggles indicate that despite their permanent residence and long-standing contributions to Ceylon's colonial success and the tea industry, Sri Lanka still regards Hill Country Tamils as unevenly belonging in Sri Lanka, and today's tea plantation workers still experience patriarchal and neocolonial forms of labor relations in which there is little potential for upward mobility, particularly for women workers. As of 2018, the highest position held by a woman in the plantation industry was that of assistant superintendent (*sinna durai*), and the woman is not a Hill Country Tamil, but a Sinhala woman whose own father was a superintendent. While she is to be lauded for breaking through the structural barriers of gender discrimination, more work needs to be done to break down the inequity of power that exists in the industry across gender, ethnic, and caste lines for Hill Country Tamils specifically. They inhabit a unique and dynamic place within Sri Lanka's heritage of coolie labor and postcolonial past, and their future is entangled in industrial investments and agro-ecological contradictions around what constitutes their long-overdue land and economic rights.

Today, many Hill Country Tamils and their families who live on the tea plantations remain landless and do not own their line room homes. While numerically and on record plantation daily wages should place them above the poverty line for households, most families experience long-standing structural forms of debt; furthermore, their wages are also affected by agricultural and ecological factors that determine labor output. These socioeconomic indicators and the difficult conditions of agricultural labor have produced higher instances of preventable medical conditions among the community that negatively affect their household income-generation capacities. Over time, generations of families on the plantations have enjoyed relatively lower levels of access to socioeconomic and educational opportunities due to the sector's long-standing exclusion from social, economic, and legal state services. These conditions of structural violence also allowed the tea plantation industry to operate and thrive over the last 150 years.

Yet Hill Country Tamils have managed to build and sustain a sense of home. Through generations of labor and investments in gender, kinship, and social relations, their notion of community in Sri Lanka moves well beyond the instrumental and dehumanizing calculus of the industry. As Rani predicted, today's Hill Country Tamil youth do not wish to become plantation workers. As of 2016, of the recorded 987,074 residents on Sri Lanka's RPC-owned plantations, only 163,068—16 percent of the resident population—were full-time workers.[49] Younger generations, dissuaded by the caste and class stigmatizations of plantation and agricultural labor, want to pursue careers and perform income-generating activities that might more commensurately match their aspirations. From participating in informal and formal labor sectors to investing in higher education, they engage in activities across a larger spectrum of labor valuation, but still do so at the intersections of gender, class, and caste discrimination. Despite these intersectional realities of precarious labor and the absence of legal assurances in many of their endeavors, their pursuits generate social and economic outputs including relational forms of dignity, monetary value, and social prestige. As such, their desires for higher incomes are not a means to a dignified end as plantation workers but a means to a potential future as equal citizens who strive for a secure place in postwar Sri Lanka and on lands they consider home.

Previous scholars have noted that Hill Country Tamils living on the tea plantations do not consider the sites to be their home, given their ancestral and migrant connections to South India. By creating connections to the plantation lands on which they reside but which a majority of them do not own, Hill Country Tamils on the estates challenge these perceptions and make visible their desires to be seen and rooted in Sri Lanka rather than India. At the same time, mobility-driven investments and transformations in work choices signal that Hill Country Tamils want to detach from the tea plantation as a site of their future labor and valuation.[50] With monetary and immaterial investments transforming houses, gender and kinship relations, and the aspirational futures of youth, they strive to distance themselves from the dehumanizing signifiers of coolie life, but they also desire an equitable place in Sri Lanka defined through the language of rights and recognition.

Overview

This book explores how Hill Country Tamils' life struggles operate on a daily basis, why they face social, legal, and economic challenges, when they are satisfied or unsettled with the outcomes of their labor and investments, and what resources they need to move forward. Its primary focus is on how a framing of such desires for dignity as decolonial can productively challenge and disrupt the colonially embedded structures and relations of labor and life, and each chapter traces a key feature of Sri Lanka's tea plantations. Within those features, I examine how Hill Country Tamils come to understand, articulate, and navigate those structures and relations through a feminist and humanistic lens. Chapter 1 outlines what is already known about Hill Country Tamils in Sri Lanka as produced within various scholarly fields. I think about what enabled former thematic foci such as structural violence, agency, and victimhood and why a move toward alternative methodologies and approaches to studying plantation life may be more commensurate and in solidarity with what Hill Country Tamils and workers want to be investigated about their lives. I then introduce a framing useful to my own approach to studying plantation life—the *poēisis* of desire—the movement and presence of desire on the tea plantations, as active sites of social change and disruption but also as sites of imperial nostalgia, industry, and consumption. I discuss how desire operates, its relation to the ethics and production of knowledge about Hill Country Tamils, and my own methodological approaches and trajectory in studying plantation life and the politics of development in Sri Lanka.

Chapter 2 explores connections between language and landscape. I examine how the language of Hill Country Tamils came to shape their labor landscapes and the imaginary of a plantation as a cohesive, remote, and industrially successful site of production. It presents an analysis of written and visual representations of Tamil coolies and estate life and labor in British and postcolonial Ceylon. In those representations, I find evidence of Hill Country Tamils' aspirations to live and labor beyond the ideals of the plantation system, and I conclude by presenting data on the future career plans of Hill Country Tamil youth who reside on the plantations but aspire to work beyond its boundaries.

Chapter 3 focuses on the representational weight of the etymological origin of the word *coolie*—the wage. It provides a brief history of collective bargaining around the plantation daily wage and how that documented past largely excludes the representational leadership, kinship investments, and gendered labor of Hill Country Tamil women. I then look into the actual wages of workers and their families and how the plantation daily wage, despite successively bargained increases through CAs since 1998, fails to accommodate the lifelong realities and kinship commitments of women workers. I conclude with a challenge to see the wage as a condition of life that compels families to aspire and live beyond it because of its sustained failure to accommodate their gendered commitments.

Chapter 4 returns to the site of the tea plantation itself, and specifically to the line room homes where Hill Country Tamils live. I draw on narratives of home, landlessness, and investment as Tamil workers negotiate and perceive their worth in kin relations, build homes on the estates, and present emerging possibilities within spoken and understood iterations of the Tamil word *ūr*, which translates to one's natal home.[51] By creating connections to the industrial lands on which they reside, Hill Country Tamils challenge and engage previously articulated conceptual and ontological boundaries of *ūr* and make visible their desire to be seen in and attached to Sri Lanka rather than India.[52] I then examine emerging housing policy schemes on the plantations and how political calls for land rights complicate what it means to claim the plantations as *ūr* and transform understandings of investment, ownership, and purchase for those who remain in line rooms and do not have equal access to these transitional reforms.

Chapter 5 moves into the more intimate ways the tea industry and women themselves articulate the value of their labor and lives through stories of their bodily experiences. It deconstructs the following phrase, which is often said among industrial stakeholders: "From the womb to the tomb, the tea estate worker is taken care of." I foreground stories of women's tubal ligations and reproductive choices around fertility and child rearing in order to complicate understandings of informed consent, reproductive rights, and family care. I then conclude with narratives of life after reproduction, namely the experiences of widows and grand-mothers. Such narratives demonstrate how state and industrial policies and concepts of care—by doing the work of hegemony to keep the industry intact—do not fully account for the shifting expectations that women experience. This chapter considers how women, as prospective mothers, wives, and caregivers, find alternative forms of recognition within their communities.

Chapter 6 builds on those incommensurabilities and alternatives by shifting to the realm of domestic and transnational rights-based praxis. I begin with the story of the 2009 deaths of two Hill Country Tamil female child laborers in Colombo and specifically interrogate the discomforting intersection of shame, labor, and human rights discourse the incident raised in Sri Lanka at the time. I then discuss how Sri Lankan state and labor policies around migrant labor specifically affect the labor and mobil-ity of Hill Country Tamil women who seek to work off the plantations as migrant domestic workers. These effects point to the working of a poli-tics of labor shaming for Hill Country Tamil workingwomen on the plan-tations; but nevertheless, women continue to draw social prestige and economic value from migrant domestic labor. Concluding with accounts of those investments, I complicate narratives of shame around intimate labor and foreground women's realities of transforming their lives through social capital gained through migrant and domestic work.

The final chapter moves beyond the tea plantation and into the spaces afforded to women's work in development and labor organizing. It spe-cifically focuses on two programs that attempt to remap the future and value of women's work. In the first, a transnational, human rights pro-gram involving young girls from the estates, I examine how success and failure are represented in the development archive as well as the chal-lenges of programming around girls' and women's rights. I then shift to examining a labor union unique for its exclusively female leadership. Unlike others, this union serves women working across both formal and informal sectors and organizes the unorganized by employing feminist and transnational methodologies in their outreach and programming.

Such forms of feminist labor organizing seek to challenge the patriarchal structures that have come to define trade union politics and praxis in Sri Lanka. However, both types of gender-based programming rely on solidarities contingent on commitments from stakeholders in and beyond Sri Lanka to acknowledge women workers' experiences and labor investments.

Ending this ethnography, I briefly discuss the political present that Hill Country Tamils inhabit as a national minority both on the tea plantations and beyond its boundaries. I ask if and how, through the lens of transitional justice, a 150-year-old tea plantation industry can survive and unfold in relation to the labor aspirations and desires of Hill Country Tamils in the postwar context. Examining the parameters of progressive policies to reconfigure the plantation's labor and residential landscapes and emergent calls for decoloniality, I ask if it is possible to see the tea plantation as a site of conscience and what potential such productive disruptions hold for Hill Country Tamils, the Ceylon tea industry, and workingwomen in and beyond Sri Lanka.

CHAPTER 1

Productive Alternatives

I SAT IN A CONFERENCE ROOM WITH A GROUP OF SRI LANKAN researchers in Colombo. It was July 2017, nearly nine years after I had begun conducting research on the plantation sector, and the researchers I sat with had several years of research experience studying the estates. We were discussing the most productive ways to approach the plantation as a site of inquiry, and the conversation turned to our methodologies: what had worked, what had presented challenges, and how best to collect data to effect the most social change in the community. Among development researchers the standard approach to studying the plantation sector primarily involved the use of mixed methods including focus groups, household surveys, management-based document collection on wages and household sizes, and interviews. But each method we discussed presented unique challenges. Hill Country Tamil participants in the focus groups were unwilling to speak in front of one another due to caste, gender, and labor differences and relations, and the likelihood of bias and controlled speech was high. Household surveys and individual interviews were difficult to schedule around laborers' long and unpredictable working hours. Most challenging was obtaining access to the estates themselves: managers had to approve questionnaires before being administered, and constant shifts in the estate management and labor force made it difficult to maintain a steady sample over continuous funding and research periods.

One senior researcher, speaking for the group, claimed it seemed as though, despite the large quantity of data coming out of the estate sector over the years, researchers were struggling to learn something *new* about the lives and experiences of Hill Country Tamils on the plantations. Her comment brought me back to a line in a research study on the estate sector conducted by the Centre for Poverty Analysis, a research organization based in Colombo. The study had been published in 2008, the year I began conducting fieldwork on the tea plantations. I had read it closely beforehand as I was preparing my own questions and methodological approaches; in 2017 I returned to the text as I reflected on my own methods and our discussion. In the study's limitations section, the researchers reflected on Hill Country Tamil participants' reactions to their study: "Respondent fatigue was clearly evident. Estates are a highly researched sector, and the respondents were not particularly interested in participating in the study. Frequently, they did so only out of habit of agreeing to requests by the management."[1] The perceived lack of learning something new about Sri Lanka's tea plantations directly relates to how Hill Country Tamils themselves perceive scholarly and development research, as well as their sense of faith and investment in outside productions of knowledge about their lives. If research was fatiguing Hill Country Tamils, what engagements might be more commensurate with what they want for themselves and their longer-term aspirations? Furthermore, if we were to look at the types of knowledge that might seem relatively marginal, untapped, and beyond the normative categories that enclose and define Hill Country Tamils and plantation life, could we locate alternative and more productive forms of knowledge?

This chapter argues that feminist methodologies and a decolonizing approach to researching Sri Lanka's tea plantations can engender new, more commensurate forms of knowledge about Hill Country Tamils' life and work experiences. The purpose of this book is not to reiterate the historical and empirical narratives that scholars have already made known; rather, I seek to locate geopolitical sources that have not been previously explored and to put these forms of knowledge into conversation with previous ways of knowing. Analyzing these forms of knowledge from a humanistic perspective supports an ethics of challenging and disrupting former structures of oppression and marginality. First, I outline what previous scholars have defined as the structuring features of marginality as well as of life and labor practices on Sri Lanka's tea plantations. Second, I explore what conditions allow the tea plantations to remain sites of authority and inequality and the need for decolonial approaches to study these sites of residence and industry from an anthropological

perspective. Third, I outline my methodological approaches to studying Hill Country Tamil workers' experiences in life and labor and the
choices I made to examine features of plantation life that matter and
meet the needs of the Hill Country Tamils with whom I worked. These
methodologies or approaches are neither perfect nor standard; nor are
they the only ways to study plantation life and the labor experiences of
plantation workers and residents; rather, they are methodologies contingent on the consent and collaboration of Hill Country Tamils themselves. I advocate that if researchers continually attend to community
interests and investments, these approaches can be potentially expansive opportunities to acknowledges sites and sources of knowledge that
may not have been previously or regularly engaged in academic research.

Hill Country Tamils on the tea plantations remain one of the most
studied communities in Sri Lanka among scholars and practitioners
in international development, public health, social sciences, and Sri
Lankan history. Anthropologists, such as Valentine Daniel, Daniel Bass,
and Sasikumar Balasundaram, use ethnographic research and analysis to demonstrate how Hill Country Tamils' heritage of dispossession
affects contemporary labor and life relations, while historians Patrick
Peebles, Kumari Jayawardena, Valli Kanapathipillai, and Angela Little
employ archival analysis to reveal how power operates within the colonial record.[2] Feminist scholars such as Rachel Kurian, Amali Phillips,
and Vidyamali Samarasinghe have marked the tea plantations as sites
of gendered labor and patriarchal subordination using social science
research methodologies such as household surveys, participant observation, and structured and semi-structured interviews.[3]

The push for a decolonial perspective on labor and life on Sri Lanka's
tea plantations has yet to be seriously undertaken as a methodological
approach, and we need to seriously consider why more scholars have not
embraced "acknowledging the source and geo-political locations of knowledge that have been denied by the dominance of particular forms."[4] The
history and place of tea production and consumption in and beyond Sri
Lanka make it difficult for those who drink Ceylon tea to embrace calls
for decolonization. Sri Lanka's tea plantations are beloved places and
national treasures, sites of prestige, nostalgia, and success. Likewise, the
commensality and rituals of preparing and drinking tea in homes,
workplaces, and at social events define Sri Lankans' daily habits and

social relations, and larger narratives about the country's transition from British colony to postcolonial nation. From being the first drink prepared and consumed in the morning to being the first offering to a visitor, tea connects individuals and allows work to continue. Tea is memorialized, commoditized, and circulated and as a consequence generates value as an object of financial, scientific, and spatial investments across corporate, ethnic, and national communities—not only in the Hill Country and across Sri Lanka but also in auction houses, cafes, export economies, and countries around the world.

What features of our lives and worlds facilitate the nostalgia of tea? What allows it to circulate and generate value within and across our bodies and places of inhabitance, and in our desires for its taste, place, and value? How might an ethical recognition of Hill Country Tamils' history and labor destabilize the plantation as a site of that nostalgia and reorient our desires for tea and its consumptive value? This book argues that structural inequalities based on caste, ethnicity, and gender make this nostalgia and desire for tea possible. These inequalities may be able to be swallowed easily, stripped away from, and distorted in the consumption experience, but foregrounding them leads to a more ethical place for the workers who experience injustice and whose labor is central to the story of Ceylon tea.

Caste, Class, and Ethnicity on the Tea Plantations

A core of this ethical foundation is acknowledging the sustained caste, ethnic, and class discrimination that Hill Country Tamils have faced in Sri Lanka since the arrival of their ancestors. This book is committed to recording and representing the expressions and language Hill Country Tamils use and understanding this community's struggles for dignity and rights as primary consequences of their caste, class, and ethnic discrimination. Caste differentiation and identification infuse Hill Country Tamils' life and labor interactions with their employers, members of their plantation resident communities, and outsiders. It was the basis of labor recruitment under British rule and also featured unevenly during repatriation of Hill Country Tamils to India when more "upper-caste" Hill Country Tamils were able to return while mostly "lower-caste" communities remained on the island.[5] Therefore, foregrounding caste and ethnic difference is critical to understanding Hill Country Tamils' ongoing experiences of marginality across their labor and social relations in Sri Lanka.

In the course of my research, Hill Country Tamils regularly mentioned ethnic and religious differences in our conversations. The Hill Country is richly diverse with respect to religious, ethnic, and linguistic variety, and the tea plantations themselves are sites of encountering difference through work and industrial relations. From incoming Sinhala or Jaffna or Colombo Tamil superintendents; longtime Muslim and Sinhala neighbors, shop owners, or estate staff; white, Euro-American backpackers; wealthy tourist visitors from Europe, India, the Middle East, and East Asia, to local Sinhala, Jaffna Tamil, Colombo Tamil, and Burgher tourists from other regions in Sri Lanka, Hill Country Tamils are familiar with encountering ethnic difference and also with being culturally evaluated by visitors and outsiders based on their distinctive identification. Anthropologists Oddvar Hollup, Sasikumar Balasundaram, and Daniel Bass note that broader practices of caste differentiation in Sri Lanka inform the markers of Hill Country Tamil ethnicity and ethnic identification. Balasundaram specifically argues that caste discrimination predominantly affects the "PPC castes" (Paraiyar, Pallar, and Chakkiliar), or the group terms that are known in India as "Dalits," though it is important to acknowledge that the latter term is not presently used to address PPC caste communities in Sri Lanka.[6]

While I heard about ethnic difference often and overtly in my research, my discussions about caste differences were more implied and many times silently understood. But when explicit, the utterances were poignant signifiers of the underlying effects of caste discrimination that Hill Country Tamils on the plantations experienced. My own positionality as a Sri Lankan Tamil American woman initially compelled me to not ask explicit questions about caste unless the individuals with whom I was speaking initiated it. It felt methodologically unethical to use leading questions and probes to insert the question of caste into conversations during which the issue did not arise organically; but if the issue did come up, I would inquire further into the dynamic of caste differentiation if my interlocutors were open to it. Part of my unwillingness lay in the fact that the Sri Lankan Tamil communities to which I am linked by blood and heritage were and remain directly implicated in ongoing forms of caste discrimination against Hill Country Tamils communities today.

On Kirkwall, where I conducted long-term research, the majority of Tamil-speaking residents with whom I spoke self-identified as being members of Paraiyar and Pallar castes at one time or another in our conversations. Utterances of caste names would almost always come up in discussions of marriage and in the search for suitable marriage partners. Only twice in the first year of research did caste come up in distinctly discriminating senses. The first instance involved rules of caste in commensality: I observed a woman worker who identified as Paraiyar refusing to drink tea in the house of an individual whom she later identified as Pallar. In the second instance, a woman who had earlier self-identified as Paraiyar was telling me about the rumored extramarital relations of a woman neighbor and commented on her Kudiyanavar *jāthi* (caste) as a reason for her behavior. In my fieldwork experience, four households in Kirkwall division were identified to me as having household members who were of the Kudiyanavar caste, which is considered an upper caste among Hill Country Tamils. Members of Kirkwall also mentioned to me that another estate division of the same RPC in which Kirkwall was situated had more upper-caste households in the line rooms. These members told me that due to the caste's upward social and economic mobility, this particular division enjoyed more wealth, resources for education, and infrastructural support across generations. On my visits to this division, I saw the evidence of this support myself. It was visible in the landscape, schools, employment positions of younger generations, and improved line rooms.

Beyond conversation, I regularly observed institutionalized forms of caste discrimination in hierarchical relationships and social practices. These ranged from observing rules of commensality to where Hill Country Tamils would stand and position themselves in Hindu festivals and rituals on the estates, to how they interacted and held themselves in public spaces such as on the bus, at political and union meetings, in NGO offices, hospitals, stores, and schools. The Tamil caste names Paraiyar, Pallan, Chakkiliar, Kallar, Kudiyanavar, and Muthuraj are based in an oppressive social and historical hierarchy of social relations. They are also terms that Hill Country Tamils used in instances of self-identification during my research, so I maintain their usages here as observed and recorded. In many contexts in and beyond Sri Lanka, these caste terms are not mere labels but tokens of sustained forms of violence, oppression, and domination that are cruel and derogatory. Furthermore, anthropology is also complicit in the production of functionalist ethnographic accounts that present these terms and their caste identifications stripped of their varied and often contradictory embodiments, investments, and motivations. Acknowledging the absence of an active anti-caste movement among Sri Lanka's Hill Country Tamils forces us to consider how and why contemporary anti-caste movements, such as those in India, Bangladesh, and Nepal, have not taken root in Sri Lanka.[7] With this lacuna in mind, my primary interest in this book is to explore the consequences of this prolonged discrimination in shaping the everyday lives of Hill Country Tamils and to draw the connection between desires to detach from previous forms of oppression and the actions of solidarity for social transformation observable in the plantation residents' lives.

Plantation Women and "Killer Stories"

The tea industry's nexus of caste, class, and ethnic discrimination is inextricably linked to the feminization and gendered division of labor among Hill Country Tamils on the plantations. Scholars have referred to women from this community in the following terms: "puppets on a string,"[8] products of reinforced social and labor inequalities,[9] agents constrained by structures of violence,[10] "bearers of cultural compliance,"[11] and individuals who shoulder "double" and "triple" burdens on their tea estates, in their communities, and in their homes.[12] Each of these descriptions represent Hill Country Tamil women on the tea plantations as carrying a weight—the weight of being strung up by patriarchal relations, the pressure of structural violence on their bodies, the burden of complying with the demands of their "culture," and the toll of maintaining commitments to their kith and kin. Human rights and media accounts about Hill Country Tamil women's experiences on the tea plantations follow similar representational modes. Statistics on maternal and infant mortality draw from quantitative research–based surveys, and individual stories are extracted as case studies from focus groups. Stories about Tamil women's being carried in the dozens by tea trucks to abandoned buildings to get sterilized against their will circulate and shock audiences with their exposures of abuse, rights violations, and stripped human agency. Public health officials report that female and male sterilizations—in the form of tubal ligations and vasectomies—are provided with monetary incentives of Rs. 500. Human rights activists and NGO workers then report that women and men favor this method of contraception, and that the economic transaction blurs the lines that distinguish force, informed consent, and choice.

These well-intended stories, too, have clear and objective ends to make a difference in Tamil women's lives and futures on the plantations: by asserting that women's rights have been violated and their reproductive futures cut short, the exposures of such grim realities aim to prevent them from happening again. The stories, however, do not explicitly discuss or present the experiences of those women who, postpartum, live with their incision wounds and blocked fallopian tubes; nor do they follow those women who continue to mother, pluck tea, and sustain their kin through their reproductive histories. Women's *desires*—the motivation or drive that opens, moves, and operates within women's bodies—seem to be more or less in the background of scholarly, rights-based, and feminist concerns, if not completely unacknowledged.[13]

In her essay "The Carrier Bag Theory of Fiction," Ursula Le Guin writes about the iterative process of human desire and its consequences as follows:

> If it is a human thing to do to put something you want, because its useful, edible, or beautiful, into a bag, or a basket, or a bit of rolled bark or leaf, or a net woven of your own hair, or what have you, and then take it home with you, home being another, larger kind of pouch or bag, a container for people, and then later on you take it out and eat it or share it or store it up for winter in a solider container or put it in the medicine bundle or the shrine or the museum, the holy place, the area that contains what is sacred, and then the next day you probably do much the same again—if to do that is human, if that's what it takes, then I am a human being after all. Fully, freely, gladly, for the first time.[14]

For Le Guin, a storyteller and novelist until her death, the carrier bag or sack was the best type of enclosure for stories that did not involve "heroes" or "killer stories" of violence, trauma, and violation that relied on some one person to save the day. Of the "killer story," she writes, "It is the story that makes the difference. It is the story that hid my humanity from me"; in contrast, she advocates for the "words of the other story, the untold one, the life story."[15] Even though Le Guin uses the carrier bag as a metaphor for the process of writing novels, there exist strong parallels between the traditional steps that a researcher takes when conducting research in cultural anthropology and Le Guin's theory of producing fiction. Field researchers are instructed to go to their respective fields, collect data, return home with their findings, and disseminate them for wider circulation and knowledge production. Cultural anthropology was built on a predominantly white, cisgender, male-dominated canon, and it is not a coincidence that "killer stories" dominated the ethnographic genre. These stories depicted the anthropologist as hero, the Native as Other, the powerless as voiceless. The traditional ethnographic form did not think about the extractive features of research, and only in the late 1990s did serious questions around the ethics and praxis of collaboration emerge. This history urges us to consider the following questions: If anthropologist-ethnographers are charged with telling stories, what kind of stories should they be telling and for whom? Is there another story beyond the killer story? Is there an alternative story that intervenes and moves but at the same time protects and restores humanity, rather than hiding it from the individuals whose stories are being told?

Cultural anthropologists in the decolonial turn know now that the production of scholarship within the anthropological canon has actively silenced and continues to silence teacher-scholars of color and intersectional perspectives that push for life stories beyond the heroics of representation and ethnographic production.[16] We also know that despite these structural inequalities and biases in citation practices, those scholars committed to an antiracist and decolonial praxis have brought forth and supported life stories and the use of methodologies that positively affect the ethnographic genre to which our profession adheres. These ethnographies conclude with potentials of transformation, places in transition, and futures unknown. They tell stories of imagined cities and aspirational moving bodies.[17] They present evidence of resilience and expansion amid loss and constriction.[18] They track the emergence of decentering publics around questions of visibility, creativity, and justice,[19] and they trace the movement of optimism, happiness, and possibility against backdrops of structural violence, racism, and patriarchy.[20] These stories have no single heroes. They describe innovation, which is a deceiving word these days, because in a sense it presumes a singular end, product, or achievement in a capitalist-technological sense. But in actuality, innovation requires multiple players, diverse reach, collaboration, connection, and human labor. These stories reach out not to move away from humanity. They embrace the unevenness of humanity, foreground collaboration, and write with an ethics of continuation rather than closure.

Sri Lanka's tea plantations and Hill Country Tamil women workers have yet to have their life stories told in such a way in cultural anthropology. Reviewing the "carrier bags" of knowledge produced about Hill Country Tamil women thus far, I found myself, like Le Guin, troubled by the absence of "life stories," with the exception Arasu's *Karuppi* and Sivamohan's *Ingiruthu*. "Killer stories" overwhelm the knowledge produced about Hill Country Tamil women's lives and long feature as the evidence of scientific and historical inquiry, development, and human rights discourse. Knowing the endings of these stories and qualitative and historical descriptions of Hill Country Tamil women fixed my a priori understandings of gender and labor practices on the plantations. But learning through ethnographic fieldwork with women on the plantations unfixed that knowledge. The stories they told me did not follow the instrumentalist narrative arcs of human rights and NGOs, where the end of the story (knowing or confirming the violation) justified the means (exposing and even shaming those violated in their defenses). Instead, women stood alongside, rationalized, and even spoke about their reproductive and life choices in sentimental terms. Troubled by these incommensurabilities, I struggled to share my fieldnotes about formerly only violating but now equally generative practices. I hesitated to characterize women's labor, their decisions, their desires—which they had valued and which had sustained their kin and bodies—as simple human rights violations, devoid of life and their bodily investments.

On the other hand, I would be lying if I said that I did not feel Siva's patriarchal stance as I approached him on the hill that day and that I did not hear the heaviness of grief and anxiety in Kāmāci's cries over Sadha's departure. But as a feminist anthropologist, I struggled to reproduce these experiences as only weight or burden through the ethnographic genre. The representation of weight alone would not do justice to, on one hand, the evident desire for movement that Hill Country Tamil women and their kin embody and inherit from their labor pasts and, on the other hand, their investments in futures in and beyond Sri Lanka. The absence of desire in former accounts of women workers left me wondering what methodologies could locate them and why they were missing from these records. I wondered how those stories would have been fuller and less flattened if women's desires had been the central focus of the story rather than their burdens. Would the shift from recording women's weight to recording women's desires make a difference in the lives of those whose stories were being retold, represented, and circulated?

This ethnography is committed to describing and recording such desires and, in doing so, explores specifically how privilege and positionality operate in the construction of former histories and accounts of Hill Country Tamils and Sri Lanka's tea plantations. Each chapter reminds readers that the struggle for dignity and equity on Sri Lanka's tea plantations and among Hill Country Tamils is ongoing and changing every day. The records and descriptions included in this monograph do not claim to be the only story of this community that has a long history of being misrepresented and stigmatized through negative stereotypes and subsequently marginalized through those narratives. In doing so, I remain committed to presenting what Hill Country Tamil women and men want to share about their lives, where they see themselves in Sri Lanka, and how they map their desires onto imperial, industrial, and national terrains of life and work.

The *Poiēsis* of Desire

On an individual level, humans map their desires to control their social relations, experiences, and futures. Desire guides human conduct and in turn urges the production of what Edward Fischer calls the "shared moral values [that] undergird economic systems."[21] Building on Max Scheler's concept of "becoming," I understand a human being to be a combination of "life-urge" and "spirit": the combining of these two forces is the manifestation of the movement from one place of being to becoming another, and the process never completes itself, but rather continues and keeps a human being human.[22] The mapping of such desires—with its unpredictabilities and diverse investments—is world making and has deep effects on the future of the Sri Lankan nation and economy in the postwar context. No longer wanting to be seen as "coolies," Hill Country Tamils are refusing to partake in agro-industrial relations and practices that signify their enclosure, and any analysis of the tea industry's contemporary economic crisis must take into account their motivations to move and be seen beyond this oppressive category.

This book argues that a process of unbecoming among Hill Country Tamils has been unfolding in Sri Lanka since the "coolie" began circulating as a viable category of labor and personhood. Personal and kin-based investments to not be seen as coolie challenge the coherence of the tea plantation as a socio-ecological form through what I call a *poiēsis* of desire. In "The Question Concerning Technology," Heidegger describes *poēisis* as the "bringing forth," "presencing," and "revealing" of something as it emerges from an enclosure.[23] To say that it is movement alone is not entirely accurate because the presence of the desire itself shifts how people think, the structures that enclose those desires in the first place, and the surrounding fields they enter. *Poiēsis* is sensed, observed, and above all resistant to reification. Embodying and enacting *poiēsis* takes skill (*technē*), or as Heidegger would write later, "*Technē* belongs to bringing-forth, to *poiēsis*; it is something poetic."[24] Skill and poetry constantly surfaced as themes in my research interactions with Hill Country Tamils and on the plantations. Children and students often wrote poetry or drew art in my fieldnote books, and I often heard men and women sing, whether during wage protests, cultural performances, religious festivals, home rituals, or to children before sleep. Each of these moments of poetry rested on the skills Hill Country Tamils had cultivated over time and had passed down through generations. Likewise, the rhetoric of the industry itself is poetic and passed down. It is strategically designed to maximize profit, and it features incremental adjustments made to sustain the tea plantation's alluring aesthetic of grandeur and success.

This ethnography is interested in how desire infuses the spatio-temporal dynamics of industry, residence, and work and how it moves in relation to its intended ends—that is, what people actually want and what it takes for them to fulfill their desires. On desire, Lauren Berlant writes, "[It is] less a drive that is organized by objects and more a drive that moves beyond its objects, always operating with them and in excess to them, with aims to both preserve and destroy them."[25] Desire, therefore, requires movement toward excess: we move past what we want and in relation to what we have. It is neither linear nor logical. Rather, it enmeshes its own subjects in contradictions, reversals, and, continually collaborative and contemplative moments.

Through *poiēsis* of desire, unbecoming coolie for Hill Country Tamils in Sri Lanka is a process of becoming a collective something not yet known. Unbecoming is polyvalent, in motion, and not yet complete. By operating in the worlding of plantation life and gendered labor relations in Sri Lanka, these desires are disrupting the story of Ceylon tea and are moving toward alternative futures of national and transnational solidarities. On the one hand, Tamil plantation residents and workers make public their refusal to give up their desires for mobility, place, and dignity and defy stereotypical narratives of their subordinated positions in Sri Lanka. On the other hand, this deconstructive work and their desires to detach from former and current narratives of patriarchy and labor present themselves as unbecoming and even unacceptable to Sri Lanka's tea plantation industry, which remains unprepared to meet their expectations at the expense of sustainability and profit accumulation. Unacceptability, refusal, and incommensurability are core features of Hill Country Tamils' attempts to secure their dignity.

This book also refuses to accept the neat, linear story of tea production in Sri Lanka. It uses *poiēsis* of desire to demonstrate how Hill Country Tamils value their work and how the struggles they engage in disrupt formerly accepted narratives of tea's success. Desires do not have clean or clear paths. They are messy, entangled in investments and inheritance, and difficult to track in relation to the objects of their pursuits. Likewise, writing ethnography is equally entangled, collaborative, and unclean. Most troubling about writing an ethnographic monograph is that it must end even though the stories and lives recorded are ongoing. The structure of what the anthropological canon puts forth as the standard and privileged ethnographic monograph demands that the author translate fieldwork experiences to text, take that which was experienced as moments of chaos, contradiction, and deficiency, and convert them into a single present continuum that is structured, rational, and sufficient. In doing so, ethnographers engage in the inevitable and required process of redaction and reduction; we manipulate time, taking someone's life and representing it in words, enclosing breaths in quotation marks, slicing experiences into vignettes, and splicing bodily experiences with the experiences of others' bodies across pages.

Responding to these demands, anthropologist Dick Powis reminds us that ethnographic research itself is "iterative" and not linear; it is not only "about writing but [also about] description, representation and record."[26] I use this perspective to frame my understanding of writing ethnography as a process that involves listening to individuals and getting their stories "right," but also taking heed that the "right" story may not fully or ever, for that matter, encompass that experience and often, may even be contradicted after an earlier confirmation.[27] This ethnography is interested in how scholars-of-color feminists, anthropologists, and activists can tell stories of work that interrogate and push the disciplinary commands of ethnography in the process. Such an ethnography—one that privileges, as Piya Chatterjee wrote in *A Time for Tea* in 2001, a "language of interruptions"—should no longer be considered experimental. It should be an ethical necessity and productive alternative when working with communities where extraction in work, life, and research is the established norm.

If the term *coolie* was and continues to be a colonial judgment, present form of oppression, and political assertion, an exploration of Hill Country Tamils' desires to move away from its frames may give us a more commensurable version of the story that Hill Country Tamils' themselves wish to tell and hear. Disrupting former narratives and representations of Hill Country Tamils and their labor reorients those willing to listen to narratives about gender and work on the plantations that move beyond binaries of structure, agency, compliance, and consent. My hope is that ethnography, in its urgent aspirations to disclose the contradictions of humanity, acknowledges the imperfections and implications of telling such a story of women's work—a story that is more than consumable, a story that refuses to end.

By reorienting the story of Hill Country Tamil women to foreground how their desires map onto the gender, reproductive, and labor relations of the tea plantations, I seek to make room for alternative forms of knowledge that interrogate how Sri Lanka's tea plantations have been researched and thought about. Responding to Kamala Visweswaran's call to recognize what kinds of knowledge get left out or do not make it into the anthropological canon in the first place, I follow South Asian feminist departures from the more traditional forms of ethnographic representation by examining the intimacies of intersectional violence and gendered forms of labor investment and inheritance.[28] I foreground the voicing of women's narratives about their desires as embedded in their kinship relations; the openness and visibility of their wounds; the unintentional exposures that accompany rights-based, political, and legal discourse and praxis; and women's refusals to settle the past injustices of their labor heritage.

Research Trajectories

From 2008 to 2009 I carried out twelve months of ethnographic research in Sri Lanka that coincided with the final months and immediate aftermath of Sri Lanka's twenty-six-year-long civil war. Between 2010 and 2012 I maintained contact with those who spoke with me during my initial field research period on the telephone and through social media and email when available, and then conducted six and a half months of research between 2013 and 2018 in the United States and in Sri Lanka on Kirkwall, in Colombo, and on tea plantations outside of Kandy and Hatton town.

In 2008 I spent one month in Colombo, where I collected development and historical documents and spoke to politicians, activists, government ministry officials, and NGO workers who were active in the plantation sector. While there, I was told that I would need to enter the tea estates with an NGO worker, which would be the best way to conduct long-term research. In this first month, I began to observe how NGOs were characterizing Hill Country Tamils and plantation life in both conversation and document-based records. I observed implicit caste- and class-based assumptions and judgments about Hill Country Tamils residing on the plantations; for those reasons, and given my own positionality as a Sri Lankan Tamil American woman whose own heritage and ancestors are implicated in the discrimination of Hill Country Tamils, I decided that I did not want to enter the estates with NGO workers, so I found a way to conduct research without an outsider or community leader escorting me.

I spent my second month of research in 2008 in Kandy, the second-largest city in Sri Lanka, located in Central Province. There I stayed in the quarters of a local plantation NGO that was one of the first of its kind in the estate sector. I participated and observed development and vocational trainings designed for a multi-ethnic rural and plantation Sinhala and Tamil youth and adults, and I met with other Kandy-based NGOs and unions that were working closely with other development actors in Sri Lanka on Hill Country Tamil plantation issues.

Following my stay in Kandy, I spent the next ten months (January–October 2009) conducting ethnographic field research in and around Hatton, a hill station town in Sri Lanka's Central Province and Nuwara Eliya district. Hatton sits at an elevation of 1,271 meters above sea level and is surrounded by tea plantations and various tourist spots. It joins with the smaller town of Dickoya under the Hatton-Dickoya Urban Council and is surrounded by RPC-owned tea plantations and a sizable number of privately owned smallholder plots, small hotels, banquet halls, and tea-drinking centers. In Hatton town I worked with local NGOs and community leaders, observing their development initiatives and participating in and observing workshops, seminars, and trainings for Hill Country Tamil plantation residents. I spent the rest of my time conducting ethnographic research among Hill Country Tamil plantation residents living on Kirkwall, one of four divisions of an estate on an RPC-owned tea plantation. In January 2009 I obtained permission from the then superintendent managing Kirkwall to conduct research on the RPC. Halfway through my initial research period he left his position, so I had to obtain a new letter from the incoming superintendent. Kirkwall estate division is approximately fifteen kilometers outside Hatton and about two hundred yards from where I stayed throughout the duration of my fieldwork. I made the conscious decision to live outside Hatton town so that I could be closer to the estates and maximize the amount of time I could spend there. The private and public buses, while regular every half hour during daytime hours, were not frequent at night, and I would often sleep in the homes of my interlocutors on neighboring plantations in Maskeliya, Norwood, Talawakelle, Kandy, and Hatton town or only come home either shortly before or well after dinner and sundown.

At the time of my initial research, Kirkwall was primarily composed of Hill Country Tamils, with the exception of a few Sinhala family

Table 1.1. *Available statistical data for Kirkwall division, 2008–2009*

Number of persons, sexes, and households	
Male	231
Female	249
Total persons	480
Total families	82
Total line rooms	107

Workforce (registered and casual)			
GENDER	RESIDENT	NONRESIDENT	TOTAL
Male	36	36	72
Female	88	53	141
Total	124	89	213

Source: Data were tabulated and given to author by Kirkwall staff at the end of January 2009.

members who were visiting the residences of their relations from time to time. When I began my fieldwork, the RPC management staff provided me the details from their records about the resident community (table 1.1).

Through community members and NGO workers, I also interacted with plantation residents and Hill Country Tamils in hill station towns and areas outside Hatton. Having witnessed the social and interactional shifts that took place among Hill Country Tamil tea plantation residents in the presence of NGO workers, I chose not to work with any escorting research assistants on Kirkwall.

Recording Life on a Tea Plantation

Emergency rule in the final months of war presented challenges for conducting field research among Tamil-speaking minorities with little to no legal assurances. The community has a long history of being suspected and questioned by security forces who doubted their loyalty to the

Sri Lankan majoritarian state and feared their support and sympathy for the LTTE. Between October 2008 and June 2009, checkpoints and cordon and searches were frequent, and during and after the war various security forces questioned me regularly as an outsider of Tamil descent. Additionally, while the state did not enforce any curfews in the Hill Country, I was advised not to travel alone after dark given the security situation and my own status as a foreign researcher and unmarried woman, and irrespective of the state of emergency, Hill Country Tamil girls and women do not usually travel alone on the road at night. Therefore, throughout my research in the Hill Country, interlocutors or known people always escorted me if traveling after dark.

Due to the heightened surveillance and state of emergency, I adjusted my research methodologies to further ensure the safety of my interlocutors. I did not conduct household surveys or collect statistical data regarding topics such as caste, marriage patterns, age breakdown, and health factors per household on Kirkwall as initially planned. After my first line of questioning by security forces, friends on Kirkwall and NGO workers in Hatton town told me that I should avoid any formal methodologies of obtaining data that could further compromise the security and safety of my worker and resident friends, and I agreed. Furthermore, the estate management asked me to not interfere with any industrial activities, which meant that I was prohibited from observing or participating in any work-related activities on site such as plucking, factory work, weeding, or accounting. Another limitation was that I also did not physically visit rubber and tea plantations in Sri Lanka's Mid and Low Country areas outside my research sites in Kandy, Gampola, Badulla, and Nuwara Eliya.

Doing this type of anthropological fieldwork under surveillance drew me toward more humanistic, decolonial, and feminist methodologies. I abandoned what I had learned earlier of the plantations and began asking the women, men, and families on Kirkwall what they wanted me to record and study. I asked them what they thought was important for me to know, and if they deemed a feature of their lives unimportant, they told me so. This was how I came to ask follow-up questions not on caste and household data, but about housing conditions, wages and debt, reproductive desires, individual labor histories, and livelihood choices. As a Tamil-speaking, non-male, cisgender woman of Sri Lankan descent, I engaged in gendered spaces and had conversations that were not ordinarily accessible to white-passing and foreign researchers and NGO workers. Much of my time was spent with workers and their families after hours and in their line room homes, kitchens, washing areas, verandas, and on worker footpaths. I conducted informal and unstructured interviews and almost always spoke with individuals while they were carrying out life activities such as breastfeeding, cooking, and cleaning. To honor the time the women and men spent with me as a researcher and what I recorded in their homes, I decided to focus on the residential and life spaces on the plantations and the features of plantation life that are often overlooked on industrial and quantitative levels. Between 2014 and 2018, I returned to Sri Lanka to conduct follow-up research on Kirkwall and with two of the NGOs I had connected with in my initial research period. These visits were quite different with respect to surveillance and security issues, as the Sri Lankan state eased certain restrictions of the wartime state of emergency regulations. In the Hill Country, the roadside checkpoints were lifted and I experienced no formal types of questioning from security forces. Nevertheless, to remain committed to the relationships and rapport that I had cultivated on Kirkwall and with community members, I continued to avoid the more traditional, survey-based forms of data collection and opted for less conventional methodologies that I will detail below. More important, between 2014 and 2017, I was able to see individuals, relationships, houses, and spaces change over time. My decision to focus on oral and life histories rather than the more quantitative or traditional case studies is a conscious choice to resist reproducing or reinforcing the imperial and industrial calculus of the industry—where wages, check rolls, and surveillance dominate everyday life and labor practices. In doing so, I am interested in foregrounding a practice of what Kim TallBear calls "inquir[ing] in concert with," so as to disclose what might be learned through relationships with individuals in engaged research over time.[29]

Research Methodologies and Data Analysis

Throughout my research, I primarily used the following methodologies: (1) interviewing; (2) participant observation; (3) body mapping and sketching; (4) photography; (5) one collaborative survey with NGO youth participants; and (6) archival document collection and analysis.[30] I conducted the majority of the research for this book in Tamil, a language I grew up hearing and speaking but in a different dialect from the dialect spoken by Hill Country Tamils. I had formally studied written and spoken Tamil in educational institutions in the United States and South India prior to 2008, so with the dialect spoken among Hill Country Tamils different from the one I had learned, I used the adjustments I had to make to build deeper connections with my interlocutors. During my research, I sparingly used a digital handheld audio recording device unless I felt comfortable enough to do so and or I was speaking with public figures such as politicians and union leaders. If I did use a recording device, I asked for verbal consent and kept the unit visible at all times. For the transcription of audio recordings into Tamil script, I hired two research assistants, both Hill Country Tamil women from the plantations; however, both women did not escort me to the plantations or in my field research activities for the reasons noted above.

For participant observation and all other methods apart from my time in the archives, I took "jottings" in a small notebook: it was a less-invasive recording technique, not as distracting, and a notebook and pen were easy to carry around, especially during walks and public events and in families' homes and more intimate spaces.[31] The technique also allowed me to be more fully immersed in my surroundings and conversations. In my jottings, I noted sensory details, emotional expressions, and language, including direct dialogue, reported speech, colloquialisms, phrases, and words that were repeated and the timing of those repetitions. I noted what emotions those words would accompany, bodily gestures and interactions between individuals, and group dynamics. I also jotted general impressions of my surroundings, how I was feeling, and when I was sensitive to new or repetitive power dynamics and gestures. Lastly, I often reflected on the fact that I was a visitor during a period of heavy surveillance in Sri Lanka as well as on the casual and everyday optics and nature of surveillance, what those dynamics brought out in the interactions of the people around me, and how they influenced my own methodological choices and limitations.

From those jottings, I generated typed and handwritten full fieldnotes and re-created dialogue through direct and indirect quotations, reported speech, and paraphrasing. Because I often stayed with people in their homes, using my laptop was not always possible, so I relied mostly on handwritten notes that I then typed and annotated with integrative and expanded memos. Throughout the recording process and to enhance my own understandings of what I was documenting, I would regularly and often ask my interlocutors for clarification. My analysis process was fairly traditional; I used open and focused coding to identify emergent themes. In 2014 I was able to bring those identified themes back to the people I had engaged during my initial research, and each chapter title and focus came from those collaborative conversations and the interplay of shared open and focused codes and theme selections.

Like jottings, photography was an integral part of my research experience and methodological approach to this study. My use of photography was not expert in any way, but it roughly followed the outlines of cultural anthropologist Ryan Anderson's methodological uses of the camera in fieldwork.[32] I used photographs to trigger my memory and fill in gaps in my jottings and fieldnotes, especially during high-activity moments such as participation in rituals, festivals, walk-alongs with community members on the plantations, and public events, and to also collect larger amounts of data from documents such as land deeds, flyers, handouts, and wage slips in shorter amounts of time. I often took solicited photographs and gave them to families as gifts for the time they took to speak with me, and I photographed residential spaces such as line room houses over time in order to track changes in the architecture and areas surrounding living dwellings. Lastly, I used photographs as a form of elicitation in my conversations and interviews, most specifically in oral histories and group interviews with families or community members. My employment of photographs prompted me to think more closely about the connections between the desired aesthetics of the plantation landscape and the ways Hill Country Tamils themselves wanted to be seen by those around them in Sri Lanka and in their communities. I paid attention to how photographs came to stand in for aspirational ideals of presenting oneself, as in my taking of portraits and bridal photographs, and how the aesthetic orderings of the tea plantations were depicted visually in the archives and marketing of Ceylon tea to visitors and local Sri Lankans alike.

Visual ways of knowing also extend to more embodied and sensory ways of knowing. During fieldwork, I used body mapping, drawing, and the analysis of art to capture the experiences and aspirations in ways beyond what the spoken word affords. Informed by an attention to what the somatic senses reveal, in what Laura Ellingson calls "embodied knowing," I also used my own body to understand the sensorium of plantation life—changes in my muscles from prolonged periods of cold and dampness, sinus infections from the changes in the climate and air pressure, the impact of stress from being questioned and monitored by security forces at the end of the war, my balance and proprioception while standing on crowded buses, the feeling of walking barefoot in the mud or on slippery or sharp stone paths, and the experience of infections and swellings in my skin from leech bites.[33] Because illness and health concerns were common themes that surfaced in the lives of many Hill Country Tamils I worked with, attention to embodiment was integral to my understanding of how laboring and caring bodies become carriers and signifiers of workers' desires and aspirations for physical and emotional security.

As described above, I initially used methodologies that resisted quantitative measurements, but when I returned to Sri Lanka in 2014 I began to think about what I could understand by putting different types of measurements—quantitative, humanistic, archival, embodied, expressive—into conversation with one another, and to consider what Linda Tuhiwai Smith calls the "five conditions . . . that help map the conceptual terrain of struggle": (1) an attention that social change must take place; (2) a "reimagining" of the world based on the deployment of different and not always tapped forms of knowledge; (3) attention to the "intersecting" conditions that allow social change to thrive and take hold; (4) the tracking of the "unstable movements that occur when the status quo is disturbed"; and (5) an understanding of the conditions of power that validate and perpetuate marginality.[34] I became interested in placing forms of knowledge that I took from archival and document-based research and more official records of plantation life and work alongside and against imagined, humanistic, and embodied expressions of struggle and aspiration. I did this intentionally to see how such unexpected intersections could produce new ways of disturbing the continuum of power that perpetuates social inequalities for Hill Country Tamils on the plantations.

The chapters that follow tend to these five conditions, knowing that when taken together, they are not the only narrative of Sri Lanka's tea plantations or Hill Country Tamils. The individuals with whom I spoke had no reason to talk to me and should have been fatigued and uninterested by my persistent presence and questions; but to my surprise they were not. As researchers rightly stated in 2008, Sri Lanka's tea plantations are overstudied places. But somewhere amid the nostalgia for tea and empire—Hill Country Tamils, and women workers specifically, had desires they wanted to share. These desires did not have clean endings—they were often messy, contradictory, and entangled in structures and histories of oppression—but they were productive alternatives that I chose to follow in concert with and alongside their storytellers. When acknowledged for what they are, and where they can potentially and creatively lead an industry, nation, and research experience, these desires have the potential to disrupt and discomfort those who are not ready to hear them play out; but they also attend to those disruptions with alternatives more commensurable with what Hill Country Tamils in Sri Lanka want for their futures in the long run.

CHAPTER 2

Unfixing Language and Landscape

CLUTCHING OUR UMBRELLAS, SELLAMMA AND I WALKED IN silence along the muddy section of a worker footpath lining Kirkwall. The nearly two weeks of steady rain had made our trek uneven. Wearing only our rubber slippers, we had to mostly look down at the path immediately before our feet in order to navigate the larger puddles and sharper rock edges that had emerged from the eroding soil. It was a little after noon and the path was mostly deserted, as those who had worked that morning had gone home for lunch. We came to a higher elevation and clearing in the viewpoint over the dam that made me look up. I caught sight of some red and green coffee berries on four overgrown coffee bushes, now looming over the horizon as trees, and they lined the perimeter of tea bushes planted below us. I stopped walking, and Sellamma stopped and looked back at me.

"Who is this coffee for?" I asked. "Only the manager [*durai*] and accountant [*kanakupillai*] pick it," she replied. "They roast it and sometimes mix it with the tea for themselves." I told her that I had never tried a raw coffee berry before. She plucked a few ripened red ones and peeled two of them for us to eat. The pulp around the bean was sticky and slightly tart. Next to the coffee trees were some overgrown and untended tea bushes.

I remarked that the bushes seemed taller and the tea leaves darker than what I was used to seeing in the fields. She motioned to them and remarked in disgust, "This place is turning into a forest" (*Intat tōttam oru kādu pōyirum*). She instinctively began plucking the darker tea leaves off some of the overgrown bushes that lined the edge of the path. As she plucked I continued to watch, and then I felt compelled to ask her which leaves she knew to pluck and how. She then began to pluck differently.

She plucked with speed—this time avoiding the older, darker green leaves and taking only the younger green ones, holding their bottoms between her thumbs and index fingers as she plucked.

After about thirty seconds she remarked, "You see this?" holding up the hard stem below one green leaf she had just plucked. "That is not okay [to pluck]. It should be discarded." "Why is it not okay?" I asked. "That one is hard" (*Atha mūttu*), she said, pointing emphatically with her index finger to the stem. She continued to pluck. When she finished, she let the leaves fall to the ground on the side of the path, and we continued our walk in the rain.

Language, Wants, and Industrial Ends

In 1878, member of the Royal Asiatic Society of Great Britain and Ireland Alastair Mackenzie (A. M.) Ferguson published the book *"Iṅgē Vā!"; or, The Sinna Durai's Pocket Tamil Guide.*[1] The guide was designed to aid English-speaking plantation assistant superintendents with pronouncing, understanding, and communicating with Tamil coolies working and living on the coffee and tea estates. I came across the book in its fourth edition, published in 1902 and fully revised and updated to reflect the cultural contours and demands of both industries. The section titled "Tea" presents a collection of nouns and verbs, unique to the actions that take tea from leaf to packaged good. The transliterated Tamil nouns and verbs, alongside their respective English meanings, appear in their colloquial forms and are spelled in English with romanized Tamil pronunciations. Following the list of words are collections of curated phrases that relate specifically to actions and content concerning the subject heading and incorporating the word list. In this section I encountered transliterated Tamil phrases akin to the plucking instructions Sellamma had repeated to me during our walk:

> Do not take hard leaves—Muttha elei edukkāthē
> Do not bring in four-leaved stalks—Nāl elei kambu konduvara wānda . . .
> Pluck only the green young leaves—Pachchei ilang kolunthu mātthiram edu[2]

Muṇḍā and Dravidian Languages, volume 4 of the *Linguistic Survey of India* (1906), lists Ferguson's *"Iṅgē Vā!"* as one of three colloquial Tamil guides published for the management staffs of Ceylon's coffee and tea planting industries. The other two, preceding the publication of *"Iṅgē Vā!"* were Rev. William Clark's *Hand-Book of Tamil for the Use of Coffee Planters* (1876) and Abraham Joseph's *The Planters' Colloquial Tamil Guide in Roman and Tamil Characters* (1872), both published in Madras. Proliferating from the mid-eighteenth century onward, these guides follow, with few significant exceptions, the Ollendorff method of learning living languages, which itself was adapted from the language pedagogy of the French transnational language instructor Jean Manesca, author of the 1834 volume *An Oral System of Teaching Living Languages*.[3]

Manesca advocated that when learning foreign languages, non-native speakers should mirror the way native speakers acquired their mother tongues: "Now, if there were a process through which the acquisition of a foreign language can be rendered easy, safe, and certain, it must be the process which nature follows in teaching us our mother tongue; for it cannot be doubted that she adopts the best means to attend her ends."[4] Manesca's "nature" was instrumental and pragmatic, and following it presented efficient conditions under which one could pursue a safe means to an assured end. Manesca deepens his justification further when he describes how the method mirrors children's language acquisition: "Do children learn their mother tongue by whole sentences? Is such the process of nature? No. Children's wants are simple, indivisible, indefinable, while whole phrases are compound, divisible, and definable."[5] If one was to take on the task of using language as a means to an end, one would need to first abandon the wholeness of the end and begin by breaking that end down to something more manageable—something more doable and certain.

His justification brought me back to Sellamma, the overgrown coffee trees, the neglected tea bushes, and the instructions she had recited. Through mastering and communicating in the language of the Tamil coolie, Ceylon's planters thought they were producing and practicing a means to an industrial end—to sustain a coherent and successful tea industry built on a resident and docile labor force. To do this, they went back to "nature" in language and practice. They took what was simple and "indivisible" and strove to give the Tamil language a presence on a definable and divisible plantation landscape. But were their methods of learning the language of Hill Country Tamil workers effective?

As I walked through Sellamma's tea estate that day, I saw that their strategy had not been as safe, easy, and certain as planned. Apart from concerted efforts to maintain the colonial nostalgia of Sri Lanka's Hill Country, today's tea plantation—when seen from within those divisibilities—does not reflect that imagined landscape. In fact, it looks quite different and incoherent—uneven footpaths, errant coffee berries, and obvious work shortages of full-time resident employees due to low wages and the stigmatization of estate labor and life. The planters' strategy of commanding and mastering the Tamil laborer through her own dialect and language—while it had measured successes in sustaining a now 150-year-old industry—was also marked by moments of rupture, doubt, and uncertainty from its inception.

This chapter looks closely at the written representations of the Tamil coolie languages and landscapes that are essential to the industry's national and global image. I examine how Tamil coolies in Ceylon came to be represented and understood in relation to both their spoken language and the industrial lands on which they resided and worked. Early written and visual records of the coffee and tea estates present the Tamil coolie as a labor commodity instrumental to the industry's success. Two features of plantation life drove this: the coolie was a labor commodity that could at once be controlled through spoken Tamil language, and the coolie was "natural labor," fixed to the plantation for the industrial ends of efficiency and profit. But on closer examination, both the language and landscape of the plantations were more unstable than the industry could have anticipated. When spoken by planters, the coolie Tamil language not only failed to fully silence Tamil workers but also failed to fully grasp the nuances of their aspirations to live beyond the planter's ideas about their future and place on the island. These industrial failures—ones that rely on instrumentality and the fragile operations of language and image-making—signify what anthropologist James Scott calls "weapons of the weak," those "everyday acts of resistance" we may miss when we focus on larger, more attention-attracting forms of protest or refusal.[6] They also foreshadow how features of coolie labor endure and resurface long after colonial rule and in the language of the contemporary tea industry as it manages an ongoing agro-economic crisis.

Despite the linguistic collapse of personhood into payment, plantation laborers in colonial Ceylon did speak, and what they said disturbed the category of the coolie as a silenced commodity. Beyond each document's stated objectives of controlling and punishing a profitable coolie labor force, the language used to command Tamil coolies reveals that planters and colonial agents were intimately aware of Tamil workers' desires to move "beyond the indenture contract."[7] The transliterated and translated speech acts that Tamil coolies utter tell us much about those desires, the industry's refusal and struggle to meet workers' needs, and the consequences of such refusals as evident in its failure to sustain a stable and profitable coolie labor force. These unstable representations constitute the unfixing of the Sri Lankan tea plantation's imperial imaginary.

Discomforting Teascapes

One of the more assertive colonial representations of Tamil coolies comes from D. M. Forrest's *A Hundred Years of Ceylon Tea* (1967), a commemorative volume dedicated to the first hundred years of tea production in Ceylon. Forrest seldom wrote of the tea plantation workers, but one passage addressed their presence on the landscape:

> The Tamil who made the long journey from his South Indian home found an environment suited to him and a standard of living which, simple as it was, surpassed in most respects what he could have hoped for in his native village. He and his wife and children enjoyed the field-work and stuck to it well, . . . looking, as an early observer noted, "like a flock of dark sheep grazing." . . . What we have seen . . . is the emergence, after all the storms and setbacks, of the typical Ceylon tea estate as a go-ahead, prosperous, and (in Victorian terms) well-balanced community.[8]

Representations of the content plantation laborer continue to "stick" today—on placards, images of women workers with their heads covered and hands in a welcoming prayer gesture stand among tea bushes to greet travelers in Colombo's international airport. Visitors to the Hill Country, Sri Lankan and non–Sri Lankan alike, often consider the plantation landscape a representational schema of colonial indulgence. Tourists trek through the plantations and watch Tamil women pluck tea leaves, never interacting with them or asking them about their lives and families. These idealized constructions aim to keep the Hill Country Tamil silent and, in Forrest's sense, a toiling, machinelike animal—a mere fixture on the landscape. Likewise, the scale of the rolling, green hills and contours of perfectly manicured tea bushes encourage spectators' appetites for the colonial aesthetics of control and beauty. On December 7, 2016, Condé Nast published the travel piece *Condé Nast Traveler*, in which author Andrew Solomon remarked on the pleasing aesthetics of taking in the tea country: "We spent two nights at Ceylon Tea Trails, with handsome bungalows above a picturesque dam-made lake. It is rather politically incorrect to be nostalgic for colonialism, but if anything is going to tempt you down that problematical path, it is this establishment, at once simple and gracious, with delicious curries, an elegant, old-fashioned tea with scones and finger sandwiches and cakes, highly personalized service by white-coated butlers, and a panoramic, undulating vista."[9]

Just as the tourist's framing of an image focuses on or excludes the Native Other, the pervasive sense of imperial nostalgia in Sri Lanka's Hill Country provides an open palette to allow visitors to selectively consume images that seldom speak against the colonial ideal. With industrial conceptions of community rooted in territoriality and place, planters and government administrators employed disciplinary tactics intended to make laborers at once mobile and immobile to suit the needs of the plantation economy.

They also aimed to create a resident group of laborers that would be at once bound to the plantation labor regime and its so-called affordances. But this ideal did not consider the reality that its members had always resented the hierarchical structure through which this concept of community had been imagined. Nor did the model of production account for the effects of postcolonial ethnic strife and economic liberalization, both of which would further destabilize the plantation enclave concept. Working within contradictions of fixedness and instability, social relations based on individual and corporate commitments and entitlements took shape and manifest in cultural practices observable today: individuals assume their roles and responsibilities as marked by gender, caste, and labor status; line rooms were built and maintained; and tea leaves were plucked, bagged, and sent to factories for production. Through this shared history of work and life as a Tamil-speaking ethnic minority, Hill

Country Tamil community on the plantations—in the formal understanding of the term—came to be.

From structuralist studies of caste[10] and kinship on the estates[11] to the broader cultural accounts of religion and politics, anthropologists have long located Hill Country Tamils in one place—physically on the plantations or displaced from their motherland India.[12] However, Hill Country Tamils residing on the plantations never fully accepted the purchase of labor security afforded by management.[13] Former scholars likened the plantations to Goffman's "total institution," and for them it was within these contained but contiguous spaces of labor and residence that Hill Country Tamils made their life choices.[14]

But more recent scholars and community members find it neither practical nor realistic to fully extend Goffman's concept to Sri Lanka's plantations.[15] Hill Country Tamil estate residents regularly partake in domestic and transnational migrant labor and utilize global communication technologies that make them very much a part of Sri Lanka's broader civil society despite their marginal status. Shifts from nationalization to privatization between 1972 and 1991 had direct effects on their community practices, livelihoods, and economic choices, and they have been citizens since 2003. Given their entitlements to receive benefits relating to language rights, free education, and government-run health services, to eclipse these realities—as the total institution concept tends to do—detracts attention from the agentive ways the community strategizes about their future in Sri Lanka and the systemic and nationalist undercurrents of the dispossession they experience. While it is worth exploring the idea of how living in a space with sustained institutional rule and no barriers might influence residents' choices and movements, what might happen if we look beyond Goffman's concept in order to foreground a far-reaching idea of community that accounts for minorities' insecurities and risks against the backdrop of the plantation and its excesses?

Hill Country Tamil community breathes and survives in the plantation's unanticipated excesses and its not so readily conceivable consequences of agro-economic production. The local community is very much on the move; it is neither static nor bounded, but dynamic and unfixable. That being said, the entrenchment of plantation institutions in colonial structures of power and domination makes it impossible to disregard the foundational "modes of response" that characterize tea plantation life.[16] These responses exhibit shared interests and experiences that bind Hill Country Tamils to one another in corporate membership and a sense of mutual obligation, entitlement, and responsibility. Given their place within Sri Lanka's broader heritage of coolie labor, their shared interests are simple: a desire for dignified recognition, survival, and place in Sri Lanka for themselves and their families. This sense of community directly informs and foregrounds the "adjustment and aspirations" of their once coolie, now minority worker community, and the continuity of their communal interests is sustaining the social and ecological crisis of Sri Lanka's tea industry. Under such conditions of labor and life, Hill Country Tamils move, work, and invest, and the tea plantation and postwar state of affairs present shifting landscapes on which the community can continually map the practical bearings of their desires.

Entrenched in systems of capital, the labor regime's control over bodily movements produced actualized consequences for the ways Hill Country Tamils perceive their worth and sense of belonging on the plantations. Quite contrary to what D. M. Forrest wrote in 1967, contemporary tea estate workers are not "sticking to the field-work well." Unsatisfied with and unable to survive on estate daily wages, younger generations of Hill Country Tamils seek to pursue alternative job opportunities off the estate that are financially more lucrative but often less secure physically and emotionally. With the language and landscape of the plantation breaking down due to the absence of labor and desire, the following sections closely examine moments where the Tamil coolie speaks and is represented in the archive, in the hope of seeing what the industry and those who so desired to sustain the plantation ideal may have missed.

The Coolie, Unsilenced

In 1902 Ceylon, an English-speaking assistant superintendent would have been given the following Tamil words in the opening pages of Ferguson's *"Iṅgē Vā!"* to help him control his labor force:

Name—pēr
Do full—mulu pēr

Do half—arei pēr

Person—āl

Speak—pēsu

Silent (be)—Pēsathē, pēsamaliru, vāypotthu[17]

In the pages to follow, he is able to elaborate on these simple words by using Manesca's methodology. Building on the Tamil word for "person" (*āl*), he could learn how to ask, "How many men have you brought?—Eththanei āl kūttu konduvanthāy?"[18] Expanding on "name" (*pēr*), he could learn how to ask, "How many men are digging?—Etthanei pēr vetrathu?" if in a situation involving road construction or field clearing. But the lessons and applications of the words are not consistent. Often times, *āl* and *pēr* are used interchangeably across gender, with no details as to when or if it is appropriate to address a woman or man in that particular context. Furthermore, specific Tamil definition entries for the English word "man" and "woman" directly contradict previous uses of *āl* and *pēr* in former hypothetical questions or statements. For instance, the English word "man" is broken down further into the categories of "male" (*āmbalē, manushan*) and "person" (*āl*), but the English word "woman" remains indivisible as either *pombalē* or *pomanātti*.[19]

The transliterated Tamil entries for the verb "Silent (be)" are also striking. As the only verb in the entire text that has three separate transliterated Tamil options, each of the three transliterations bears a different literal and contextual translation from the other. But the guide makes no mention of these nuances. In context, *pēsāthē* translates to "do not talk" and contextually is a negative imperative that commands one to not speak in the moment. *Pēsamaliru* is either transliterated incorrectly or printed in error, as the correct transliteration should be *pēsāmaliru*, since the long *ā* is a negative signifier meaning "without." This verb, when spoken, translates to "be (there) without speaking" or "do not say anything" and is more polite, meant for someone you care about or to whom you are close. Lastly, *vāypotthu* translates to "shut your mouth" or "shut up." Like *pēsāthe*, it is a powerful command; indexing the mouth, it suggests that the addressee has been talking too much.[20]

Such entries and idiomatic phrases reveal how industrial modes of instrumentality—and by extension, the project of living language learning—were deeply flawed, contradictory, and ambiguous in their delivery and content. Take, for instance, the following hypothetical exchange with a laborer regarding pay negotiations over picking coffee:

"I'll give cash for over two bushels—Rendu busalukku mēle (edutthāl) kei kāsi koduppēn."

"Sir, if we have to take two bushels to get our name, we must go to Haputale, for there's precious little coffee elsewhere—Eiyā, pērukku rendu busal edukka vēnum ānāl Apputhalē pakkam pōha vēnum, yēn endāl vērē pakkatthilē kōppi sutthamāy kedeiyāthu."

"Chu! Shut up!—Chi! Vāy potthu!"[21]

This scripted exchange is striking in three ways. First, it demonstrates that the idea of the wage, much like the idea of the laborer as a person, was conceivably and actively negotiated and contested between laborers and their planter employers. Here, the planter attempts to bargain with the laborer for *kei kasi* or "money in the hand"—a wage supplement for anything picked over two bushels. The laborer's response is to reference not only the valuation of his labor (i.e., two bushels to have a name), but also the reality that what the planter is offering is not only monetarily unappealing but also industrially unrealistic on the said estate. Second, the laborer tells the planter that he "must go" (*pōha vēnum*), confirming that movement again was a stable feature of the industry, but also that planters anticipated and knew this. Third, the exchange ends with the desire to "silence" the coolie. But upon reading the effective shutdown *Vāy potthu!*, the phrase's effective force is unconvincing; even if uttered from this rehearsed exchange off the page, all "Shut up!" tells the reader is that the planter refused to accept what the coolie had to say. The planter's commanding of the coolie to shut up, while maybe successful in silencing him then and there, may not have been strong enough to remove the laborer's discontent with the payment and convince him to stay on the estate.[22] In the guides, the presence of the dissatisfying wage, or *kūli* (without necessarily writing or saying *kūli*), tells us more about how traces of simmering discontent and anxiety were embedded in the rifts of the plantation and its language of control.

Planters' refusals to hear laborers' desires and plans also surfaced in their referencing of the landscape. In the guide, a common command when a planter suspected idleness, resistance, or mockery from a worker was to "send her to the lines," and this command appears for both men and women laborers who were perceived as disrupting the plantation order. In the exchange below, this type of command appears in the context of a woman standing "idle" in the road:

Who's that laughing? "Sirikrath'ār? Laughs who?"
Send her to the lines. "Lāythukku pōha sollu. To the lines go tell."[23]

The exchange suggests that the planters did not think of the line room as anything but a punitive space. On the one hand, to send a woman to the lines was to send her home without pay as punishment; on the other hand, to send a woman to the lines was to send her to her home, to her family, relations, and neighbors, in whose company she would most likely continue to laugh but more importantly strategize about how to live. What is telling is that the planter, in being instructed in coolie Tamil to shut down the conversation, is not afforded the opportunity to understand *why* she is laughing. His command of "sending her to the lines" is both punitive *and* negligent; it succeeds in momentarily purifying the plantation landscape visible to him but, in doing so, contributes to the building of community and worker solidarity among Tamil residents. What the planters failed to acknowledge was that Hill Country Tamils' attachments to the landscape did not include the industry's aspirations but rather the labor- and place-driven aspirations of a worker community building their lives in Ceylon.

Natural Labor, Unfixed

Alongside coolie language learning, planters and industrial stakeholders also perpetuated myths of the laborers' attachment or nonattachment to the land in other writings. In his 1880 private diary, Alfred Duncan, a British coffee planter in Central Province, details a story about Karupen, his Tamil "beef coolie," the name given to a male Hill Country Tamil laborer whose job it was to walk with a wooden chest on his head to carry beef, other meats, and assorted luxuries to and from hill station towns and the superintendents' private bungalows on the plantations. In the entry "My Beef Coolie," Duncan narrates Karupen's story as follows:

I find that my beef coolie is a man of great determination of character and not to be trifled with. . . . In a quiet part of the road a Singhalese man of unprepossessing appearance, suddenly appeared before him, and ordered him to set down the box whilst he inspected the contents and [to] choose therefrom those things which would be agreeable to his wife and little ones. The beef coolie was compelled to submit, but it would appear that, when taking the box down from off his head, he launched it forward, striking the Singhalese man with great violence on the face, and actually bearing him to the ground with the force and weight thereof. . . . Karupen seized the stick which he always carried in his journeys, with both hands, and began to batter the ruffian. . . . In telling me of his adventure, Karupen said he thought it would be as well if I gave him a pruning knife, to carry along with him. . . . I have given him the knife, and I feel confident that my beef and bread will be defended by Karupen to the last. . . . It is almost needless for me to remark that, after finishing the account of his adventure, the worthy man smiled upon me and asked for some *vepunuy* and *chelvai kasie*, and it is also almost useless to say that neither money nor margosa oil were given by me on the occasion. Karupen has been many years with me, and the roof of his head has now a hard bump on it from constantly carrying a heavy beef box. He speaks of paying a short visit to his country this spring, but, when the time comes, I do not think that he will have the heart to entrust my provision box to another.[24]

For Duncan, Karupen gained "just notoriety" through an act committed as a laborer not in the intimate enclosures of the planter's bungalow or the carefully monitored coffee fields, but in the public market—a space he was compelled to enter as a worker. The norms of handling stranger sociality apply in such unenclosed spaces of labor, and these spaces were not off-limits to coolies given their journey from South India and well-documented internal migrations between estates, to Colombo, and abroad as accompanying domestic labor. What Duncan omits in his representation is that Karupen knew well the norms of navigating public spaces in Ceylon; his own knowledge constituted not only his labor but also his sense of being and his desires to make claims to and in Ceylon. Instead, Duncan confines his laborer's desires to his labor alone and confidently claims that he would want to stick to his job. But even he himself recalls that the hardship of being the beef coolie stuck to the bodies of those workers who performed the required tasks.

The hardship of the beef coolie would come up again in Mary E. Steuart's *Every Day Life on a Ceylon Cocoa Estate* (1905). Steuart, the wife of a coffee planter, describes the following instance when a beef coolie who was meant to travel and bring the goods from Kandy town refused to carry out the task:

> Later in the evening one of those scenes took place which are the perpetual worry of a planter's life. A cooly has to go twice a week into Kandy to fetch our provisions, which he has to carry home on his head in a ventilated tin box. The orders are all written by us in a book called a "beef book," this he takes with him. Obviously we must have food, but we are sixteen miles from Kandy, the nearest market, and it is not an enviable task to walk thirty-two miles returning with a heavy load, and the coolies much dislike it. On this particular evening the "beef coolie" flatly declined to go, and threw the beef book on the floor of the kitchen. Of course, such a breach of discipline could not be allowed. My son was told, he sent for the delinquent, who could not be found in his Lines. Messenger after messenger, having been dispatched without any result, at last Rob said, "Well, if he doesn't come to-night he will be punished much more severely tomorrow."
>
> Soon after he appeared having been hiding in the branches of a jak tree. Needless to say, he was punished, and ended like a naughty child in being very repentant, and saying he would never refuse to go again. These natives have to be treated exactly like children, and managed with a perfectly just, but very strict rule, they take advantage at once of any laxity of discipline and only respect a firm hand. They appear never to resent punishment when their conscience tells them they deserve it.[25]

Like Duncan's, Steuart's narrative misses key features of Hill Country Tamils' desires by correlating workers' receiving their punishments with loyalty and acceptance. Like Duncan, she, too, acknowledges the beef coolie's hardships and even witnesses his public resistance and refusal. But as the worker refuses, she underestimates him and reduces him and the other "natives" to children, making them more divisible and alienated from their actual conscience, such that they would believe they deserved the punishment. By making coolies more divisible and alienated from their social relations and more fixed to their oppression, both Duncan and Steuart fail to see how workers' desires exceed the limited scope of language that workers shared with their employers.

While these intimate coolie narratives misrecognized their desires, other colonial depictions were struggling to fix the coolie to the natural landscape. In 1900 Henry W. Cave, member of the Royal Asiatic Society, published *Golden Tips: A Description of Ceylon and Its Great Tea Industry*. The volume comprises twenty-five chapters that detail the geographic bounds of Ceylon's tea industry on the island, but only two deal exclusively with tea production and one with the life of the Tamil laborer, titled "The Tamil Coolie." Cave begins the chapter with the usual euphemistic description of Hill Country Tamils' migration and eventual settlement in Ceylon. But the passage soon takes a peculiar turn as Cave describes future generations of Tamil coolies:

> Now that children have been found to be well fitted for the work of leaf plucking he finds it useful to preserve his progeny, and little brown urchins of both sexes from the age of five earn their ten and twelve cents a day. . . . These children if not reared upon tea are indeed brought up amongst the bushes. No sooner are they born than they accompany their mothers in the work of plucking. It is an amusing spectacle for the stranger to see them, literally small gangs of suckling humanity basking in the sun upon mother earth, or upon the cumblies of their parents spread out for them upon the estate paths, or amongst the bushes where the work of plucking is going on . . . these small details of native life have their bearings on the future prosperity of the industry, however trivial they may seem.[26]

Accompanying the description is a grainy photograph captioned, "Small gangs of suckling humanity." In the image's foreground, four infants and toddlers are positioned on what appears to be cumblies (blanketlike cloaks) on a dirt path much like the one on which Sellamma and I had walked. Seven women workers stand amid tea bushes in the background. One woman holds a small child dressed in white, and other women stand alone as they balance wooden baskets on their covered heads. In the worlding of plantation life, Tamil women and their children are presented as natural and fixed labor, and this mythical entanglement of life and labor was critical to the ways planters and those observing plantation and coolie life sought to justify the means to their industrial ends. Cave places women laborers and their children at the intersection of nature and humanity. Production of life on the plantations was the production of laboring life. Reminiscent of Manesca's methodology of returning to the simple and indivisible in order to master and control, such details were critical to the industry's future success. Babies became "little brown urchins" raised among the bushes, and plantation labor was their destiny. Their wages, like their bodies, were divisible to the smallest degree. However, such a planned fate and industrial end were neither assured nor certain, and Cave claims that it is the aspiration of the laborer that in fact would lead to the demise of the plantation industry:

> It must be born in mind that a little too much education and unaccustomed luxury would unfit these children for their calling, or indeed for anything. Freedom they will always enjoy under British rule; but a just and almost paternal control, and a hand almost sparing in the direction of philanthropy are best suited to their needs. . . . The ill-advised provision for the poor in England above referred to is perhaps not quite analogous, but its effect was the destruction of industrial self-sufficiency. The outcome of treating the Tamil estate labourer in like manner, too considerately, would be laziness and industrial degeneracy.[27]

For Cave, the coolie way of life promised "freedom" and therefore was a right to be enjoyed. In a technical sense, planters separated coolies from the enslaved on this count of being "free," when in reality the bonds of relational debt kept Tamil laborers working in exploitative conditions. But by calling this exploitation freedom, Cave paints an image of philanthropy stripped down to only the basic needs of humanity—needs suited for industrial profit—namely the reproduction of human laboring life fixed to the plantation. Control was justified as a means to an end because it was "just" and "paternal" and would allow Tamil coolies to experience just enough humanity to produce and reproduce a laboring progeny; but it would never extend far enough to capture workers' aspirations to live, rear children, and labor beyond that landscape. The planters knew the limits of their modes of governance and provisions for Tamil laborers being considered "philanthropic," but Cave fails to acknowledge that Tamil workers, too, knew well the limits of such "freedom" and desired more than what the planters had imagined for them.

Industrial Recursions

According to Sri Lanka's Export Development Board, with the exception of 2014, Sri Lanka has been the third-largest global exporter of tea, following China and Kenya since 2007. As of 2017 it is the fourth-largest producer of tea in the world, generating approximately 320 million kilograms per year, with its tea plantations spanning across over 194,000 hectares (approximately 749 square miles).[28] The emblem of Ceylon tea is a golden lion, the same image featured on Sri Lanka's national flag. In 1965, two years before the hundredth anniversary of tea production on the island, Sri Lanka, then Ceylon, became the world's largest exporter of tea. When the country was renamed the Democratic Socialist Republic of Sri Lanka in 1972, the Sri Lanka Tea Board campaigned to keep the name of its product, "Ceylon Tea," justifying their sentiment as follows: "The cost of promoting and establishing an unfamiliar new brand—'Sri Lanka Tea'—would be ruinous. Though opposed by some who demanded a complete break with the colonial past and a new start for the country, industry leaders managed to persuade the socialist government then in power to permit the continued use of the name Ceylon to refer to the country's most famous product. Tea from Sri Lanka would still be marketed as Ceylon Tea; a priceless world brand had been saved."[29]

The consumptive prestige of "Ceylon Tea" also manifests in the ways industrial actors speak about Sri Lanka's distinctiveness in the global market despite its declining productivity and profit. In 2014 I was walking alongside the tea bushes of an up-country estate with a field officer working on an RPC plantation in Central Province; I asked him what made Sri Lanka's tea so special in the international market. He told me that Sri Lanka was mainly known for its orthodox process of production— whole tea leaves are plucked by hand (not machines), withered, rolled, oxidated (or left out to dry with monitored humidity levels, which determine the bitterness), and then dried. He took pride that on his estate, the CTC method—Cut, Tear, and Curl, which includes the above steps but uses a machine to crush the tea leaves (and therefore they need not be whole and can be extracted from the bush by a machine)— was not being used at that time. He lamented the fact that now, given labor shortages and fierce global competition in the tea export market, Sri Lanka's plantation companies were resorting to CTC and machines in line with the markets of Japan, China, and India and not relying on women's deft, delicate fingers to pluck their tea leaves.

Facing these pressures, it was no surprise when, in March 2015, nineteen of Sri Lanka's twenty-three RPCs reported a loss of Rs. 2,850 million (roughly $21.43 million) in 2014. Citing a combination of high labor costs and low labor productivity among plantation workers, the Planters' Association responded to workers' demands for higher wages with the following statement: "The industry's survival is now up to them [the workers] . . . the plantation industry must thrive in order that we can give opportunities for earning and livelihood sustenance for over one million people that are resident and whose quality of life will depend on the relative fortunes of the plantation industry. If the industry collapses, where would all these people go for employment in order to sustain their livelihoods?"[30]

Charging Hill Country Tamils with the responsibility to stick to plantation labor signals to the darker underbelly of broader discursive practices of sustainability and care within Sri Lanka's tea industry. This language, however, is not new and speaks to the persistence of colonial practices that remain "vitally active and activated."[31] But just as Hill Country Tamils know well the language of command and industrial landscapes that they themselves maintained, they also know well the language of their ancestors' duress on the continual and often ambiguous spectrum of exploitative labor. The language of oppression, like the language of illusory causality and perpetual crisis, also sticks. But is it possible for both languages of desire to thrive among today's Hill Country Tamils and their children?

Mapping Desires

Today, although they call the tea plantations their homes, Hill Country Tamil youth desire to unfix their labor futures from the industrial language and landscapes of the estates. In late August 2015 I surveyed a group of fifty-one Hill Country Tamil young women (N = 29) and men (N = 22) between ages sixteen and twenty-seven years old (average = 19.5 years) living on tea estates in southeastern Badulla district. The household sizes of the participants ranged between two and nine individuals (average = 5), and twenty-two of the participants said they were preparing for their General Certificate of Education (GCE) Ordinary Levels (O/Ls) or Advanced Levels (A/Ls) examinations in estate schools. The rest of the individuals were either unemployed or working in temporary or informal contractual labor. I conducted the survey during a full-day meeting that a local trade union had organized focusing on youth educational and future career aspirations. The program's goal was to motivate Hill Country Tamil estate youth about career choices and to then educate job-seeking youth about the resources at their disposal. Outside speakers presented on local government and state services for job seekers, including certifications through vocational training institutes, the local Pradeshiya Sabha, and computer and technology training courses, and a local female police officer gave a presentation about women's and children's labor laws and rights.

With the exception of one young woman, all the participants had listed either one or both of their parents as tea estate workers, but when asked to list what they aspired for their own careers, not a single participant mentioned the tea estates. Twenty-seven of the fifty-one youth (53 percent) wrote that they wanted to become teachers; four said that they wanted to go into some kind of job in the finance sector, ranging from accountant to bank teller. After that, self-employment, medicine, and law were the top desired categories, with three youth listing career aspirations in each. But the survey revealed other career aspirations as well. Youth were also aiming to become auto mechanics, carpenters, tailors, police officers, nurses, bus drivers, journalists, social workers, and athletes.[32]

That more than half of the participants aspired to be teachers was not surprising; across Sri Lanka, the desire to be a teacher is quite common given the colonial legacies of instilling value, social mobility, and status on educational standing.[33] On the estates, of all the career aspirations listed by participants, teachers and teaching have long been institutionalized within the plantation labor system. Before any formal education

Table 2.1. Percentage distribution of population aged five years and above by level of education and sector, 2016

SECTOR	NO SCHOOLING (%)	UP TO GRADE 5 (%)	PASSED GRADE 6–10 (%)	PASSED GCE O/L (%)	PASSED GCE A/L (%)	PASSED DEGREE AND ABOVE (%)	SPECIAL EDUCATION (%)
Sri Lanka (nationwide)	3.3	23.5	44.1	15.3	11.1	2.7	0.1
Urban	2.4	19.3	40.4	18.4	14.7	4.7	0.1
Rural	3.1	23.5	45.0	15.1	10.8	2.4	0.1
Estate	10.1	39.6	41.8	5.4	2.6	0.4	0.1

Source: Household Income and Expenditure Survey (HIES) Final Report, 75.

ordinances that required the establishment of schools physically on estate grounds, either missionaries or planters themselves taught Hill Country Tamil children on the estates in *kankāni*-run "line schools."[34] While estate children accessed these forms of education unevenly across gender, labor, and caste lines, with preferences given to the children of estate staff, in a Durkheimian sense, placing educational facilities physically on the plantations was instrumental to sustaining a strong and cohesive residential labor force.[35] With the Rural Schools Ordinance of 1907, educational development on the estates increased, but even then, schooling on the plantation was separated and treated differently institutionally; unlike the rural sector, where teachers were government appointees and schools were designated according to revenue districts and elected village school committees, the estate schools were the responsibility of the plantation superintendent, who was required to furnish "vernacular education" for children ages six to ten years and "to provide and maintain a school room."[36] Even Ordinance No. 1 of 1920, despite attempting to centralize government management of estate schools, still maintained a differentiation between estate schools and schools in the rural sector. Given the scant governmental support and the paternalistic hand of planters and *kankānis*, teachers became respected fixtures on the plantation, through contiguous residential, kinship, and hierarchical social and labor relations, and primary role models for estate residents. Furthermore, higher education is an aspiration for many plantation residents because a good number of Hill Country Tamil youth do not attend school after taking their O/Ls. For instance, the 2016 statistics for school attendance within the estate sector are strikingly disparate when compared to the rural and urban sectors (table 2.1).

Teaching jobs are also considered prestigious because it is harder for Hill Country Tamil youth to obtain the economic resources to pass their A/Ls, and those who do are considered role models within their estate communities. These economic disparities reflect in the data, as the estate sector has the highest percentages for the number of individuals five years and above who have no schooling and for the number of individuals who have only completed fifth grade when compared to the other two sectors.

Complementing the survey results, meeting organizers then broke the participants into groups according to their career aspirations and asked

2.1.   The dream map of self-employment created by a group of young Hill Country Tamil men at a career workshop

them to construct visual representations of their goals in response to the following prompts: What steps would they need to take to get there? What were potential obstacles and challenges? What would their final state of achievement look and feel like? Each group then presented their drawings to the entire group with a brief explanation. In the group geared toward self-employment (*suyaththozhil*), a collection of unemployed young men who had been out of school since their O/Ls drew six steps toward achieving their dream (figure 2.1). A single goat in a shed became a family of goats grazing on green grass. From there they drew a building structure, which, they explained, was the house they could purchase once they had accrued enough capital from their livestock business. With that revenue, they would then purchase different types of vehicles that would in turn build up to the purchasing of buses. Finally, the business would be a self-owned transportation company that would rent, hire, and lease private buses, vans, three-wheelers, and motorbikes.

Because there were so many aspiring teachers, the organizers created four different groups around that goal, and each presented different dream visualizations. Two groups depicted their career maps as transformations from larvae to butterflies. The third drew human figures in various stages from childhood to adulthood with animations of examination achievements, certifications, and universities above their heads. The last group, aspiring to hold government teaching jobs, drew four ships sailing up a steep staircase towards their goal of a government teaching position (figure 2.2). Each component was a different color and coded with the following words: the orange stairs were "ordinary life" (*sātharanam*), the purple A/L ship was "gratitude" (*nandri*), the green ship (their government teaching job) was "great gratitude" (*miga nandri*), and the red ship, tipping below a large gray boulder, was coded "to falter or be unsteady" (*thalladu*) with the English words "university results," "economic," "family," and "society" below the boulder. At the top of the staircase they wrote the English word "win" below an image of the sun.

Mapping is an aspirational activity that reveals what Hill Country Tamil youth want for their futures and how they perceive their life trajectories. From the accumulation of self-sustaining wealth to the

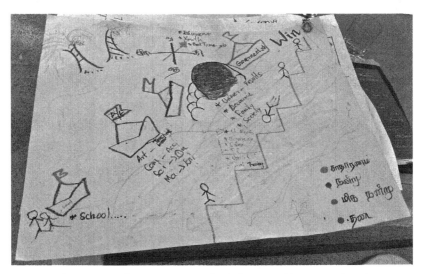

2.2.   The dream map of government teacher jobs created by a mixed gender group of Hill Country Tamil youth at a career workshop

navigation of systems and institutions beyond the plantation, Hill Country Tamil youth know well what is available to them as Sri Lankan citizens, but these activities also reveal the structural and social limits they face. When asked what obstacles or challenges would prevent them from achieving their goals, 86 percent (N = 44) of the group listed "financial or economic problems," and 35 percent (N = 18) listed family problems, ranging from the absence or death of a parent, domestic violence, and the lack of parental support or guidance. One respondent, an eighteen-year-old woman who aspired to be a doctor and whose parents were both estate workers, wrote the following: "My parents are both working on the estate, so unlike them I need to study, but to do that, we will need to spend a lot."

At the same time, desires for self-employment suggest a neoliberal impulse—the conviction that the private sector can successfully pick up the welfare support of the state. Coming from a community whose well-being has been so mishandled by the plantation industry, government, and other communities in Sri Lanka, it is not surprising that youth were voicing these desires, and it speaks to recent postwar trends of predatory microfinance schemes and debt accrual in the country's North and East. Critiques of microfinance are not new to Sri Lanka or South Asia. Given that self-employment and loan schemes will continue, a silver lining of identifying self-employment as an aspiration of Hill Country Tamil youth is that labor organizers of the reserve labor force—the force not in school and not working—can challenge and serve as a potential antidote to the exploitation and corruption perpetuated by profit-hungry stakeholders.[37]

Beyond a family's estate-based income, governmental and infrastructural issues also exist on the estates. In the month following the youth career workshop, I participated in and observed a meeting that a local NGO organized to provide capacity building around accessing local government services to resolve estate infrastructural issues. In the meeting, participants completed a community mapping exercise that the NGO then used to assess the estate's identified needs, which were numerous (figure 2.3). The members drew maps of their estate communities and in red marked the places and locations that were troublesome, problematic, or needing repair. They identified potholes in the roads, illicit liquor being sold in the lines, leopards in the adjacent forest area that made getting firewood dangerous, double-barrack line rooms that were cramped and

2.3.　A community map created by Hill Country Tamil residents highlighting infrastructural and social issues on a tea estate in Gampola, Kandy Province

had poor water and sanitation, and even a newly erected Buddhist *pansala* (living quarters for Buddhist monks)—an anomaly on the landscape given that the majority of residents on the estate were not practicing Buddhists.

From an evidence perspective, the maps provided concrete data by locating the specific wants of a residential community and using those wants to achieve an end—making the residential landscape of the estate more livable and dignified according to government and social service standards. The self-articulation of these wants also excavated legal and extralegal practices of industrial authority and in doing so interrogated the larger histories of creating a productive but cohesive plantation landscape. Planters had capitalized on creating landscapes that were remote, to which only a coolie—as "homo rusticus," or one incapable of civilization—could remain fixed. But in the end, the very cultivation of the plantation's remoteness forced Tamil laborers and their descendants to move and "unsettle themselves and others" with their desires for a less remote, more livable residence.[38] By mapping and identifying those wants, Hill Country Tamils break up that imagined landscape and destabilize the industrial ideals that capitalized on the fixedness of their labor and bodies.

Enclosing the Coolie

In July 2014 I visited the Tea Plantation Workers' Museum and Archive on Old Peacock Estate in Gampola. The museum opened in 2007 and is a member of the International Coalition of Sites of Conscience, a nonprofit organization and network of over 230 member sites of conscience and memory, including trauma and loss, around the world.[39] Over a period of thirty years before the museum opened its doors, Hill Country Tamil plantation workers and their families had donated their personal belongings and those of their ancestors to the care of the museum director, Periyasamy Muthulingam, a longtime activist and advocate for Hill Country Tamils and plantation workers. The museum sits in stark contrast to the Hill Country's touristic landscape, factory tours, and tea boutiques and also in contrast to Sri Lanka's more technical sites of industrial knowledge such as the Ceylon Tea Museum or Tea Research Institute in Central Province. At present, it is the only space in Sri Lanka dedicated to the history of plantation labor within the tea industry, and it was built up through community-based donations from Hill Country Tamils. Given its focus, it consciously focuses on themes of displacement, migration, violence, and resistance, rather than themes of cohesion, rootedness, beauty, and complacency. It also caters specifically to local communities *and* foreigners; there is no entrance fee (it is donation based), and the labels for the items are in Tamil, English, and Sinhala.

From 1920s cooking utensils and incense holders to the original passports and citizenship applications saved from repatriation, the donated items are housed in four rooms adjacent to a nineteenth-century line room that has been preserved and furnished to give the feeling of how Tamil workers and their families would have lived at the time. As I walked through the museum's rooms, I came across one item in particular that drew me back to Henry Cave's text and image. There, enclosed and hanging in a glass case, was a donated brown, lambswool cumbly, similar to the ones on which Hill Country Tamil infants had been laid down while their mothers worked above them plucking tea (figure 2.4). The glass it was hung up behind reflected the citizenship and immigration papers and workers' union songs exhibited on the opposite wall, making the cumbly difficult to focus on—but it was there.

2.4. A donated lambswool cumbly cloak, traditionally worn by Hill Country Tamil women pluckers during fieldwork. Here, it is enclosed in glass reflecting the citizenship applications of stateless Hill Country Tamils on exhibit at the Tea Plantation Workers' Museum and Archive in Gampola, Sri Lanka.

In my conversations with Sellamma and other retired women, beyond serving as blankets, cumblies were primarily used to protect workers from the elements, as they kept women warm while they plucked. In the latter half of the century, plantation managements stopped issuing cumblies for pluckers and shifted to plastic rain coverings, which many retired workers told me they detested. As one of Sellamma's friends once remarked to me, "If you still had a cumbly, you should save it because it was the best protection." Now, here it was, hanging in a glass repository. Perhaps the children and grandchildren of the cumbly's owner no longer needed to wear it; or perhaps its owner had decided its best use—its best end in the story of coolie labor in Sri Lanka—was to be preserved for locals and foreigners alike to see it with a conscience and to honor the heritage it embodies.

Since the arrival of their ancestors to Ceylon, Hill Country Tamils have been constantly caught up in the language and landscaping of capital accumulation, labor control, and natural fixation. Such imaginings "collapsed the person into payment" and stripped plantation workers of their humanity.[40] "Coolies," if controlled, could work with efficiency and silently on the plantation's green, rolling hills and if so, the industry would remain generative. The painstakingly thorough and anxiety-ridden presentations about what laborers might do, what they might not do, and what they might not do well explicitly link to the way the Tamil language—specifically a constructed "cooly" Tamil language—disrupted, operated, and circulated within the plantation's daily activities and yet remained instrumental to its productivity and survival.

The "cooly" Tamil guides reveal much about how colonial and industrial stakeholders, while stripping workers of their humanity, remained anxious about their very humanness. Where and when would they laugh? How should they pluck? How much could their bodies carry? Their anxieties were so high that commentators on their embodied labor and lives were moved to liken them to urchins, animals and "machines" that could work with efficiency and in silence among the tea bushes at a distance. But we ought to be reminded that even though "machines that manned the booming capitalist economy . . . became gods of a sort, alien technological gods," laboring humans on the natural landscape—namely women who plucked tea leaves with their bare hands—kept the industry alive, not machines.[41] Perhaps that was Cave's imagining of the "small suckling gangs of humanity"—to imagine the coolie as autochthonous labor, an alienated people sprung from the earth and not from women's wombs, as fixed rather than on the move.

The current language of Hill Country Tamils and their own perceptions of the plantation landscapes on which they reside articulate desires that leave the category of the coolie enclosed, for it was never instrumental to how workers themselves saw their labor, investments, and place in Sri Lanka. Their aspirations for dignified careers and languages of recognition—as means to ends that are not yet achieved—are still on the move, and go beyond the excesses of the plantation landscape and what it can afford them. These desires discomfort the conscience of the Sri Lankan nation and the current teascapes of the plantation—sites at once celebrated and stigmatized, and which continue to grapple with the degenerative effects of imperial nostalgia on industrial dreams.

CHAPTER 3

Living the Wage

THE RECOGNITION OF A YOUNG GIRL'S COMING OF AGE OR FIRST menstruation is known colloquially among Hill Country Tamils as *vayacu catanku* or an age attainment ritual. The ceremony and celebration constitute the first major introduction of a Tamil girl-turned-woman to the larger community and signifies her eligibility for marriage. In September 2009 I witnessed and documented the *catanku* of a friend's niece on an estate about twenty minutes by train from Hatton town. The celebration spanned over two days and, as confirmed by my friend, the maternal uncle, cost her family nearly Rs. 50,000 ($435.65). Costs included a hall rental for the celebration, materials for the home-based ritual, catered meals for two days, photography and video (including a professional album), and three different sets of saris and jewelry for the young woman. The girl's parents were estate workers, and her paternal uncle, who was working in Qatar, was also a primary financial contributor to the occasion. When I arrived at their line room for the event, I noticed that their home stood out from the others around it; when I asked about these differences, my friend told me that the extra facilities, such as a fridge, gas cooker, retiled front sitting room, and glass-encased armoire, had all been financed through her uncle's migrant remittances.

During the reception I sat with Rajesh, a young boy from Kirkwall. Seventeen years old then, Rajesh had stopped attending school and was working in a shop in Colombo. He had taken leave from work and come back for the *catanku* because his father was another of the young girl's maternal uncles living on Kirkwall. I asked him what the standard monetary gift (*moi*) was for relatives and estate community member attendees. He told me that family members must give at least Rs. 500

($4.36) in cash but that they could give whatever else they pleased as long as the *moi* was placed in a sealed envelope with the family's name, estate name, and address written on it for reciprocity purposes. Because his family was a closer relation, they had given the girl a gold ring, which Rajesh had purchased in Colombo and brought back with him for the occasion.

I shared with him my observation that Rs. 500 was a lot for workers to give for one celebration. At the time, it was ninety-five rupees more than the total wage that one plantation worker could earn for a day's work. He told me that it had to be that way because the cost of the *cat-anku* would put a significant dent in the family's savings. The *moi*, he said, would help the family recover. He then said something that made me pause: "You know why they do a big *catanku*, Akka? It is because, now, most young girls do not get married like before with their parents finding a boy for them, watching for caste, and whatnot. Now, it is either a love marriage or elopement, so the family figures that this will be their only chance to show and celebrate their daughter's virtuousness so publicly. The *catanku* has become more important than the marriage."

This chapter examines how the plantation wage, pay structure, and labor economy fail to fully accommodate the gendered commitments and life expectations of Hill Country Tamils. It explores how residents perceive and value their earned wages and how forms of situated knowledge of kinship investment and attention to the colonial and industrial entanglements of wage valuation help contextualize families' histories and shared aspirations for economic security. Drawing from archival and historical evidence, I reassert the distinctive political and economic marks that feature in household income generation and spending practices on the estates, and I trace the 2009 CA negotiations that coincided with household expenditure practices that I recorded. This tracing reveals the connections between labor dispossession and the intractability of the daily wage to demonstrate that pressures of debt directly affect Hill Country Tamils' familial relations and investment decisions.

For Tamils in and beyond Sri Lanka, intergenerational reciprocity and intermarriage serve as practices of strength building for community structures and also cement caste-based and gendered networks of exchange and status.[1] On the tea estates, the patriarchal leadership in caste groups relies on practices of intergenerational reciprocity and religious and estate-based life cycle rituals to solidify their status.[2] Within this frame, material and ideological delineations of male and female spaces, gendered divisions of household labor, and ties between plantation labor and reproductive practices directly inform Tamil women's kinship experiences.[3] While prospects and rituals of marriage across generations serve as signifiers of strength and solidarity, not having the economic resources to observe these rituals strains kinship relations and households as they struggle to survive. These intergenerational rituals and the persistent commitments Hill Country Tamils have to marriage reveal what Thiranagama refers to as the "preexistent and stable foundation[s] of nonpolitical 'cultural life.'"[4]

Building on this foundation, I argue that the inextricable link between Hill Country Tamil kinship investment and the historical politics of the plantation wage redefines waged labor as a fragile endeavor and condition of life that Hill Country Tamils take on in order to survive and gain prestige in their communities. Rather than focus on the continuities and tenacity of ritual practices and gendered expectations of reproduction, I focus on the contingent relationship between kinship relations and shifting labor and wage valuations within Hill Country Tamil families. For women, specifically, life rituals and practices of fertility such as age attainment, pregnancy, and motherhood are not only necessary vehicles for broader forms of social recognition but also gendered acts of obligation within structures of kinship. More important, these life commitments significantly affect the trajectory of a family's economic security and standing. On the plantation daily wage, Hill Country Tamils who are employed as full-time workers are not able to live on the wage according to what they want for their families; therefore they turn to other forms of employment that, in turn, transform traditional forms of kinship relations in the long run. Seeing waged labor as a politically informed condition of life allows us to contextualize and not discount the plantation sector's deep roots of political and economic inequality. It also brings to the foreground the additional and contradictory burdens, anxieties, and pressures that Hill Country Tamils take on when they move, work, and strive for a sense of dignity beyond the plantation wage and across generations.

Methodologically, this chapter pulls at the historical frameworks of violence that have come to be associated with counting. Quantitative data and numbers in the tea industry and on the plantations operate and are operationalized through human and waged agricultural labor. Asking people about their finances is never a comfortable experience, and when I began research on Kirkwall I embraced my instinctual reluctance to obtain quantitative data out of fear of reproducing the racist and extractive impulses of colonial data collection and analysis. But through deepened relationships with families and in the time I spent in kitchens, living rooms, shops, and social settings in residential spaces on the estates, the people with whom I spoke shared the wage-based and microeconomic data I present here. Because the women and men with whom I spoke showed me their pay slips and explained their life choices to me, I decided to look more closely at what stories numbers could tell about how workers value the money they earn from wage labor: where it went, and how it was managed to negotiate life choices around debt, work, education, migration, marriage, and family. Because of this meeting point, I am hopeful that the following use and analysis of numbers can provide researchers new ways to approach the study of plantation life and the waged labor integral to its sustainability.

Calculating the "Negligible"

The social and economic constraints of the plantation wage system I observed in 2014–15 has underpinnings in the historical and political relationship between the question of minority representation and legislation around the plantation wage prior to independence. With independence a real possibility by the early 1920s, Ceylon nationals had begun to contemplate the role minorities would play in a newly representative Ceylonese state. In 1919 the Ceylon National Congress (CNC) took shape as a political association of elite Ceylonese individuals from different backgrounds to advocate for their political stakes in the British colony. Though initially multiethnic by composition, the CNC had by 1922 become increasingly dominated by Sinhala majoritarian interests. Ceylon Tamil Congress member and Sri Lankan Tamil Ponnambalam Arunachalam, the CNC's inaugural president and a staunch supporter of a multiethnic, cooperative Ceylon polity, had withdrawn from leadership, and the unofficial minority interests of the Legislative Council had began to manifest in weak political alliances subject to the manipulations of British colonial administrators holding positions as official members.[5]

In August 1922 the CNC sent a telling memorandum to the principal secretary of state for the colonies, Winston Churchill, in which the body expressed collective concern over the question of minority representation in Ceylon: "In regard to the minorities, the Congress has repeatedly put the question as to what their separate interests are as distinct from the interests of the country generally. This question still remains unanswered and will never be answered for the obvious reason that they [the minorities] have no separate interests . . . having secured all they wanted and even more, the minorities are now asked to sit in judgment on the form and strength of the representation to be given to the country generally of which they are comparatively a negligible factor."[6] Such conditions allowed Ceylonese colonial subjects, looking up to the horizon of sovereignty, to pivot their desires for the nation on the denial of distinctive minority interests; for in their minds the minority—in this case, the Hill Country Tamils working and sustaining Ceylon's thriving tea industry—were, ironically, considered a potential threat to the yet-to-be-formed nation.

On April 17, 1923, less than one year after the CNC told Churchill that Ceylon's minorities had "secured all they wanted and even more," the colonial secretary issued an order to hold an inquiry into the wages and cost of living for estate laborers. The report, prepared by R. Jones Bateman, director of statistics, was published on August 3, 1923, and covered April–May of that year. The methodology of the study drew from the survey pool of the 1921 census, which, at the time, stated that on 2,367 estates, 493,944 "immigrant Tamils" and 54,579 Sinhalese constituted Ceylon's estate population.[7] Specifically, the inquiry was charged with collecting the following particulars per the copy of the survey form sent to estate superintendents that year.

1. Total net cash paid out to the labor force and its dependents, etc.[8]
   (a) Balance pay earned during the month after deductions for the rice, dhoby, etc.
   (b) Other earnings, i.e. head money, bonus, payment for overtime, cash work, contract work, etc.

(c) Gifts of money made during the month, "santosums"[9] to women after child-birth, to newly arrived coolies, to non-workers, etc.[10]

The inquiry also asked estate superintendents to provide data for the average "daily strength of the labour force," "average number of non-workers" or dependents on the labor force including children and the elderly, and "goods supplied or services rendered to the labour force and its dependents for which no payment is made, or for which deductions are made from wages." This last category included bushels of rice which the estate supplied as food rations and also cumblies (as seen in chapter 2) for workers to wear to protect them from the harsh elements during work. Lastly, superintendents were asked if they supplied the labor force with "free quarters," "free firewood," free medicine and medical attendance," a "barber," and "dhoby" and to then approximate the average number of gardens that coolies used for their own cultivation on the estate.[11]

The survey tool itself and the data collected demonstrate that the colonial government and planters were interested in extracting the fullest amount of profit from their coolie resident labor force, but its extraction was even more intimately attuned to the gendered commitments and obligations that workers had to their families and communities. In the report, Bateman also describes the payment system for estate coolies. The fixed daily rate differed for men, women, and children; he takes note of "piecework," overtime, and contract work, though with respect to bonuses he reports, "There seems very little uniformity on difference estates . . . [which] makes it impossible in most instances to say definitely how much money any particular cooly has earned in a month."[12] Bateman goes on to highlight the many "advantages" that coolies enjoyed for free, including benefits that were not technically "free" but rather entitlements to workers that estates were legally required to provide them. One such entitlement was education (e.g., Ordinance to Make Provision in Rural and Planting Districts for the Education of Children in the Vernacular Languages No. 8 of 1907) and medical aid (Wants and Diseases [Labourers] Ordinance No. 9 of 1912). Labeling such benefits "free advantages" is a striking inclusion as it does not accurately capture the educational attainment levels and realities that coolies were experiencing on a national level at the time. Furthermore, calling a legal entitlement that is supposed to be free and afforded equally across the entire island an "advantage" is unethically misleading because it was clear that coolies were not advancing in colonial Ceylon. In fact, they were at the center of debate among Ceylonese elites to be disenfranchised and deprived of their citizenship rights, an idea that became a reality upon independence.

The biases evident in the data collection and analysis make Bateman's formal conclusions predictably complicit with the industry's interests: the figures "indicate[d] a fair degree of prosperity in the labour force."[13] More compelling than his conclusion, however, is how he failed to address what is not explicit in table 3.1. First, while the average daily labor force increased by 6,198 coolies (roughly 1.8 percent) from April to May 1923, Bateman does not address the Rs. 83,706.82 increase (nearly 54 percent) in *santōsums* gifts declared during the same period. Second, Bateman

Table 3.1. *Abstract of returns received from estates, 1923*

TOTAL NET CASH PAID OUT TO THE LABOR FORCE AND ITS DEPENDENTS	APRIL 1923	MAY 1923
(a) Balance pay earned during the month, after deductions for rice, dhoby, etc.	Rs. 1,546,741.39	Rs. 1,842,014.42
(b) Other earnings (i.e., head money, bonus, payment for overtime, cash work, contract work, etc.)	Rs. 825,983.88	Rs. 852,053.82
(c) Gifts of money made during the month, "santosums" to women after child-birth, to newly arrived coolies, to nonworkers, etc.	Rs. 155,211.45	Rs. 238,918.27
Average daily strength of the labor force during the month*	338,990	345,188
Average number of nonworking who are dependent on the labor force**	92,401	94,281

Source: "Report on an Enquiry into the Wages and the Cost of Living of Estate Labourers," 10.

* This number includes sick coolies and other temporary absentees and does not represent merely the number actually working each day.

** Children too young to work and old men and women.

took this data set and analyzed it alongside May 1923 data about the coolie's dietary needs (which he found compared "favourably" with the jail diet and the diet of the working classes in Bombay), remittance amounts from India via money orders from 1922, data from savings banks on select estates from June 1922, and expenditures on clothing, festivals, special occasions (which he estimated occurred at most only once or twice a year), and jewelry. Lastly, he used the 1921 census data on age and sex to make claims about family constitution and marriage that would ultimately justify his conclusions. He argues that with marriage or cohabitation "almost universal" and the rates of age and gender the same as the 1921 census, the likely average family size was five persons.[14] This conclusion assumes that males and females above the age of fourteen were sexually active, in marriages or cohabitating, and ultimately reproducing. Moreover, the data does not account for elderly populations who might have still been working; rather, they, too, along with the sick and absent, were included in the average daily "strength" of the labor force.

Despite self-professed rigor and, of course, declared gratitude not to the coolies but to the Planters' Association and the superintendents for providing the data on Tamil coolies' wages and needs, Bateman and his methods were, to say the least and to use his own words, "rather clumsy."[15] But the report does give us one moment—prior to collective bargaining and labor organizing in the plantation sector—where the industry and government attempted to account for Hill Country Tamil workers' gender and kinship relations and their desires. But both stakeholders ultimately skewed these crucial factors in their computations and justifications for the sake of maximum profit. Coinciding with Indian independence movements, the Indian National Congress had already sown seeds of agitation about the welfare and wages of Hill Country Tamil plantation workers with the government. The inquiry and report demonstrate the ways the government used data on workers' wages and their nonworking lives to keep the plantation industry profitable and to diminish the potential of minority representation in a soon-to-be independent Ceylon. In 1927 the government implemented the Minimum Wages (Indian Labour) Ordinance No. 27 and established the Estate Wages Board to fix plantation pay, but these legislative acts did not involve any significant forms of labor organizing from the trade unions or worker participation.[16] More important, neither the government nor the industry thoughtfully considered the gendered realities of workers' lives and their familial and community expectations.

Bargaining in a Labor Regime

Excluded from early Sinhala and Tamil nationalisms, Hill Country Tamils found accessible but flawed modes of political representation in trade unions. The Trade Unions Ordinance No. 14 of 1935 institutionalized collective bargaining practices in Sri Lanka.[17] The first Collective Agreement (CA) in the plantation sector was signed in 1940 between planter representatives (the Employers Planters' Association of Ceylon, Ceylon Estate Proprietary Association, Ceylon Association in London) and estate trade union representatives (Ceylon Indian Congress Labour Union, Ceylon Indian Workers' Federation, and All Ceylon Estate Workers' Union).[18] From 1940 to 1998, estate unions collectively bargained with plantation employer representatives through the end of colonial rule and into nationalization. Privatization of the plantations in 1991 brought the current signatories—the Employers' Federation of Ceylon (EFC) and the three representative unions—the Ceylon Workers' Congress (CWC), Lanka Jathika Estate Workers' Union (LJEWU), and Joint Plantation Trade Union Centre (JPTUC)—into negotiations for the first CA signed among them, in 1995. The three union signatories were designated as representatives of the entire plantation labor force because their collective memberships constituted the majority (nearly 75 percent) of tea and rubber plantation workers in Sri Lanka at the time. The CA document covered the plantation workers' wages and also outlined plantation employment regulations, employee benefits, estate facilities, and union and worker grievance procedures. Furthermore, the entirety of the CA document would be up for renegotiation every year and was to be reevaluated and resigned every three years.

In my first year of fieldwork, I participated in and observed community and union events surrounding the renegotiation of the 2009 collective wage agreement. The 2007 CA had allotted plantation workers a Rs. 200 daily wage,[19] a Rs. 20 daily price share supplement, and a Rs. 70 daily attendance incentive.[20] During field research, union representatives demanded that the daily wage be increased to accommodate the rise in cost-of-living standards. The remuneration package of the 2007

CA expired on March 31, 2009, without any decision regarding the renegotiation of the contract's content. According to union and media reports, the RPCs represented by the EFC had repeatedly refused to offer a wage raise, citing the looming global economic crisis and consequent financial loss.

Following its expiration, the RPCs and trade union representatives held talks for five and a half months in 2009, but to no satisfactory outcome for either party. During this time, estate laborers worked on the plantations without a contract. Acknowledging that workers needed some sort of wage raise, the RPCs offered a 12.5 percent increase on the current total wage (Rs. 326). The unions rejected their offer and called for a basic wage raise that would parallel the 55 percent cost-of-living increase that had taken place over the previous two years (2007–9).[21] When the RPCs refused their demands, the unions called for no less than Rs. 500 for the basic wage on the basis of humanitarian grounds and cited the 2007 World Bank poverty assessment report in support of their position. The RPCs offered Rs. 330 and then Rs. 360, but the unions would not accept their offers. At this point the unions decided to take collective action. All unions initiated a "work to rule" or "go slow" campaign from September 7 to September 16.[22] The unions called for the president to intervene, and one Tamil-language protest poster captured the community's frustration perfectly: "Kūttu oppantamā? Kūththu oppantamā?" (Is this a Collective Agreement or a folk-dance agreement?). According to D. M. Jayaratne, then minister of plantation industries, the 2009 go-slow campaign cost the RPCs over Rs. 800 million (roughly $7.27 million) in losses.[23] Negotiations came to a head and, in the end, the EFC and three union representatives signed the Collective Agreement No. 14 of 2009 on September 16. The signed and agreed-on total daily wage for plantation workers was set at a cumulative Rs. 405.

Non-signatory unions such as National Union of Workers (NUW), Up-Country Workers Front (UWF), Democratic Workers' Congress (DWC), and Ceylon Workers' Alliance (CWA), however, rejected the agreement; they claimed the 2009 CA was illegitimate because it had failed to include the full representation of estate workers during negotiations. These unions also felt that the government should have intervened on the grounds that the 2009 CA violated International Labour Organization (ILO) Convention No. 98,[24] which Sri Lanka had ratified on December 13,

1972.[25] Furthermore, they stated that the three CA union signatories represented no more than 60 percent of the plantation workforce at the time of signing and were therefore unfit to make decisions for the entire plantation worker community.[26]

Lastly, the non-signatory unions stated that the Rs. 405 (28.4 percent) increase on the total daily wage would not be enough to meet cost-of-living demands, not only because it did not match the rise of inflation but also because the price wage supplement and daily attendance incentives were not guaranteed sources of income. Plans to reinitiate the go-slow campaign following the conclusion of mid-October 2009 Tīpāvaḷi festivities were set but never mobilized. Thus workers remained under this binding agreement until May 31, 2011, and began receiving their new wages on September 16, 2009.

Given the events leading up to and during the signing of the 2009 CA, the lingering sense of betrayal and resignation felt among plantation workers regarding union leadership signaled a general pessimism about the ability of the unions to represent the people. In mid-June 2009 I met with a group of unionists and community leaders who met to discuss the CA negotiations. Their frustrations focused on the fact that the negotiations were held behind closed doors and had not incorporated the views of local *talaivars* (estate-level union leaders) and other outside members. One veteran unionist raised valid questions about the transparency and dynamics of participation more generally: "What about the *kīzh makkaḷ* [lower-class or bottom people] and those in civil society? Were they satisfied? Was there an open invitation [*azhaippu veḷippāṭu*] to them? In my experience, they will ask for Rs. 450 and when they get 350, they will say it is enough [*pōtum*] without thinking. They used to milk the cows by hand. Now they use machines, which extract both the milk and blood from the cow. This was how the past collective wage agreement was done. This wage struggle is like a disease for the plantation workers [Inthak kūttup oppanta pōrāttam peruntōttat thozhilālarkaḷukku oru noy mātiri]."

Other unionists and activists, calling out the pattern of male-dominated negotiations, felt that the 2009 CA was a prototypical display of the hegemonic masculine politics of opportunism, a stepping-stone for unionists-cum-politicians to secure votes for the next election, and an agreement between Colombo's *mutalāḷis*, or money-making business owners. Their frustrations also extended to the signatories after the sign-ing. In September 2009 a CWC representative even admitted that the signatories felt "cheated" by the way the RPCs handled the negotiations and felt as if they were forced to make a decision based on false disclo-sures of company profits and investments. Given that the CA would not expire until March 31, 2011, Hill Country Tamil estate workers and their representatives were compelled to reflect on these missed opportuni-ties and formulate new strategies to demand their social and economic rights.

The next agreement, signed two years later, did not improve the negotiation process or wage struggle. Signed on June 16, 2011, Collective Agreement No. 22 of 2011 raised the plantation daily wage from Rs. 405 ($3.70) to Rs. 515 ($4.70).[27] Although reflecting a 27 percent increase, the raise did not match January 2011 media reports citing that Sri Lanka's cost of living had risen nearly 200 percent since April 2010.[28] Politicians like then DPF leader Mano Ganesan, though not an official signatory, protested the RPCs' substandard offers but also recognized the economic impact of collective bargaining on the industry's survival: "We need at least 1,000 rupees per day for a decent life . . . if we demand more, the tea industry will collapse."[29] His remark highlights the conundrum that unions representing plantation workers in a state of economic crisis and postwar economic reconstruction perpetually face: the plantation sys-tem needs to keep workers' wages low to retain maximum levels of pro-duction and profit. This desire, however, simply does not satisfy workers' needs—or in Ganesan's words, their hopes for a "decent life." Anxiety over the wage (*sampalam*) and, more important, its lack thereof (*sam-palam pattātu*) is crucial for rethinking Hill Country Tamil perspectives on how community hinges on the existential sense of insecurity and desire for a dignified life.

The failed attempts to secure a living wage between 1998 and 2016 (table 3.2) bear similarities to the biased miscalculations of the 1923 wages report. What were Hill Country Tamil workers' representatives and employees failing or refusing to see about the realities of their employee constituents' lives and desires for their families?

On the plantations, the early trade unions strove to inform workers of their labor rights and mobilized them around various work-related grievances but they became increasingly politicized through the question

Table 3.2.   The daily plantation wage as negotiated and agreed on through Collective Agreements, 1998–2016

YEAR	BASIC WAGE (RS.)	PRICE SHARE SUPPLEMENT (PSS) (RS.)	ATTENDANCE ALLOWANCE (AA) (RS.)	CASH PLUCKING SUPPLEMENT (PER KILO) (RS.)	TOTAL POTENTIAL DAILY WAGE (RS./USD)
1998	95	6	n/a	n/a	101 ($1.55)
2000	101	6	14	n/a	121 ($1.57)
2002	121	14	12	n/a	147 ($1.53)
2004	135	20	25	7	180 ($1.78)
2006	170	20	70	12	260 ($2.50)
2009	285	30	90	12	405 ($3.53)
2011	380	30	105	17	515 ($4.66)
2013	450	30	140	20	620 ($4.80)
2016	500	30	200	n/a	730 ($5.01)

Source: Compiled from Collective Agreements between Employers' Federation of Ceylon and representing trade unions, Ceylon Workers' Congress, Lanka Jathika Estate Workers' Union, and Joint Plantation Trade Union Centre, 1998–2016.

of statelessness, disenfranchisement, and the minority question. The politicized and patriarchal structure and tactics of the unions often left women workers underrepresented and larger and more powerful unions, such as the CWC, became highly fragmented on organizational levels: caste discrimination prevented lower-caste workers from attaining upper-level positions, and female laborers felt alienated from traditionally male-dominated positions of leadership.[30] These factors contributed to the unions' inability to effectively represent a diversifying minority community and created internal rifts and a lack of trust between constituents and their unionist-cum-politician leaders.

This gendered lack of trust came up in my conversation with Sivapākkiam Kumaravel, one of the first female leaders of the Ceylon

Indian Labour Congress (CILC) in the 1940s. Ninety-three years old, she spoke with me on the telephone about her union career in May 2012, and we met at her home in Kandy in August 2015 and again in July 2018. As a nineteen-year-old, Sivapākkiam joined the CILC and later the CWC, becoming one of the first leaders of the union's women's wing. In 1941 she was the first person to raise the demand for a six-hour workday for women plantation workers to accommodate their lives as mothers and household caregivers, and in 1946 she was the first person to demand a separate trade union for women. Peri Sundaram, cofounder of the CIC, had supported her campaign for a separate women's union, she told me, but it was longtime CWC leader S. Thondman who rejected her demands.[31] Sivapākkiam remained a women's wing leader in the CWC until the early 1950s, writing for one of the first newspapers for workingwomen, working from 5:00 a.m. to 6:00 p.m. daily to mobilize members in the field, rallying women for the group's historic 1946 march in Nuwara Eliya, and later attending the Commonwealth Conference in 1950 alongside India's first prime minister, Jawaharlal Nehru, and his daughter and later former prime minister, Indira Gandhi. But S. Thondaman's quest for power and his manipulation of bottom-level workers forced her to leave the CWC in the early 1950s. About his life and her work, she told me in 2012, "His life as a representative of the people was 100 percent a lie! It was all about money for him. He took all of the money of the people and for crores and crores of money bought buildings and businesses in India to enjoy for himself. In our women's committee, we worked on the ground with the depressed and suffering people. Thondaman's history we shouldn't remember."[32]

Plantation union leaders like S. Thondaman are hegemonic filters that have come to define much of Hill Country Tamil possibility through their visibility, politics of patronage, and bargaining power as politicians.[33] Sivapākkiam's call for scholars and activists to reimagine the history of union leadership on the plantations—much like a closer look at the skewed data of the 1923 wages report—reminds us that the history of plantation labor often silences women's desires and commitments. But it is often difficult to locate that silence in colonial and industrial records full of evaluations and judgments about their lives. From statistically accounting for all children above the age of fourteen as reproductively viable to counting the ounces of salt, anchovy (*nettali*), and dhal (lentils) a "cooly" would need to eat in order to survive and labor to contemporary calculations of deficit, productivity and profit—despite countless calculations and divisibilities—the plantation wage and its guardians and defenders have consistently failed to account for the gendered realities that women workers face.

Bearing Debt in the Womb

I began finding this missing evidence when I sat down with Siva in his kitchen around the fire after he had finished a long day of casual work on Kirkwall in August 2015. A thirty-eight-year-old father and husband, he listed to me how much his teenage daughter's *catanku* had cost him last year:

> Payment for the *dhobi* (washer) to wash the home: Rs. 600
> Invitation cards: Rs. 15,000 (for three hundred cards)
> Ritual items for the house ceremony: Rs. 5,000
> Reception hall rental: Rs. 25,000–35,000
> Reception guest meals: Rs. 60,000 (Rs. 200 per meal)
> Cook for meals at the house ritual: Rs. 30,000 (Rs. 100 per meal)
> Hired bus (from Hatton to the estate): Rs. 12,000
> Van: Rs. 1,000
> Flowers and decorations: Rs. 3,000
> Video and photography: Rs. 14,000
> Hired drummers and musicians: Rs. 8,000
> Clothing for the girl's maternal aunt and uncle: Rs. 25,000
> Extra wood for cooking at the house: Rs. 1,000
> Painting of the house: Rs. 5,000
> Total expenses: Rs. 203,600–213,600 (2–2.1 lakhs or $1,885–$1,978)[34]

The expenses had come up because it was the tenth day of the month. His wife, Sarasi, a full-time plucker on Kirkwall, had just received her monthly salary for July: sixty rupees, or forty-five cents at the time. When I asked her why it was so low, she told me that work was "slow" that month so she had only worked for about fifteen days. But upon further examination of her pay slip, I saw extra deductions from her salary for two additional loans—one from a private bank and one from the

RPC—for roughly Rs. 3,000 ($27.77) each. Her salary, without any deductions and including her standard benefits and welfare deductions, would have been above Rs. 9,000 ($83.33).

I asked her about the loans in front of Siva, and he explained that they were still paying off the two-lakh loan that they had taken out for their daughter's *catanku*, which took place last year. Even with a return *moi* of one lakh, they were still unable to pay off the loan, given its accruing interest and the daily wage of Rs. 620 ($4.80) at the time. The loan burden had pushed Siva to stop working on the estate: he had joined other men from Kirkwall in tea smallholding work about an hour-long bus ride away, for a daily cash wage Rs. 900 ($6.62).[35] As we sat around their kitchen fire, somewhat deflated from reviewing their family's expenses, Sarasi crumbled up her pay slip, laughed, and said, "What are we going to be able to do with sixty rupees? Buy our daughters some biscuits for the week?" Using sarcasm to mitigate what was a dire situation, she captured what we were all thinking: the plantation daily wage could not accommodate the life she and her husband wanted.

I returned the next day with questions that I had not yet anticipated because of my own hesitation to use the quantitative methodologies of the industry. I asked to see her pay slips. She showed me the ones she had saved—twelve slips dated between May 2011 and July 2015—which taught me about her income as a full-time plucker (table 3.3). For each of those twelve months, the RPC on which she was employed offered between twenty-two and twenty-five days of work. For nine of those pay periods, Sarasi worked the 75 percent of the available days offered and for that work, she received a daily attendance allowance. When I asked her why she had not been able to work the necessary days for the other

Table 3.3.   *Sarasi's average days worked, earnings, and deductions, May 2011–July 2015*

Average number of working days	19.95 days
Average of total earnings	Rs. 12,545.75 (US$89.06)
Average of total deductions	Rs. 10,956.40 (US$77.88)
Average net income	Rs. 1908.33 (US$15.44)

three months, she told me it had been because a family member had been sick and she had had to bring food to them in the hospital or, in the case of her young daughter, who had a serious illness, had to stay overnight at the hospital. For some of the days, she told me, she did not go because her body was tired, the rain was too strong, it was too cold, or she did not want to work. Plucking work (*koluntu velai*), she told me, was hard on her body; as the only family member working full-time on Kirkwall, she needed to not push herself too much because without her income, her family would have almost nothing coming in and no retirement funds. Sarasi's pay slips also showed me her family's larger history of debt apart from the two loans I had seen in her August 2015 pay slip. Over the twelve pay slips, she had made payments to banks and other private, plantation-associated moneylenders that ranged between Rs. 450 ($4.10, May 2011) to Rs. 5,900 ($44.84, June 2015) each month. When I asked her the purpose of those loans, she explained that each had been for a specific item or project—her two teenage daughters' *catanku* celebrations, a new television when her family's twelve-year-old unit had finally broke down, repayment of another informal loan, and the thirty-day ceremony for her sister-in-law's newborn child.

Sarasi's experiences with debt are not uncommon in the Hill Country. Between 2011 and 2015, the national poverty line in Sri Lanka rose from Rs. 3,244 to Rs. 3,888.[36] In Nuwara Eliya district, where Sarasi lives, the poverty line increased from Rs. 3,313 to Rs. 3,922 during that same period.[37] With the national poverty headcount index at 4.1 percent in 2016,[38] the estate sector reported a poverty headcount at 8.8 percent for the same year, the highest in the country, surpassing the urban and rural sectors.[39] Likewise, 73 percent of households in the estate sector were in debt, above both the rural and urban sectors.[40] In my research I would hear of and see signs of ongoing loans and debts that Hill Country Tamil workers were experiencing while trying to live and support their families on the plantation daily wage. Debts were to a host of actors and institutions—from a local electronics store in town to informal debts paid through microfinance schemes or pawning with local stores for food items or cash. Talk of debt on the estates revealed that a combination of undesirable working conditions, low wages, and difficult life experiences—both expected and unexpected—had made the plantation wage unlivable and debt a condition of everyday life.

It became clear to me why, under such economic conditions, the *catanku* ceremony was so significant for the girl's family and their future. To be able to host the event and present your daughter was to be able to show the larger community that your family could live beyond a wage designed to keep you within lower social and economic brackets. The public life ritual not only affirms the girl's gendered potential but also her family's economic strength and investments. On a pragmatic level, the hosting of the *catanku* also had significant social implications for a family's generative future. When I asked a middle-aged woman and mother of two young boys on Kirkwall why the age attainment ceremony was so important, she said, "Everyone knows there is a girl in the house that can be married. If not, they [meaning the community] do not know who can be married." Serving as a girl's sign of entry into a new world of social possibility, the *catanku* is celebrated as a token of a family's capacity to regenerate and engage in networks of kinship, marriage, and reproduction. It also serves, in a Durkheimian sense, as a structured event that binds and brings society together, as opposed to those structural inequalities—labor, caste, and ethnicity—that cut into and potentially tear communities apart. A Hindu Tamil mother of three, who had just hosted a *catanku* for her fourteen-year-old daughter in 2014 on Kirkwall, expressed this sense of a shared coming together best: "If you don't hold a ceremony, then no one would know, and my girl would go unnoticed. We do it so that we can be content [*cantōcam*]. Without it, a marriage cannot be set." The last part of her comment motivated me to further examine why Hill Country Tamil women and families were describing this life cycle ritual as a necessary form of social recognition and how practices of waged labor affect those gendered commitments.

Echoing Rajesh's comment in 2009, on more than one occasion women, when talking about the *catanku* with me in 2014, would call it a marriage (*kalyanam*). Comments about how the *catanku* reflected how well a family was doing socially and economically often accompanied these verbal slippages. In July 2014, I sat in the front parlor of a worker's line room, along with a group of women aged between fourteen and sixty, watching the "*catanku* piece" (a Video CD) of a relative's ceremony. While watching the video, I observed how the visual representation of the occasion elicited in the room memories and comments about standards of beauty and economic status. A fifteen-year-old girl, a first cousin of the attained girl, said, "She looks beautiful, sha," observing the beauty of the honoree; in turn, the cousin's mother remarked how much healthier and bigger she looked then, watching herself pose with the family for photographs; a grandmother, the neighbor of the attained girl's family, then commented about how the family had put on a grand reception. It was clear that the *catanku*, in its representational force, was able to stand in and generate prestige for the family's potential and actual social and economic standing, even well after it had taken place.

After the piece finished, the mother of the fifteen-year-old cousin, who had also attained age in 2014, brought out the two saris her daughter had worn for the occasion. She and her husband had only had enough money to have a *catanku* for their first daughter but not for their second, who attained age shortly afterward. They still needed to pay the videographer Rs. 4,800 in order to get their Video CD and photo album, so they did not have any photographs of the occasion yet. She then asked both of her daughters to wear the saris for me; after a frenzied fifteen minutes of doing their hair and makeup, she asked me to take photographs of them dressed up so that she could have them for prospective husbands in the near future.

But as Rajesh said in 2009, planned marriage prospects and lavish wedding ceremonies were becoming less and less assured on the estates due to migrant labor practices. Many younger women I knew who had already attained age as teenagers in 2009 were either newly registered (without a *tāli*), mothers of infants, or in "love" relationships with migrant worker Hill Country Tamil men within their age set when I met them again in 2014. When I asked them how they had met their husbands or boyfriends, most told me they had met their partners within geographic proximity of their workplaces in shops, garment factories, and private homes in Colombo or other major towns. Marriages set or proposed by parents had now been increasingly replaced by love found in non-plantation labor markets across religions and outside plantation and caste-based kinship networks. Such unions are not parents' first choices for their daughters, but the necessity of migrant labor and the shift to employment outside the estates had resulted in a sensed decrease of proposed kin marriages.

While some love relationships cause temporary tensions and estrangement, they also produce new forms of pragmatic strategizing among parents to better secure their daughters' futures. Hill Country Tamil parents often told me how they would accommodate "love" in the form of "proposed love"; parents would put the idea of love into their daughter's head about who would be traditionally proposed for marriage—perhaps a daughter's maternal uncle's son or her paternal aunt's son. As one mother of a recently attained girl told me in 2015, "We have someone in mind [for her] but we know that love is more common. So little by little we speak about how she should feel love for him. She now has developed love for him, and when the time comes, they will get married." In some instances, unions of proposed love among kin resulted in early, premarital pregnancies and registrations without *tālis*; while the pregnancies initially created familial tensions around the stigma of premarital sex and early pregnancy, kin would quickly have a registration performed with no large ceremony and, as I observed, family members and the larger estate community would welcome and cherish the children conceived in those unions.

As three accepted practices of kinship and marriage, the *catanku* as the "new" marriage, love relationships in formal and informal economies of migrant labor, and "proposed love" directly reflect the failure of the plantation daily wage to accommodate Hill Country Tamils' life aspirations. By foregrounding the public expectations of marriage and fertility for young women, these practices reflect that a young woman's worth on the plantations is ultimately recognized through her capacity to sustain and reproduce life for her family so that they can maintain their economic security through kinship investments. These practices also reveal how the wage unfolds materially in and among households on the estates and through its capacity to constrain and challenge households to live beyond it, transforming familial trajectories and community evaluations of a woman's worth.

Beyond the *Kūli*

The biases of the 1923 wage report and the incapacity of the wage to accommodate women workers' lives reveal how the plantation's clinging to economic models of compensation create three interconnected illusions about tea plantation work in Sri Lanka—livability, negligibility, and viability. First, colonial agents and planters created and cultivated an optics of livability on the estates: they justified meager wages as a means of creating a healthy, productive residential coolie labor force. Second, the minority politics of pre-independence Ceylon built up the discursive illusion that as stateless minorities, Hill Country Tamils were "negligible"; they were treated like a threat to the nation's strength and yet necessary to its economic survival. Third, the patriarchal politics of patronage of the trade unions created an illusion of viable labor on the plantations for workingwomen; as the only recognized form of Hill Country Tamil worker and minority representation, their politicization constrained them to a national history of negotiating for an unlivable wage.

These illusions circulated in political discourse and thrived. In the form of calculations, statistics, and extractive practices they also assumed legal and industrial authority in the colonial and postcolonial politics of minority rights. The economic models on the plantation also have unexpected kinship with Sri Lanka's formal and informal economies of migrant, intimate, and immaterial labor. They live well beyond the wage valuations and timeframes of a kilo, day, and month of work that workers have experienced and inherited over generations. In these afterlives, these models inform individuals' obligations to one another but also make emerging possibilities of citizenship, education, and gendered mobility more appealing to workers and their families. But as Laura Bear and her colleagues warn, "Such conversion devices do not produce reality . . . [they] erase particularity and sever objects, people and resources from their contexts . . . but do not determine sociality."[41] For Hill Country Tamils, the past and present strain of waged labor is a condition of life because of its relationship to living economies of dispossession and the interpenetration of that dispossession into the reproductive labor and kinship investments that individuals take on to sustain their relations of care.

While the above stories suggest more surplus in movements of value between reproductive and productive labor, it is important to remember that a focus on movement often occludes key features of lending and borrowing—that of absence and debt. In Sri Lanka, the amount of debt among Tamils in the North and East is at an all-time high.[42] The postwar proliferation of microfinance, self-entrepreneurship, and social-impact moneylending programs has contributed to the increase of debt in these regions, and scholars Lamia Karim and Debarati Sen (studying these programs in Bangladesh and Darjeeling, respectively) demonstrate how they embody the extractive, neoliberal, pull-yourself-up-by-your-bootstraps model of development and social change.[43] These systems claim to create value at every step of the supply chain but, on closer examination, make invisible structural and socially embedded forms of inequality. The scale and depth of debt of Tamils in Sri Lanka's North and East now financially exceeds those debts shouldered by Hill Country Tamils on the estates. But scholars and activists can learn from the estate sector's historical and lived stories of wage valuation to identify what economic relations, power differentials, and social vulnerabilities these extractive development programs tap into as they lead individuals, families, and generations into unmanageable futures of indebtedness. As evident in the colonial wage valuations, contemporary household debt accruals, and colonial number crunching of coolie wages, the language and mechanisms that circulate and support coalitions of stakeholders across public, government, development, and private businesses make these justifications stick; asking why they stick and what actors allow them to operate and take hold requires strategizing a dismantling of such coalitions. In their place, we must look to new forms of solidarity among community members, cooperative societies, and power-sharing initiatives that can not only alleviate the debts Tamils face but also restructure how valuations from waged labor shift between reproductive and productive labor and the impacts of those shifts on workingwomen.

In the finances, pay slips, and intimate contexts in which workers engage, women and men in the Hill Country want to live and navigate their social relations beyond what the wage can afford and do not want to be known by or for their plantation work. But the political history of that wage largely structures what and how they invest in their relations; the work they do in their social worlds, as seen in their calculations and reflections, actively strives to disentangle their relations from these negative connotations and embrace more desired conditions of existence. The plantation wage as a condition of life demonstrates not only the failure of the wage to live on its own but also the persistence of women workers' and their families' desires to continue to live. As Griffith, Preibisch, and Contreras claim, living the wage is "creative and unique" but "wage-labor relations are nearly everywhere and across time, similar."[44] The cycle of capital accumulation is on repeat and, as evident in the successively unsatisfying CA plantation wages, history will repeat itself. As seen in the above colonial records, the industrial language of wage negotiations often eerily resembles the justifications of white British planters. In planters' minds, conditions of "free" labor meant giving "coolies" just enough compensation so that they could live to labor, knowing well that what they offered was not enough for workers to live with dignity. The aspirations and desires for dignity that Hill Country Tamils voice suggest that the minimum is never enough. It is a condition of life whose logic of inhumanity they continue to struggle with, swallow, and accommodate. Attending to Sri Lanka's historical and dynamic relationship with waged labor as a condition of life allows us to see how workers and their families accommodate that language and heritage, how both infuse their present circumstances and the movement of their investments.

CHAPTER 4

Building Home

SAROJA, A YOUNGER MIDDLE-CLASS PROGRAM COORDINATOR AT the local NGO office I was visiting in Hatton, asked me what I had done over the holiday weekend. It was the Monday after the Sinhala and Tamil New Year celebrations in April 2009. I had spent Saturday night on Kirkwall in the line room home of a worker whose relative had returned from Colombo for the festivities. When I told her, she immediately began to warn me about staying in the lines and called them "backward" spaces—unventilated, unhealthy, crowded, and unhygienic. Michael, the former director of the NGO who was visiting from out of town, overheard our conversation and jumped in with frustration: "The line room is like a prison! Only when you leave do you see the disadvantages of living there. You cannot grow—socially, mentally, physically—it is a debilitating system. You can give someone a house, but will it be a space where he or she can grow or will it just be a facility?"

The conversation was uncomfortable and unsettling. While I knew that Michael's frustration stemmed from his fight for better living conditions on the estates, I also recalled the home in which I had slept and the family members who had welcomed me into their space. Mindful of Michael's intentions and the context in which Saroja spoke as a middle-class, upper-caste woman not living in the estate lines, I felt that the families with whom I had spent time—the families who call their line rooms home—had been stripped of their humanity. How was it that life had continued to grow and live in such debilitating spaces? Judith Butler and Athena Athanasiou write, "The power of dispossession works by rendering certain subjects, communities, or populations unintelligible, by eviscerating for them the conditions of possibility for life and the 'human' itself."[1] Michael's words seemed to have done that. By denying the existence of life enclosed in the line room, he had made Hill Country Tamils' homes and their lives "unintelligible," improper, and inhuman. I found myself brushing up against a representation of dispossession that did not accommodate the generative signs of life, investment, and desire I had observed. With dispossession on the plantations contingent on the reproduction of Hill Country Tamil labor, life in the line rooms forces us to consider the human-environmental connections that workers cultivate within the industrial-residential spaces they have called home since the arrival of their ancestors.

This chapter examines the relationship among labor, investment, and home on the tea estates in order to present a broader conceptualization of the Tamil term ūr, or what Tamil speakers around the world come to understand as a representation of one's "home." E. Valentine Daniel defines ūr as a "territory that is (1) inhabited by human beings who are believed to share in the substance of the soil . . . and (2) to which a Tamil can cognitively orient herself at any given time."[2] The utterance of the word, he contends, is contextually "idiocentric" and inherently relational: its signification depends on the speaker's position at any given time and space and whom the speaker addresses.[3] Whenever I would meet someone during fieldwork, I was asked, "What is your ūr?" My response would vary depending on where I was, where I was heading, and to whom I was speaking. On the plantations, questions of ūr bear a unique weight on the speaker. Knowing one's ūr gives those who hear it a sense of not only where the speaker considers home but also, potentially, what the speaker has done, where they may have worked, what their ancestors have done, and where they stand within hierarchies of caste, class, and labor. The term—to use Paul Kockelman's phrase—"at once enclose[s] and disclose[s]" one's standing in the world.[4] Diane Mines examines this discursive tension as it plays out in the public distinction between ūrmakkaḷ (the tax-paying village people) and kuṭimakkaḷ (Scheduled Caste laborers or service-providing families) in South India.[5] Mines found that ūr could represent the whole village and that those who lived in the village could call it their ūr; what the ūrmakkaḷ did, for instance, during Hindu festival times would come to stand in for the benefit of the entire village in a metonymic sense. Mines builds on Daniel's enclosing ūr by focusing on a more disclosing ūr. For Mines, ūr is motile—it moves alongside social and political relations across intersections of caste, communal action, and social power.

Sharika Thiranagama also focuses on the more disclosing ūr in her research among internally displaced northern Muslims whom the LTTE evicted from Jaffna in 1990. She argues, "Attachment to ūr thus provided a belonging that superceded present political possibilities [and] ties that continued to exist despite the severing of their right to return."[6] In this context, ūr can be lost, idealized, and claimed—even if material and sociohistorical signifiers suggest otherwise. This is an especially useful framing for the Hill Country Tamils whose heritage is marked by land and labor dispossession that lives in workers' memories and is passed down over generations. If ūr is not always contingent on others' beliefs, legal rights and praxis, and political action, then how do landless citizens who continue to inhabit the industrial-residential landscapes of the tea plantations experience it?

Expanding on the above iterations of ūr—the enclosing and disclosing, motile, and lost—this chapter explores what it might mean to integrate Hill Country Tamils' heritage of industrial labor and dispossession into anthropological debates on home. The stories and analysis to follow recalibrate the weight of ūr as a signifier of material and affective rootedness to industrial landscapes. Practices of building homes and the values associated with labor and investments in sustaining those homes embody what Keith Basso calls the "interactional work" of articulating connections between landscapes and vested individuals.[7] Hill Country Tamil plantation residents take on building homes and investment practices in their line rooms, and those practices directly challenge the coherence of the tea plantation. In doing so, they expand formerly accepted understandings of ūr to acknowledge the intersections of labor, industry, and personhood that inform workers' experiences of dispossession.

Like the "places of being" that Elizabeth Dunn describes among refugees in camps, the residential spaces on Sri Lanka's tea plantations are filled with "connections and links disrupted and damaged but still existent"; in order to live, Hill Country Tamil tea plantation residents create and build their homes out of constructed spaces that were formerly incommensurate with their life desires, and they transform them into practiced places that can accommodate their aspirations.[8] But unlike the refugee's remaking of worlds in the camps after catastrophic disasters hit, worldmaking in Sri Lanka's tea plantation line rooms is not a complete remaking of the life once known but a gradual, imbricative undertaking. This process has been taking place since the settling of Hill Country Tamils as resident wage laborers in makeshift huts and other laborer dwellings on Ceylon's coffee and tea estates. Today, the colonial construction of the plantation line room, or *layam*, today stands as a living artifact of this bricolage process and also as material evidence of the uneven nature of landlessness for marginalized agricultural and migrant laborers. Of the lines rooms, Sivamohan Sumathy writes, "home, the layam, is a mark of one's political subjecthood and subjectivity."[9] At the same time, workers actively seek to delink from the tea plantation as a site of their future labor, and their desire to distance themselves from the plantation presents material and affective evidence of imperial deconstruction, industrial instability, and political reform on its landscapes.

This evidence also challenges former anthropological claims that newer generations of Hill Country Tamils affirm ūr as any place other than Sri Lanka proper—namely India, a place unvisited by most Sri Lankan–born Hill Country Tamils today and mostly sensed through media technologies, song, and cinema. Instead, Hill Country Tamil plantation residents embody a sense of place that is built, put out into the world, and made visible through both material and cognitive investments in the plantations and their desires for dignity, home, and the good life. But this sense of home sharply contrasts with everyday perceptions of class and hierarchy in human rights and development discourse, as evident in Michael and Saroja's open condemnations of line room life. Cordoned off as lower-caste and lower-class spaces that stunt human growth and constrict human agency, tea plantation line rooms are often defined as enclosures of what Nathaniel Roberts calls "biological impurity [and] immorality."[10] Given these representations, state policies often seek to transform the lines rooms into spaces more commensurate with transnational development principles of human rights and dignity, but within limits that maintain the industry's sustainability and productivity. Keeping these reforms in mind, the line rooms, when renovated, become practiced spaces where workers and their families produce and consume ūr, but they also bring to the surface the tensions and incommensurabilities that layers of alienable industrial labor, state reform, and rights-based aspirations have produced over time.

Locating Ūr

In 2015 I sat down with Sellamma, her nephew Kumaravel, and his wife, Devi, in their line room home over tea and asked them, "What is your ūr?" Sellamma immediately said, "Abbottsleigh," the estate division about five kilometers away, where she was born in 1957. Kumaravel said, "Kirkwall division, Portswood Group, Hatton." Devi, said that Cinnamanvetti Tōttam (small trenching hoe estate) in Kotagala (about twelve kilometers from Hatton) was her *piranta ūr* (natal home) but now, after marriage, her ūr was Kirkwall. Their responses evolved into a longer conversation. "Wherever I go, I say I am Kirkwall," Kumaravel told me. Devi, who had worked as a domestic in Saudi Arabia for three years, interjected, "If I am in Saudi, I say Sri Lanka or Hatton depending on whom I am talking to. I say Kotagala if I am here [on Kirkwall]. If I am in Kotagala, I say I am here [in Kirkwall]. He [pointing to Kumaravel] says Kirkwall because he has not been to Saudi and has always lived and worked here." I asked Sellamma where her father, who had passed away in 2011, would have considered his ūr, knowing I had already asked him this very question, while he was still alive in 2009. Born in Pattukkottai, Tamil Nadu, he had traveled to Ceylon in the early 1940s as a four-year-old. He began working as a twelve-year-old on Lochiel estate, outside Dickoya town, which is situated about halfway between Kirkwall and Hatton. After marriage, he moved to Kirkwall with his wife and family to find better work. Until his death in 2011, he lived there with his extended family of children and grandchildren and never held Sri Lankan citizenship, only carrying a faded paper slip from the plantation management that verified his residency on Kirkwall. Sellamma confirmed what he had told me earlier in 2011: "My father would say Lochiel, the estate where he had gone to from India and worked on as a child."

Our conversation mirrored the spatiotemporal fluidity that anthropologists studying concepts of ūr and belonging among Tamil-speaking communities in South India and Sri Lanka have already documented.[11] Officially, Hill Country Tamils living in the line rooms would not appear to have ūr on the plantations; the soil or earth, in the plantation's original state, was never shared by a consistent group, but by a dispersed community of laborers sustaining and responding to the needs of colonial, state-run, and private economies. This lack of consistency with the soil became even more poignant during a Hindu funeral I attended in September 2009, when the body of the deceased woman plucker was not buried on the physical grounds of plantation itself but alongside the main road to Hatton in a designated and available place that had been selected by the estate committee. Hill Country Tamils commonly bury their deceased as opposed to cremating them according to caste and Hindu practices, but it is important to note that this particular management did not provide workers or residents any designated burial grounds on the estate grounds. While the 1899 Cemeteries and Burial Grounds Ordinance No. 563 regulates burial practices and designates the provision of cemetery grounds, the tea estates were unevenly kept up to code and only select tea estates were provided designated burial grounds for Christian and Catholic residents. Residents of estates without these provisions would often tell me about their concerns over the burials of the deceased. More often than not, they would be required to bury their dead along open roads and other liminal and public spaces, and these spots were less enclosed and more susceptible to *pey*, the Tamil term for unsettled or evil spirits.

For older residents, the plantations do not fit the definition of one's natal home. Sellamma was not born in the line room she currently lives in, but on the estate where her mother and father worked previously. During repatriation to India, her sister went to the Nilgiris in Tamil Nadu, and the two siblings had not spoken to or seen each other since. When I would ask her and others on the estate, "What is your ūr?" I never got a firm orientation to a particular location and would hear more fluid stories of mobility and work histories. In this way, ūr had come to be felt and known through kin- and labor-based networks that were built on wage labor and concretized through histories of migration, displacement, and market-based changes in Sri Lanka's economy. I also never heard Hill Country Tamils deny that ūr was in Sri Lanka or confirm it to be in India. Their insistence that ūr was in Sri Lanka mirrors how other Tamil-speaking communities who are deprived of home in Sri Lanka speak of ūr as a "materially emotive way of reckoning belonging" despite that belonging going unrecognized by others.[12] Valentine Daniel states the following regarding Hill Country Tamils' claim of ūr: "Every Tamil, by definition, has an ūr of his own. . . . To this day, even the Tamils of Indian origin whose ancestors settled in the hills of Sri Lanka in the nineteenth century to work in British-owned coffee, rubber, and tea plantations claim to have an ūr of their own, back in India. As many as eight generations of these Tamils have lived and died on these plantations, but they do not consider these plantations as their own ūr. So, its truth would have been one of those already always-confirmed truths."[13]

Throughout my fieldwork, Hill Country Tamils expressed that they considered the plantations to be their ūr, and their claims to the plantation soil as home challenge us to reconsider former criteria for ūr, belonging, and home investments. What exists for Hill Country Tamils on Sri Lanka's tea plantations is not the truth of ūr "already always–confirmed" but one that must be continually confirmed and reinforced by workers' desires for the good life and the potential of the industry to actualize those futures.[14] Sri Lanka's plantations workers' claim to ūr is built and its single end or standard object is a *home*—which, in socio-legal terms, was and continues to be effectively denied by normatively accepted markets of exchange.

Industrial Ūr

In July 2015 I was walking with Sunil, a thirty-eight-year-old Sinhala field accountant on Kirkwall. Originally from Bandarawela, Sunil left his former career in the armed forces in Batticaloa to work as an estate field accountant in Badulla eighteen years earlier. He came to Kirkwall for a salary raise nine years ago and settled with his wife and three daughters in the estate's staff quarters. During our walk, he admitted that his Tamil was better than his Sinhala, as he had worked and interacted daily with Hill Country Tamil workers now for more than half his life. When I met his wife and three daughters for lunch later that day, they, too, spoke to me and to one another in Tamil. They also attended Hindu festivals, and worshipped the Hindu god Ganesha to protect their staff quarter home (which they did not own).

I asked Sunil where he considered his ūr to be. He said that Bandarawela was his *piranta ūr*, but that this place, Kirkwall, was his *conta ūr*, a term best translated as "one's real home."[15] Despite not being of the same caste or ethnicity as other Hill Country Tamils who also consider Kirkwall to be their *conta ūr*, Sunil did bear signs of being in his real home beyond the traditional definitions I had been familiar with, such as his fluent Tamil, now-unsure Sinhala, and his intentional interactions with the estate landscape. As we walked back to the main road on worker footpaths, he paused out of respect as we passed the roadside shrines to the Hindu deities Muniandi (guardian of the estates), Rōtamuni (deity of estate factories), and Māriamman (goddess of rain and curing of diseases). Over the last 150 years, workers had constructed and maintained these shrines to not only protect but also seek comfort in what happened to their bodies, the land, and the industrial components designed to sustain them.[16] On my numerous walks with workers along the tea bushes or footpaths, we would always pause and pray at each shrine, even if the workers I was with were not practicing Hindus.

Beyond feeling connected to the land, Sunil had close relations with the workers he supervised. This closeness became most clear when he attempted to move up to assistant superintendent in 2015, a promotion that the Kirkwall workers I spoke to wanted him to have because they trusted him and because he treated them fairly. But, in the end, the company rejected his application due to internal politics, and he felt forced to seek a more lucrative job and move his family to an estate outside Central Province. In the midst of having to uproot his family yet again and dejected from not receiving the promotion despite his eighteen years of industrial experience and nine years of work on Kirkwall, Sunil described to me, in a mix of Tamil and English, how he had lost faith in the plantation system: "Of the sixty women workers on my check roll, only twenty-four or twenty-eight will be coming. They [the women who pluck the tea] do not like to work. There is no solution and we will continue to see a labor shortage with this new generation. They are not like the older ones from before. They are more educated. One's work should be genuine. Right now, plantation work has no respect [ippat tōtta vēlai mariyāthai illai]. The companies should make it as such."

The lack of respect to which Sunil referred has real consequences for the tea industry but also for workers' desires to detach from a labor system that refuses to provide them with dignified work. On an industrial level, the RPCs pride themselves on being one of few tea industries still using human labor to pluck; yet the reality is that machines may be the only alternative sources of extraction given the worsening labor shortage. In 2014, I heard rumors that a former manager had been transferred and demoted for putting black dye in the tea, which he allegedly did because he was not meeting the standard industrial expectations for quality of product. In 2017, workers on Kirkwall told me that management had begun using tree-cutting and pruning machines as well as electric leaf-cutting shears. As I walked with Sunil that day, he commented on such acts of desperation and lamented at how productive Kirkwall could be—if only the planters would recognize and reward the actual connections that Hill Country Tamil workers had made with the land.

The Motile Ūr, Revisited

While dispossession was a key feature of their lives, all the men and women with whom I spoke still felt rooted to the land on which they resided and worked. The difference between resident and visitor became all the more apparent early on in my fieldwork. On the days I traveled into Hatton from my residence, I would wait for the bus on the roadside opposite where I stayed. One day in early January 2009, shortly after I had arrived for research, I had to wait for the bus for more than twenty minutes. I stood on the side of the road reading some Provincial Council campaign posters and candidate ballot numbers that had been canvased and chalked into the rocks that lined the edges of the slopes leading to the plantation fields. During the twenty minutes I stood there, I did not see one person walk by me on the road nor any three-wheeler or car. Furthermore, since I had been waiting below the cliff of a slope, I could not see anyone working in the fields above me. The bus eventually came, and I climbed onto it and continued my research in town.

Later that afternoon, I went to Kirkwall and stopped by Sellamma's home. After asking me what I ate for breakfast and lunch—not uncommon for elderly women to ask younger women in Sri Lanka—she asked me what I had done in town. I told her that I had met with a few NGO staff members, and I asked her how she knew where I had gone. She told me that she had seen me waiting for the bus while she was taking a break from her housework and chatting on the stoop of her friend's line room veranda, which was adjacent to her own home. The lines of that particular division of Kirkwall sit at an elevation of approximately 3,700 feet, and the road on which I was waiting was about fifty feet below and a little over a quarter of a mile to the east of them. I had not seen anyone, but Sellamma had seen me. My presence as a visitor—manifest in my posture, skin color, clothing, and mannerisms—was recognizable to her even from that distance. Living on Kirkwall for more than fifty years, she, as a participant in plantation group life, knows the rhythms and textures of the place to which my presence was a new addition. Self-conscious of my outsider presence on that January afternoon, I would later sit with Sellamma on the stoop in the months and years to follow, watching that same road and its unsuspecting travelers from above.

The incident seemed minor in the moment but presents a significant entry point for challenging previously held assumptions that Hill Country Tamils on the tea plantations have no rooted sense of belonging to places or territories in Sri Lanka. It also serves as evidence that acquiring knowledge of a place in situ and making a place intimately known to oneself requires an embodiment and sense of time *over time* and an established commitment to interact with the industrial and residential landscape such that emotional attachments inform one's social relations. By nature, these attachments often elude institutional, industrial, and state-run documentations of residence but reveal themselves in the more quotidian "lower frequencies" of dwelling and work on the plantations.[17]

In early August 2015 I experienced another "lower frequency" moment like the one above. I was visiting a local *pūcari* (local-level Hindu priest) with Sellamma and her brother, Mūrthi, at a Māriamman temple on an estate about five kilometers from Kirkwall in the direction of Hatton town. While traveling by private bus was the only economically feasible option at the time, it was time-consuming and uncomfortable, as the private buses only came every thirty minutes and were often filled to capacity. Nevertheless, after our meeting ended, Sellmamma, Mūrthi, and I waited for the bus for ten minutes in the rain. When it still had not arrived, Mūrthi suggested we walk by foot through three estate divisions back to Kirkwall.

We began our journey home on a path not discernible to visitors, on what remained of older worker footpaths that Sellamma and Mūrthi had used when they were working on the estates over thirty years ago, which linked all the estate divisions within the plantation group. Now largely unused, the paths were overgrown with grass and at one point seemed to stop, ending on the outskirts of an open, marshy field. Mūrthi then identified where the path continued across the field. We walked barefoot through marsh, with leeches between our toes, to get to the other side. About three quarters of the way home, we stopped at a wooden lodge in the forest areas of a neighboring estate. Twelve years earlier, Mūrthi and three workers had built the lodge for high-level male estate staff, managers, and foreigners. As we walked around the lodge, he showed me each bungalow as well as each chair, table, and fixture he had carved out of wood. We had tea with his male relation who oversaw the kitchen and visited a small spring, where we were able to wash off our feet, which were soiled and pruned from the rain and mud. As we continued, the rain stopped and the sun came out briefly. We cut through the tea bushes on uneven stone footpaths for pluckers. It seemed as if we had been walking for quite a while, so I asked Sellamma the time. She told me it was fifteen minutes to seven. I asked her how she knew the time since she had not been wearing a watch or carrying a phone. She said, "I can tell what time of day it is by looking at the light of the sun on the tea bushes." I pulled out my phone. She was right. It was a skill she had developed during her years as a plucker—telling her when to go home to breastfeed her child, take a tea break with other workers on the road, and walk back to her house at the end of a day's work.

4.1. Walking with Mūrthi on old worker footpaths, through estate divisions, on our way back to Kirkwall estate in 2015

We continued our walk, passing by clusters of line rooms, stopping for more tea in the homes of relations, and then finally reaching Kirkwall's temple below their line. After we ate dinner I prepared to leave, and Sellamma placed a small piece of fully burned but still warm wood from her hearth in my palm. She called it a *karikattu* and instructed me to hold it until I reached my home and then throw it outside of my room once I crossed the threshold. The *karikattu* would protect me while I was walking on the main road between their home and mine. She would not need one because this was *her* ūr, she said. I was not from here; therefore, it was not safe for me to travel in the dark without some form of protection from her home's hearth. We walked back in the dark on the main road, and she and her son left me outside my door. I threw away the *karikattu* and walked inside as they turned around and walked back home.

Diane Mines describes ūr as a "motile discourse" Tamil speakers use in a place while moving within and in relation to it: "[it is] not verbal or graphic but motile . . . they define it by walks, they talk around it, walks that are said to encircle . . . or go 'by way of' the ūr."[18] These walks also effectively mark the boundaries that could then include or exclude those who fall inside or outside the ūr.[19] This framework allows us to see that despite the circulating myth that the plantations restrict and bind Hill Country Tamils, estate residents have always enacted mobile ways of belonging. In fact, their mobility has enabled them to create a sense of place in Sri Lanka and not in India. More compelling, ūr for Hill Country Tamils extends beyond natal or resident tea estates. Walking through the three estate divisions with Mūrthi and Sellamma, I witnessed that their sense of knowing the place was not restricted to Kirkwall but extended to those undetectable and un-taxable spaces outside the jurisdictions of the plantation market.

As a "motile discourse" ūr is not always found in words or plantation landscapes, but in embodied human interactions with the soil and natural elements that make the plantation a place of being in the world. It is contingent on plantation residents' capacity to move—an experience of dispossession easily forgotten, but one that exists and complicates the operations of rights-based movements for land, housing, and citizenship. This ūr in motion also suggests that all places on a plantation do not exist solely for labor extraction and workers' exploitation. Labor is the very discourse through which workers like Mūrthi and Sellamma communicate their sense of being with the soil and other geological, nonhuman forms. This sense of being echoes what Julia Elyachar calls "tacit knowledge"—the "unsystemized, unverbalized forms of knowledge that were integrated into the body itself."[20] This knowledge surfaced in Mūrthi's pride while he toured us through the built structures of the wooden lodge he had carved, in Sellamma's telling time by the strength of the sun on the tea bushes, and in her shared belief in the power of the once burning, still warm *karikattu* as we walked from their line room home and through the darkness of the main road. These moments reflect a sense of being-with-the-place that is brought to life through memories, labor, and physical manipulation of the soil—a human and natural condition and an unpredictable reality of industrial dispossession such that retired and casual workers could find, follow, and tread on a path that was no longer a path.

Terraforming Ūr

The evidence and presence of ūr were also prominent in intimate domains on the estates—namely, in the line rooms where workers and their families live. In February 2009 I sat with Ramaiyi, a fifty-seven-year-old retired plucker, on the stoop of her line room home on Kirkwall. To the left and right of Ramaiyi's home live members of her extended family, a total of twenty-two people occupying four rooms. Past the front threshold of her house is the original twelve-by-seven-foot room where Ramaiyi, her daughter (who was twenty-six years old at the time), and two of her three grandchildren sleep. When she was younger, Ramaiyi would work on and off as a tea plucker but also earned additional income as a domestic worker in Colombo. In 1998 Ramaiyi was plucking when she had an accident and had to stop working full-time. She became a domestic to support her family of eight at the time, and when we met she was taking care of her grandchildren at home. When her son married in 2000, she took out the money she had earned from domestic work in addition to her estate work pension. With those funds, their family added an extra room onto their line room behind the original enclosure. In this room they built a makeshift, separate kitchen and storage area, and in the back of the room they kept their Hindu altar and a double bed, where her son, his wife, and their last child, then an infant, would sleep.

At the end of Ramaiyi's line live her younger brother, Chandran; his wife; and his sixteen-year-old son, who had dropped out of school as a teenager to work in Colombo in a shop. In 2007 Chandran took the money saved from his son's earnings and bought materials to split the main road pipe to carry water up to their entire line. He then added a private garden and bathing area to the back of his line room. Seven months into my fieldwork in 2009, Ramaiyi's family decided to further add on to their original line room. This time they used money that her daughter had earned as a domestic in Colombo and built a private, tented washing area similar to the one Chandran had constructed. Each year that I returned to Kirkwall between 2014 and 2017, I saw that Ramaiyi and her family had renovated their line room again and again. The first renovation took place in 2013, in preparation for her first granddaughter's age attainment ceremony. They built a small study and storage room on the anterior of the main room (figure 4.2) and a hallway and separate kitchen room with a small window on the left anterior of the main room, along

4.2.   Ramaiyi's renovated line room in 2014 showing a newly constructed anterior study and storage room as well as a constructed hallway leading to a separate kitchen room and private, tented, outdoor space for bathing

with laying down large slabs of stones for better traction in the private washing area. The last renovation was in 2017, when they converted what was once the smaller study room into a larger bedroom that could fit their double bed. Other renovations throughout the years included three extra rooms plus a separate kitchen and the expansion of their tented washing area that included a private tap connecting to the split water line that Chandran had brought up from the main road in 2007.

In 2014, I asked Ramaiyi how they had financed the first round of renovations. Ramaiyi's son was listed as a casual worker on Kirkwall, but in actuality he was a full-time worker for a tea smallholder an hour-long bus ride away along with other men residing on Kirkwall. Ramaiyi had also gone back to agricultural work after 2009 as well, this time as a casual laborer for a smallholder in the same area as her son's employer. Each day mother and son would travel two hours roundtrip together and come back with a combined net salary of Rs. 1,400 with two of three of their meals paid for, a considerably higher compensation than what they could receive working on Kirkwall.

In August 2015 I celebrated the Hindu auspicious occasion of Ādi Pūcai with Ramaiyi and her extended family, including her daughter's in-laws from an estate in Maskeliya. We spent the afternoon making sweets, and when it got dark we went into the front room, which was the twelve-by-seven-foot space that had been their original line room. It was a special occasion—Ramaiyi's daughter, who got married in 2012, was having two gold coins fastened along the sides of the pendant at the center of her marriage necklace, or *tāli kodi*, a turmeric-dipped thread, symbolizing her union. The occasion was also bittersweet. Ramaiyi's son and daughter-in-law were to have provided the two gold coins last year but could not do so because of their household expenses and debts. Given that her daughter had already given birth to two children after marriage and had no gold coins, her daughter's mother-in-law from Maskeliya paid the Rs. 8,000 so that she would not have to transition through another Ādi Pūcai without the completion of her *tāli*. Later, as we prepared to serve the dinner, Ramaiyi's daughter-in-law lamented how upset she and her husband were that they could not provide the gold coins as kinship custom had dictated. But at least, she told me, because of their work income and investments in renovating their home, they were able to host the entire family for the auspicious occasion. That night, the twelve of us slept on the floor in the main room in one line, while her visiting in-laws slept in the private bedroom with Ramaiyi's toddler grandson. We slept in the room that was built by them for the specific purpose of accommodating their lives, rituals, and generative possibilities.

Former South Asian and anthropological concepts of postcolonial and market-based territoriality, home ownership, and investment do not adequately accommodate the practices of home building that I observed on the estates. Landless Hill Country Tamils who do not own their residences on Sri Lanka's RPC-run estates are not waiting for the government or development to feel a sense of ownership of the spaces they consider home. Instead, they actively seek out and secure more dignified lives, and their labor is deconstructing the ideals of a standardized plantation workforce and landscape. This process of terraforming is a pragmatic task taken on by Tamil plantation residents who recognize that the allotted line room spaces are uninhabitable and unaccommodating to the fullness of the lives workers wish to lead. Realizing this, they terraform lands that they do not own and find alternatives to transform these spaces into places more commensurate with their aspirations. What is left is a new artifact of home—a practiced space built by labor that falls neither within former conceptions of ūr nor within practiced notions of ownership, investment, and belonging in Sri Lanka. It is a concept of home more inhabitable and more compatible with Tamil plantation residents' needs and desires.

Anthropologists studying labor and its effects on belonging have noted similar home-building practices on plantations.[21] Sarah Besky argues that plantation houses in Darjleeing's tea gardens—as "outgrowths of the colonial line"—are forms of "fixity," "inheritance," and "containers for a history of reciprocal, nonmonetary relationships of care among workers, the land, and the management."[22] Similarly, Andrew Willford, studying the transition and inevitable death of Malaysia's rubber plantations, describes how former Tamil laborers did not want to leave the estates and missed the "comforts or decorations of home" in their new urban flats.[23] The crucial difference on Sri Lanka's tea plantations, however, lies in the instability and unevenness, rather than in the stability or constancy of a belief in the management's capacity to provide and foster a sense of home among workers. Instead, workers *themselves* use what Igor Rubinov calls "migrant assemblages" to make "livelihoods livable" and industrial spaces more homely.[24] In the cracks, layers, and shifting foundations of each line room home that I visited, a material assemblage and archive signified the cash flow and value of residents' labor histories; and yet the product of those labors are investments in spaces unowned but practiced as home over generations of work. Terraforming directly calls out the *nonreciprocal* rather than reciprocal investments that plantation workers put into their unowned lands and homes. It also demonstrates, as Mark Hauser found on Dominica's colonial sugar plantation enclaves, "how people [specifically enslaved laborers] mobilize surplus for their own ends."[25] This distinctiveness urges a reimagining of labor dispossession on the tea plantations that accounts for the tripartite relationship between Tamil forms of personhood, income investment, and civic belonging in Sri Lanka.

Contrary to Michael's claim, life does exist in the line rooms, and the fluid structures of the spaces are signs of not only sustained dispossession but also emplaced connectivity. Workers perform rituals and prepare and eat food, and the line room is not a permanent structure but a site of "knowing a place through labor" and "care for others."[26] This was evident in the gradual, structural modifications to Ramaiyi's home, the handling of her daughter's *tāli* ceremony, and Chandran's infrastructural renovations. These built environments and investments to make industrial landscapes livable raise questions about what it means to claim home on the plantations and to call Sri Lanka's plantations ūr.

Ūr in Transition

Terraforming as investment is significant because the majority of Hill Country Tamils living on the plantations do not legally own the line rooms where their sense of ūr is claimed. Their residence is contingent on one person per household maintaining full-time employment status on the plantation, such that if a family decides to pursue off-plantation employment full-time, the family would be rendered homeless. In 2005, future president Mahinda Rajapaksa's election manifesto, *Mahinda Chinthana*, proposed to give a "new life" to the plantation community by providing housing development assistance to move toward an ownership structure through housing loans and in-kind grants.[27] In 2006, the Ministry of Nation Building and Estate Infrastructure Development, working within the UN's MDGs (Millennium Development Goals) and with assistance from the UNDP (United Nations Development Programme), unveiled the National Plan of Action (NPA).[28] In this plan, the government committed to construct 160,000 single-family housing units for plantation workers and to provide a soft loan of Rs. 125,000 ($1,170) per household with a 7.5 percent annual interest rate in addition to an in-kind grant of Rs. 125,000 for construction materials and expenses.[29] As the ministry outlined, the program's objective was to replace the "very obsolete housing stock which is unfit for human habitation."[30] Citing the high interest rates, mounting labor shortages, and lack of time available to workers to build their own houses, plantation unions and political leaders lobbied the government to change the proposal. The ministry then introduced new housing schemes, experimenting with lower interest rates, twin housing structures, and beneficiary contributions through unskilled labor in pilot projects throughout the sector.[31] In accordance with the UN MDGs and UNDP mandates, the 2006 NPA proposed indicators to complete half of the project by 2010 and the entirety by 2015.

Before Sri Lanka's 2010 presidential election, the incumbent, President Rajapaksa, renewed the commitment despite the fact that the housing project had not met its projected goals. This time, he vowed to make the plantation community a "house-owning society" and that "instead of present line rooms, every plantation worker family [would] be proud owners of new homes with basic amenities by the year 2015."[32] Between 2010 and 2015, however, political turmoil, unmet promises for national reconciliation, and economic development in the North and East took priority, and the government made little progress in the plantation sector.

In January 2015, after ten years of broken promises, candidate Maitripala Sirisena, soon to be president, announced that "steps [would] be taken to provide ownership and proper housing to plantation workers instead of their current confinements in line rooms."[33] After his electoral victory, the Sirisena government adopted this principle in April 2015 and committed to build 377 single-family houses (each on seven perches of land) for low-income beneficiaries who qualified for the housing program through an application process and required membership shares in the Estate Worker Housing Cooperative Society (EWHCS).[34] Through this program, eligible beneficiaries could enter the housing project under the following stipulations. First, the worker could not partition or divide the land and could only sell the land to the EWHCS, which is run by the plantation management and whose president is the plantation manager. Second, in order to own the house, the worker had to be a full-time employee of the RPC connected to the purchased land. Most critical, at the time of the program's development, the government owned the land on which the RPCs were running the tea plantations according to the 1972 Land Reform Act. During the transition to privatization, the government gave the RPCs the land on long-term leases. Therefore, plantation workers and the houses they are eligible to own are confined to a plantation value and labor market, which the RPCs oversee and restrict in relation to national and global market land values.[35] With loan payments and interest rates high and RPC wages low, even those workers eligible to enter the housing program find it difficult to survive economically. During my visit to a plantation outside Kandy in 2015, workers told me they were renting their "owned" houses to casual workers for extra income and preferred to live in the line rooms with their kin because it was more affordable. Furthermore, even those workers who had paid their loans in full had yet to receive land titles or deeds to their houses from the management-led EWHCS. While obtaining deeds to government-supplied lands is an issue for many Sri Lankans, that the unmet promise of a deed came to stand in for what was the first taste of land rights and home ownership on industrially productive soil for Hill Country Tamils is uniquely concerning in the context of the community's former disenfranchisement and statelessness.

By 2016, the Ministry of Estate Infrastructure and Development had been renamed the Ministry of Hill Country New Villages, Infrastructure, and Community Development.[36] A new National Plan of Action on the Social Development of the Plantation Community was released for 2016–2020 with a goal of constructing fifty thousand houses in the timeframe and support for securing title deeds for homeowners on the estates. On December 6, 2016, the Cabinet of Ministers responded to a proposal made by Palani Digambaram (Ministry of Hill Country New Villages, Infrastructure, and Community Development), Navin Dissanayake (Ministry of Plantation Industries), and John Amaratunge (Ministry of Land) to "provide freehold and bankable lands of 7 perches each for legal residents and to release identifiable lands from plantation companies and other public institutions."[37] In February 2017, the government of Sri Lanka, in conjunction with three ministers from the Tamil Progressive Alliance (TPA), provided land ownership to residents in Hauteville Estate of Agarapatana Regional Plantation Company, installing mailboxes and setting residents up with individual addresses.[38] On August 1, 2017, the Ministry of Hill Country New Villages, Infrastructure, and Community Development again proposed a revised action plan to the Cabinet of Ministers to grant ownership of houses constructed between 2010 and 2016 in Nuwara Eliya, Badulla, and Kegalle.[39]

The financial commitments in these housing plans are not limited to regional and national stakeholders. Under the UN-Habitat rehabilitation initiative, which began in 2010, the Indian Housing Project in the Central and Uva Provinces (IHP-CUP) was implemented through a memorandum of understanding between the governments of India and Sri Lanka to construct four thousand houses on RPC-owned tea plantations as a part of the Indian Housing Project's overall commitment to provide fifty thousand houses in postwar Sri Lanka.[40] On May 12, 2017, Indian prime minister Narendra Modi, during his visit to Sri Lanka, made a speech in the hill station town of Norwood, about twelve kilometers away from Kirkwall. To a crowd of about thirty thousand Hill Country Tamils, he announced the construction of an additional ten thousand houses under the IHP and various other development commitments that the government of India pledged to give the estate community. In his speech he remarked, "You have made Sri Lanka your home. You are an intrinsic part of the warp and the weft of the social fabric of this beautiful nation."[41] Given the uncertainty and flux of Hill Country Tamils' land and housing rights on the plantations, the euphoria around his visit and speech, as journalist Meera Srinivasan notes, was "not only misplaced but also has the danger of reinforcing hill-country Tamils as passive beneficiaries rather than rightful citizens."[42] One part of Modi's speech was true: Hill Country Tamils living on the tea plantations had made Sri Lanka their home. However, they have done so largely through their own gendered labor and work investments into lands and dwelling structures that are not legally their own.

In these three iterations of the "new life" housing programs, one constant remains: Hill Country Tamils are given the promise of land ownership, home investment, and purchase in the absence of a true public marketplace. These endeavors raise significant concerns over the current line rooms in which plantation residents have cultivated a sense of home and in which they have invested their labor and time. The line rooms on Sri Lanka's RPCs, despite new legislation placing them in state categories of territory and governance, are still not fully regarded as such; and yet they are subject to local forms of state policing, militarization, and surveillance. Under privatization, the line rooms were considered the responsibilities of the RPC business enterprise and were detached from Tamil and Sinhala village concepts such as the Tamil *kirāmam* or Sinhala *grāma*; with the government maintaining and determining these village boundaries, the line rooms were legally inscribed outside state jurisdictions of care but still subject to forms of state governmentality.[43] For example, section 33 of the Pradeshiya Sabha Act No. 15 of 1987, only repealed in December 2017, excluded plantation residents from receiving services from local government councils (Pradeshiya Sabhas). Prior to the repeal, these local government councils did not have access to plantation lands for development purposes without management approval, despite estate residents' tax and fee contributions to those very same councils.[44]

Given this condition of taxation without village inclusion, Hill Country Tamils' ūr on the plantations maintains its distinctiveness from the Tamil concept of *kirāmam*, as highlighted by Daniel: "If lost, a *kirāmam* has a value, and hence, is recoverable as a commodity in a capitalist market. Or, if whatever else of value it may represent is lost, other things of equal value can replace it. This is why a *kiramām*, as a revenue unit, provides a measure of its own taxation. An ūr, strictly speaking, cannot be taxed . . . the loss of an ūr, a place, the practices of which constitute its identity as a place, cannot be worked into an exchange market because it is priceless."[45] Here, Daniel defines the value of ūr as not "marketable" but "intrinsic" or "priceless" in the context of Hill Country Tamil's extended landlessness in Sri Lanka. But current state-run housing projects, promotions of purchasing value-restricted lands, and taxations of workers who live on untaxable lands blur these previously held distinctions. What is left is a sense of ūr on the plantations that is not as easily defined by socio-legal categories of territory and governance but politically entangled within postwar reconstructive efforts marred by continued militarization and majoritarian politics.

Despite the absence of land and housing rights, estate residents' breaking down and building up of the lines rooms and renting of their "owned" houses suggest that ūr as we knew it—the "ūr that was already always there"—no longer fully accommodates the life practices and sentiments of Hill Country Tamil communities' connectivity to the plantations.[46] While ūr maintains its sense and strength in Tamil forms of world making and mobility in and beyond Sri Lanka, the built plantation line room where that ūr is felt is not always there; it is not autochthonous. Rather, it is constructed—like the rooms added to Ramaiyi's home and the shrines to Rōtamuni and Muniandi maintained inside muster sheds; it is tended to—like the hearths on which we cooked for Ādi Pūcai; and it is embodied in human values that are not only rendered "priceless" through rituals but also deemed marketable through relationships of exchange, capital, and investment.

Ūr, Buried

At 7:30 a.m. on October 29, 2014, a three-kilometer landslide buried sixty-three line room homes on Badulla's Meeriyabedda estate in the island's southwestern plantation areas. In what was then called Sri Lanka's worst natural disaster since the 2004 Indian Ocean tsunami, 830 Hill Country Tamil plantation residents were internally displaced, sixteen died,[47] and approximately 150 line room homes were buried.[48] Reports later confirmed that the NBRO, which monitors the island's natural disasters, had issued the original warning the day before, but the Disaster Management Center in Badulla district had not disseminated the bulletin in time for the evacuation of plantation residents.[49] After the disaster, Hill Country Tamil politicians and unionists adamantly raised the issue of housing rights in their campaigns. President Rajapaksa visited the internally displaced in the days after the disaster and promised them newly constructed single-family homes within three months. The Sri Lankan Army took over the decommissioned Makanda Tea Factory to accommodate the sixty-three families as a part of that plan; in the factory, residents lived in makeshift conditions while construction for their new homes began.

In January 2015, in response to intense pressure from Hill Country Tamil leaders, the incoming Sirisena government announced that the Meeriyabedda survivors were to receive 550-square-foot single-family houses on seven perches of land on a full grant basis. The Meeriyabedda housing plan was adopted and integrated into Sirisena's hundred-day work program and fully supported by Hill Country Tamil politicians who hoped to maintain their parliamentary seats in the upcoming August 2015 elections. But the hundred days came and went, and as of July 2016 the internally displaced families still lived in Makanda Tea Factory; by July 2017, all the survivors had been resettled, but NBRO's final technical report of the resettlement process cited multiple instances of lacking coordination, infrastructure issues, and mismanagement.[50]

The Meeriyabedda landslide embodies what Elizabeth Povinelli calls geontopower—the blurring of life and nonlife to enable how power relations come to be justified through practice.[51] In the end, the plantation soil—the substance that Hill Country Tamils had called and felt as their ūr—had buried and destroyed their homes, lives, and market investments. The slipping of the land was a nonethical act but had ethical origins and ends. These types of geontological crises are not new to Sri Lanka and will happen again given the market demands of the plantation industry and the sector's long history of affecting Sri Lanka's geological landscape through years of mono-cropping and soil erosion.[52] In the event of such future crises, what resources will it take politically and socially to rebuild and sustain Hill Country Tamils' sense of ūr on and beyond the plantation's fragile grounds?

In the summer of 2014 I returned to Kirkwall, a little more than a year after Cyclone Mahasen hit Sri Lanka. Having the most impact on the Northern and Eastern Provinces, the cyclone also hit Central Province with flooding, rain, and landslides; the surrounding plantation and urban areas of Hatton and Dickoya had also been hit, resulting in the loss of three lives in one family, damage to several line rooms and owned homes off the estates, and significant property loss. During my visit, I went to Letchumi's line room, only to see that the back wall of her renovated kitchen add-on had partially collapsed. She was retired, and even with her daughter-in-law working full-time and her son employed as a mason in Colombo, her family had no extra money to finance the repairs, and it became clear that the estate management would not repair the damage even if it was their responsibility. The wall remained collapsed in 2015 and in 2016; by 2017, with additional loans and her son securing a job with a higher salary in Colombo, they had repaired the wall themselves. The likelihood of losing one's home throws into sharp relief the limits of well-intentioned and far-reaching housing and land rights policies for the plantation sector's currently landless civilians. Although political representatives, community leaders, and plantation companies promote and provide conventionally legal forms of housing and land rights to estate residents, such rights are not evenly enjoyed or guaranteed in the context of the tea industry's own economic sustainability and crisis. As seen in Letchumi's situation, working families are the primary investors in the security and strength of their line room homes.

Ūr *Activa*

Hannah Arendt's *vita activa* takes three basic human activities—labor, work, and action—as the core "conditions under which life on earth has been given to man."[53] Each activity is a means to an end. Labor produces life, work produces "permanence and durability," and action produces "the condition for remembrance, that is, for history."[54] Each activity is guided by different temporalities of displacement and production. Labor's products—life as experienced in my meals with Ramaiyi's family or my walk with Sunil—are consumed right after production; they are fleeting and cannot be ported or stored. Work, on the other hand, is more mediated and displaced; it is done with our hands. Its products—human artifacts—can endure unforgiving environments. While they are meant to remain on earth for human beings to enjoy in the long run—much like the wooden cabin Mūrthi built—they, too, can be destroyed.

But Arendt's sense of action is most unsettling. It requires an experience of intersubjectivity—subjects being among subjects in a public sphere. Through action, we present words and deeds for the sake of making the patent visible to those within our ever-changing web of social relations. Our words and deeds are not wholly predictable and cannot be destroyed or taken back once released into the world. We make promises, we forgive, but we often forget our speech acts and their consequences. In this sense, action's products—history and how other subjects remember us in this world—appear to be the most displaced and *displacing*; they require a continual practice of mutual recognition and trust that our words and deeds will be seen on our terms in the end. As Arendt argues, in our modern life, processes of bureaucratization—as seen in the recursions of the plantation industry and postwar land and housing policy reforms—reduce our action to work and our work to labor, such that everything we produce—our identities, worldly things for our kith and kin, and our environments, both built and natural—are subject to impermanence and destruction.

In August 2017, to intervene in the 150-year celebrations of the tea industry, the Centre for Policy Alternatives stated boldly in a report about the line rooms, "This house is not a home."[55] But my conversations and time spent with residents who live, eat, and invest in their homes made this phrase, like Michael and Saroja's comments back in 2009, hard for me to accept. While having a deed, address, and mailbox are legitimate rights that all Hill Country Tamils living on the plantations should enjoy as citizens, what does it truly mean—*what does it do* to the person who inhabits and invests in their home—to tell workers—women like Sellamma, Ramaiyi, and Letchumi—that generations of their families' work did not in fact create and sustain a home? These speech acts are not born of ill will; rather, they rightly call out the intergenerational injustices of depriving a minority community of land and housing rights over a sustained period. But they also do not account for the workers' investments that transform unlivable, inhumane spaces into livable homes. This passing over should make us stop and consider what constitutes building homes across ethnic, class, and caste differences, and how the government and industrial stakeholders evaluate these practices in relation to histories of injustice and dispossessed labor in Sri Lanka.

By arguing that Hill Country Tamils in fact experience home within dispossession, these stories locate their place in Sri Lanka as contingent on their desires to transform the plantation's malleable landscape. In the postwar context, such claims—that Hill Country Tamils have ūr—are not apolitical; instead, they make visible the rights-based claims of minority workers to a place that was designated to flourish through their very labor exploitation. Such claims to ūr on industrial soils also force us to consider that Hill Country Tamils have always embodied a built and motile sense of "here" since their ancestors' arrivals. One must contemplate the range of actual and conceivable consequences when minority

Hill Country Tamils make their sense of ūr visible to the Sri Lankan nation, and the ontological possibilities they present to imagine dispossession on generative but precarious terms. When Hill Country Tamil life and passion for the good life become visible to the nation, the story is rarely felicitous or on terms that plantation residents themselves have put forth. Most often than not, the stories are of landlessness, displacement, the incommensurability of rights-based praxis, and unfinished industrial abandonment, as seen in the case of Meeriyabedda or Michael's stigmatization of line room life. But these stories of enclosure can also disclose the more intimate, passionate, self-sustaining projects in which Hill Country Tamils continually invest.

Attention to the building and making visible of ūr on the plantations does not seek to downplay or displace concrete forms of labor and civic dispossession. Rather, it centralizes them within a Sri Lankan nation, tea industry, and agro-industrial landscape that have been continually challenged by their unjust treatments of this minority community since their formations. What we see on Sri Lanka's tea plantations is an uneven and unpredictable playing out of Hill Country Tamil plantation residents' desires to challenge those injustices and to sustain life, feel a sense of permanence in the world, and create histories that represent their community as more than durable, disposable labor. By claiming their ūr on the plantations—exposed, unearthed, and unowned—Hill Country Tamil plantation workers are disrupting the cycle of their subdued representations. They are refusing to be a nonhuman group, and staking a distinct home for themselves in the nation—as Others not undone.

CHAPTER 5

"From the Womb to the Tomb"

IT WAS EARLY FEBRUARY 2009, AND DILLON AND I HAD JUST finished an afternoon cup of tea outside Hatton town. "From the womb to the tomb, the tea estate worker is taken care of." He spoke confidently and quickly in English while pointing to the green, rolling hills of a nearby estate where he had once worked as a superintendent. After retiring from his position and up until his death, Dillon was working as a tour guide. Every day, he took tourists through the Hill Country's estates so that they could learn about tea cultivation, production, and taste. The estate we were looking at sat on the base of a large crest of a hill; using the scene, he began calling out specific landmarks for me on the horizon. Still speaking in English, he continued:

> When a woman worker gives birth, she is given maternity leave and a midwife. When she goes back to work, she can leave her infant in the crèche right there [he pointed to a small rectangular building near rows of workers' line room homes]. When the child is ready to go to school, he or she can get a free education up until the fifth standard right there [he pointed to a longer rectangular building]. Their homes [he moved his fingers to a set of rectangular barrack-style lines] are within short walking distance from work [his index finger moved up the hill to the factory and the lines of tea bushes below and above it]. Finally, when she dies, the management will even pay for her tomb and funeral expenses.

5.1.   A sketch of Gunamalar's sterilization scar she made in my fieldnote book during our conversation in April 2009

From the Womb

Gunamalar, forty-two years old, recalling her sterilization in April 2009:

> I have three boys—fourteen, fifteen, and eighteen years. I had the "operation" fourteen days after giving birth to my last son, who is fourteen years old now.[1] It took place in an estate clinic, not a government hospital. They opened me here [she lifted her sari to show a cross-like scar and then drew it in my fieldnote book; fig. 5.1]. Afterward, my body felt like it was on fire. I had to pee in a bag and walk slowly. I did not like other forms of contraception like the pill because they cost too much and ones like the injection make you fat. With this procedure, there are no problems, and you receive money. For us, it is good. We have no money. It is difficult. If another child does not come, it is easier. No house problems then.

To the Tomb

August 2016. It was two days after the one-year anniversary of Dillon's death. Two days before he died in August 2015, while getting ready for a full day's work he began experiencing piercing chest pains and shortness of breath and was rushed by his friend to the hospital. While there he was in better spirits, even joking with the nurses and refusing to lie down, insisting that he could sit upright in bed. But he then died unexpectedly the day after he was admitted.

I was sitting with his daughter and his friend, looking at old photographs they had recovered while clearing out his home a year after his death. Dillon had rarely spoken about his family; he only discussed tea, its health benefits, its taste, and how not to ruin all three with milk. He spoke also of the plantations he had managed and his fondness for and appreciation of his workers. Knowing the focus of my research, he would tell me often how much he loved going to the marriage and age attainment celebrations of their children on the estates. At his wake in 2015, I stood beside his lifeless body while elderly Hill Country Tamil women, workers who had plucked under his supervision but were now retired, came in wailing, lamenting his sudden death and calling him *cāmi* in Tamil, a term of endearment Hill Country Tamils often use and whose original meaning is "god." Older Hill Country Tamil men, also now retired, came in wearing crisply ironed shirts and holding large umbrellas and canes at their sides; they had tears in the corners of their eyes but stood stoically as they stared at his body, which was once upright and full of life but now small and enclosed in wood and white satin. His daughter, as lines of workers, colleagues, and acquaintances passed by his body to pay their respects, leaned over his body, stroked his forehead, and remarked to me, "How peaceful he looks. Like he is finally at rest. He worked too hard."

While Dillon was reticent about his family, his daughter eagerly filled the silence he had left behind. As she spread out the photographs on the floor, many of which had water damage, I saw his father and mother for the first time in sepia prints taken during his childhood. In one of the photographs, his mother, a young Hill Country Tamil woman, wore a checkered sari, light blouse, and jewelry. She was smiling into the camera as she held an infant child. Dillon's daughter and my friend could not tell for sure if the child was Dillon or his younger sibling, but they guessed it was Dillon given his mother's youthful appearance. To her left stood Dillon's father, a tall, older white man wearing a light-colored shirt unbuttoned three-quarters of the way down his chest. He, too, was smiling, standing close to his wife and child, their bodies turned slightly inward toward one another. The child looked away from the camera, clinging to the folds of his mother's sari. The photograph was not formal; it was an intimate portrait of their family and life as parents, and there was genuine happiness in their eyes and smiles.

Until that day, I had never seen or heard anything about Dillon's parents. Only after his death did I discover through his only daughter that his mother had been a young Hill Country Tamil woman, the daughter of an estate overseer, who had worked for his father, a white superintendent. They married when she was just a teenager, and she gave birth to three children, Dillon and two siblings. Dillon's daughter told me that her father would tell her that when his mother and father would go to the nearest hill station town to do shopping for the family, she would sit in the back of the bus with the rest of the Hill Country Tamils while her father would sit either in the front of the bus or travel in a separate vehicle with other white planters. Dillon's mother died when he was in his twenties, and when I asked how, my friend told me that she had once heard Dillon say she had a "womb problem."

As we sifted through more photographs, I caught sight of another family portrait, this time of an older Dillon, perhaps as a late teenager, with his mother and father. In this portrait, the image of his mother's face had been scratched away with what appeared to be a sharp enough object to leave only a small hedge of canary yellow lines where her face had been. His daughter observed my eyes pause on the attempted erasure and quickly moved the photograph to the bottom of the pile. I sensed that she did not want to talk about it, so we continued to reminisce about her father and his life.

Suturing Reproduction

Sri Lanka's tea plantations are actives sites of hegemony, a stabilizing "crystallization of leading personnel" and their "exercises [of] coercive power" across intersections of gender, race, ethnicity, class, and labor.[2] This crystallization, like the process of manufacturing photographic images, is unstable to begin with. Through a host of different factors the crystallization becomes more stable over time with the right resources and knowledge, but requires constant attention to detail and forms of care cultivated through human investments of time and labor. On the fragility of hegemony Vinay Gidwani writes, "The work of hegemony is always unstable, never seamless, and never able to erase the traces of its labors."[3] Gidwani's hegemony is grounded in the term *suture*, and in particular Michèle Barrett's reading of Laclau and Mouffe's work on hegemony's suturing of a "body politic whose skin is permanently split open, necessitating the ceaseless duty in the emergency room for the surgeons of hegemony whose job it is to try and close, temporarily and with difficulty, the gaps."[4] To suture is to do more than close or seal an opening; it is work that requires attention, intimacy, and skill. The seal is not permanent and will soon reopen. Without the work of suturing, our threads would be left unstitched, our seams open, our wounds exposed.

Within the plantation's seams, I came across these open wounds, and one particularly entered my fieldwork in Gunamalar's story of her tubal ligation surgery (what she called the "operation"). The government of Sri Lanka's health survey in 2006–7 estimated that of the 64.2 percent of married women in the estate sector that used contraception, 61 percent of them used modern methods of birth control; of that group, 41.1 percent used female sterilization as a modern (and permanent) solution.[5] This demographic was approximately three times larger than its counterparts in the rural and urban sectors, which were surveyed at the same time.

In my conversations with middle-aged and older Hill Country Tamil women, I would come to learn that Gunamalar's story was not unique. And like Gunamalar, other women who had undergone the operation would keep their wounds open by retelling their stories, even after they had been sutured and scarred years before. Tasked with writing ethnography, I initially did not know what to do with them. In style, language, and embodiment, they fell out of place with every other narrative I had heard about female sterilizations on the estates.

Before Gunamalar, I had never had anyone from Kirkwall or the tea plantations pick up my pen and draw in my notebook to supplement what they were telling me. As she recounted her experiences, I temporarily forgot the hegemonic language of consent, compliance, rights, and victimhood—which tells you what you did not give, what you bore, what you did not have, what you suffered. This is the language of policy reform, poverty, and structural violence—the language of "killer stories" with which I was familiar and through which Hill Country Tamils had come to be known. Instead, her story of embodiment, fertility, and reproduction became a counter-suture to the inhumanity, through which the language of empowerment insidiously operates. As a narrator, she refused to stay quiet and still. Instead, she pointed, enacted, and grounded the experiences in her body and surroundings. Her story, like Dillon's phrase, was at work.

This chapter presents the opening, closing, and afterlives of wounds. I examine how the language of women and of state and industrial policies manage and make sense of workers' reproductive capacities and embodied experiences. In the folds of stories of young fertile women, sterilized mothers, and retired workers on the estates, Dillon's phrase "from the womb to the tomb" waits to carry out the work of Gidwani's hegemony. When assembled and stitched together, the six words strive to make seamless and enclose the lifelong contributions that Hill Country Tamil women make as mothers, wives, and caregivers, but most importantly, as agricultural workers. They presume a certain kind of permanence: if you, as a woman worker, follow this life plan, from the womb to your tomb, you will be taken care of. But as seamless as they are—as much as they try to confine a woman worker to the bounds of industrial care—they are not strong enough to seal and erase her reproductive labor and investments.

What keeps women and their kin's wounds open are narratives of life work and reproduction, which women themselves recall and articulate. The accounts in this chapter acknowledge the work of hegemonic discourse around women's reproductive capacity—what they are perceived to be capable of as women with respect to their fertility, their desires to have children, and their labor and kin contributions after giving birth. What the narratives of industrial care seek to suture and seal, I seek to keep open with counter-sutures that bring to the surface women's embodied reproductive labor. In doing so, I ask how keeping wounds open makes space for workingwomen to be seen alongside the industrial strategies that work to manage their bodily experiences.

Planning Productive Labor

Three major economic phases in Sri Lanka's plantation history shape the development of health-care administration and practice for Hill

Country Tamil estate workers. From 1880 to 1972, care of plantation workers' bodily health, though officially the responsibility of the government of Ceylon, fell to the private plantation companies. However, after the nationalization of the plantations, services like health care, sanitation, and welfare on the estates were solely overseen by the government, which resulted in some positive changes within the sector, including the building of more government hospitals. But problems such as language barriers, lack of identification, and escalating civil violence persisted, hindering Tamils living on the plantations from fully accessing their medical and bodily rights.

Privatization in 1992 again placed the well-being of plantation workers under the care of the plantation companies. Recognizing the transitions estate workers had made during nationalization, the RPCs, in conjunction with the government of Sri Lanka and select plantation trade unions, created the Plantation Housing and Social Welfare Trust in 1992.[6] Later renamed the Plantation Human Development Trust (PHDT), this social service unit currently serves as the mediating organization that manages services for plantation workers, including housing, educational training, social welfare, and health programs.[7] The transition to a privatized estate sector was not without problems. According to a 1995 report by a plantation NGO, even basic needs such as access to water, housing, and toilet facilities were not updated and hospitals and estate dispensaries were not given the same supplies and services afforded to the rest of the country's population.[8] In 1997, the government acknowledged these disparities and created the Ministry of Estate Infrastructure and Development to allocate funds for further development of the estate sector.[9] In the third phase, the government of Sri Lanka outlined the health priorities for plantation residents, as put forth by the UNDP and MDGs-supported 2010 and 2015 NPAs for the plantation sector, and in 2015 the government began transitioning the state's gradual takeover of all estate medical services and facilities.[10] Even so, health services are not easily accessible to workers given their long hours and the lack of transportation to government-based hospitals from remote estates.

These three phases demonstrate that shifts in management have direct and negative consequences for the ways Tamil women could enjoy their reproductive rights in the context of family planning and sexual health. They also laid the foundation for understanding how the government, estate managements, and institutions of surveillance cultivate a delicate relationship among human need, technologies of knowledge production, and agentive capacity for Tamil women making "choices" about their reproductive futures.

Specific administrative, legal, and socioeconomic factors contribute to the disproportionately higher numbers of female sterilization among Hill Country Tamil women on the estates. On an administrative level, reprivatization and a lack of defined infrastructure on the plantations obscure exactly where legal responsibility lies in assuring women plantation residents' health care and well-being. While the RPCs employ the estate medical assistants and midwives, these health professionals also carry out the programs that fall under the PHDT, which is managed by the government, RPCs, and plantation trade unions. This confusion also leads to key players in health management having conflicting interests. Most prominently, the estate midwife, who is responsible for between two thousand and five thousand women, is not only given annual sterilization quotas by both the plantation management and PHDT but is also rewarded with additional financial incentives for every woman who receives a sterilization procedure under her care—an occurrence that estate medical personnel and crèche attendants verified for me during fieldwork.[11] Such quotas and incentives could, for obvious economic reasons, influence the midwife's encouraging of Hill Country Tamils under her care to get sterilized. Furthermore, these incentives pose the risk that midwives will perform their professional duties in a manner that leans toward advocating for sterilization over other, more temporary forms of contraception, a point made by a crèche attendant on an RPC estate with whom I spoke in 2014. The combination of economic insecurity, lack of awareness, and administrative quotas and incentives put forth by the RPCs and PHDT validate and inform the midwife's communication to married and reproductively capable women workers that female sterilization is a "necessity" for the benefit of their family's social and economic well-being.

With the need for sterilization established, state and plantation institutional actors deploy hardened technologies of production and practices of surveillance to effect larger percentages of female sterilizations among Tamil women and their families in the plantation sector. One key site where these technological transactions of knowledge take place is in the midwife's visit to the woman before, during, and after her pregnancy. Contrasting the privacy of medical clinic visits, home visits that midwives in Sri Lanka make to women's line rooms on the plantations are more public, as they take place in the late afternoon or early evening when everyone returns home from work and school. Transmitting medical advice and authoritative forms of knowledge in such places that are not only not private but bordering, if not adjacent to, a woman's place of employment, may very well enable such conversations to end with the "decision" to get sterilized over other forms of temporary contraception. These technologies are not so bluntly authoritative or isolating, but in fact community-driven and kin-based; the midwife often uses this intimate time in the household to transmit knowledge to the woman about her body and educate her surrounding kith and kin about her future bodily utility for the betterment of the entire family and wider plantation community. As anthropologists Bambi Chapin and Daniel Bass note, women's reproductive choices in Sri Lanka are often not privately informed or judged; rather, their actions are infused by a host of perspectives and judgments from male kin, medical professionals, policy makers, and politicians.[12]

"Like a Cross"

I encountered this type of surveillance and judgment in 2009 in the home of Devi and Veeriah, casual laborers for smallholders and private gardens in the surrounding area of their resident estate. It was 4:30 in the afternoon and their daughter-in-law, Subāmini, a full-time plucker, had just given birth to her third child seven days earlier and was home meeting with her midwife, who was conducting a scheduled postnatal home visit. To accommodate their growing family of six, Veeriah had expanded their twelve-by-seven-foot line room to incorporate a private kitchen space in the back, out of which he and his son ran a liquor bar to supplement their household income.

I walked in as the midwife was leaving and sat with Subāmini on the bed as she breastfed her daughter. Veeriah was in the back area serving liquor to some men who had walked in before and behind me, but when he saw me he took a few minutes to sit with us. Devi told me that the midwife had scolded Subāmini for giving birth to three children in a little over four years and counseled her about the operation. She then left to the kitchen to make us all some tea. Twenty-four years old, Subāmini was worried because she knew that the qualifying age for tubal ligations was twenty-five and that she would need to wait and find an alternate form of contraception until she was eligible. She told me she was considering an IUD (she called it "the loop"). Veeriah interjected that she should use the loop until she turned twenty-five, at which point, he said, she should definitely get the operation. He turned to me, saying, "I am getting old. Soon my wife and I will have to retire and will not be able to support my son and his family. We do not need any more children in this house." Returning from the kitchen, Devi gave us all tea, sat down, and reflected on her own sterilization experience as a young mother:

> I was twenty-three years old when I had the operation after my third child. When I got the operation, I was with twenty other women or so in a hostel—one room. Back then it left a bad scar, like a cross. [She then drew the x mark in my fieldnote book.] Following the operation, the stitches separated and the wound got infected. I was in the hospital for one month after. Since then, my body has been weak. I get stomach pains often and my back has become hunched. I feel unfit, even after all this time. She [nodding in Subāmini's direction] should go in for the operation when she turns twenty-five. Now she is using the ūci ["injection" or Depo-Provera shot] every three months, but it is giving her problems—her body is cold, she cannot work, and she feels achy all the time. She wants to have it. She cannot afford to have more children. Camāḷikkavillai [She cannot cope with it]. Then it was differ-ent. My mother had eleven children. Now, two or three is more than enough.

She gave my fieldnote book back, and we continued drinking our tea. In the first year of fieldwork, Devi, through oral histories that I recorded with her, would often tell me that back then was a different time. Of her mother's eleven children, she was the third-eldest child, and when her younger brother was born her family began having money problems. After fifth grade, her older sister stayed at home to care for her younger siblings. When Devi finished fifth grade, her parents sent her to Colombo to work as a servant in the home of a family. She told me, with a smile, "I was scared when I first arrived, but they treated me well. I did not do any cooking. An older Tamil woman from the estates was there to do those things and to care for the children. I was given clothes to wash, I swept the house, cut onions and other small vegetables, and in return they fed me and gave me clothes and a mat to sleep on outside the kitchen." Her parents were paid a monthly salary of Rs. 250 a month at the time, and she would continue to go back and forth between Colombo and her estate home until she was fifteen, eventually coming back to get married, work on the estate, and raise her own family.

Devi's story is not singular. Of her eleven siblings, four of her sisters had also gone to Colombo as children to support their family, and in my ongoing field research every household of lower-caste Tamil plantation workers I visited on the estates had had at least one middle-aged or elderly household member who had either worked in Colombo or on the estates when they were children. Other former child laborers also spoke to me fondly and even affectionately about their familial contributions as Colombo domestics. Stories of female sterilization like Gunamalar's were not unique either. After she shared her story with me, I began extending my pen to other women during our conversations about their "operations" and fertility, and they, too, began drawing "crosses" in my field notebook. They would lift away their saris and point to the spaces of their abdomens below their navels—to incision scars that were too faded for me to see on their skin.

The operation stories that I recorded did not follow the objectives of human rights discourse nor did they fit the representations of Hill Country Tamil women I had read about in scholarly narratives of reproduction. Instead, they challenged those boundaries to reveal how embodied and intimate experiences of gendered labor and reproduction had sustained generations of industry and kinship investment for Hill Country Tamil workingwomen. Human rights discourse and Western forms of feminism focus on a woman's individual bodily rights; often those rights are stripped of the context of structural violence, kinship investment, and women's own aspirations and valuations of their own time and labor. The statistical evidence of female sterilizations in the estate sector was not capable of standing in for the conditions workingwomen were describing—namely their historical experiences with structural violence at the intersections of gender, caste, class, and age that led them to have tubal ligations. As Gunamalar told me, oral contraceptives were costly and the timing of taking pills was not conducive to household and estate work schedules; likewise, injections like Depo-Provera had side effects on women's bodies such as weight gain. Another decisive factor for electing to have the operation among the women with whom I spoke was the financial incentive, which for some amounted to between a third to half of their monthly salary, which was already lowered by long-standing debts and standard salary advances. Within the context of the estate sector's relatively high rates of household poverty and lack of upward economic mobility, it became clear why women could justify their decisions to receive monetary compensation for their choice of a permanent form of birth control.

Questions of choice and agency raise valid concerns about the marked gap between international rights discourse on reproductive capacity and the way women articulate their choices on the ground. In September 2009 I spoke with Tanya, a legal advocate and human rights activist in Colombo, about this gap and the complications it presents in the struggle for women's reproductive rights. Working in the field of human rights for over ten years at that time, Tanya claimed that while some progress had been made since 2000 regarding female sterilizations on the estates, the issue still came down to the hypocrisy of the woman's "choice" within such transactions: "People think of forced sterilization and the word *forced* makes us think of images of women being carried by tea lorries into empty buildings and getting sterilized by the dozen against their free will. This used to happen, but now the meaning of forced has changed. Forced is not necessarily without consent. What does consent look like? If a mother is given eighty-four days for her first and second maternity leaves and then forty-two days for her third, does this difference not mean anything? How is consent being taken? That is where reproductive rights need further examination."[13]

Her comment brings attention to the need for feminist scholars to reconfigure the relationship between reproductive capacity and the enjoyment of reproductive rights among workingwomen from marginalized communities. While institutions and health personnel tout the necessity of "informed consent" in the name of ensuring women's right to "choose" female sterilization, informed consent is not a vessel empty of information; rather, it teems with technologies of power that are able to convince larger political and economically productive worlds of the transaction's integrity. For example, midwives and other plantation officials may convince the woman that she had no other choice but to get sterilized given her social situation of poverty and immobility, thus absolving them of any legal accountability. This occlusion makes it difficult for Tamil women on the plantations to locate the freedom in their "choice," and renders the concept of "informed consent" unviable outside the community in which it must be situated in order to thrive as a right to exercise. The diminished exchange value placed on a third pregnancy further invalidates informed consent as a valid transaction; the change to forty-two days' leave as opposed to eighty-four influences a woman's decision and desire to undergo a tubal ligation and works to justify her feelings of being content with her "choice." Additionally, an incentive of Rs. 500 (roughly $3.14) in exchange for completing the sterilization procedure further buries the notion of "informed consent": the "informing" is conditioned by state and institutional desires for ensuring the maximum output of economic production within a declining and state-subsidized national plantation economy. As a provincial director of health services was recorded saying in a Ministry of Health meeting on the state of the estate sector's health, "If [the] estate community is given education and good health, they will move out of [the] estates, and there will be no labour force."[14]

With the exchange value of having children and stripping wombs of their reproductive capacities set, women on the plantations think of their generative possibilities in the transactional language through which such procedures are communicated to them. It should be noted that men, too, are offered sterilization options during midwife home visits, but in the form of vasectomies for financial compensation. Sasikumar Balasundaram notes that this procedure is often refused because it tends to undermine men's feelings of masculinity, but I encountered men in my research who had undergone vasectomies alongside their wives' tubal ligations after second and third pregnancies.[15] Ramasamy, for instance, a thirty-one-year-old father of three and full-time estate worker, underwent a vasectomy soon after learning that his working wife had become pregnant for the third time in seven years of marriage. I asked him why he had done it, since his wife had told me she had had the operation after delivering her third child. He said he did it so that they could eliminate any worry about having any more children and for the financial incentive, because it would help pay for his daughter's school expenses. His decision reveals that family planning policies go well beyond women's physical wombs and reach into the decisions that ultimately determine a family's social standing and economic trajectory. These dynamics of constraint and desire also require deeper investigations into the archaeologies of such transactions on the body and how women workers on the estates reflect on the process of sterilization throughout the remainder of their lives.

Reproductive Afterlives

How a woman recalls her life experience as a mother, wife, and caregiver actively works to give meaning and place to her reproductive history in the present. Like Devi, her older sister, Ramaiyi, with whom I discussed line room renovations (see chapter 4), often used her memories to make sense of and find her place on Kirkwall as a retired plucker and grandmother. Born in 1952, Ramaiyi is the oldest of eleven children (eight girls and three boys). Her father was born in Vandavasi, a town in Tiruvannamalai district near the northwestern coast of Tamil Nadu in South India. After migrating as a young boy to Ceylon, he worked on the plantation as a mason and married her mother, a plucker on another estate, according to his caste and parents' arrangements. Neither of Ramaiyi's parents had citizenship under the Citizenship Act of 1948, given that both their fathers were born in India. Additionally, neither her siblings nor she were able to obtain citizenship in the form of National Identity Cards until they got married to men who were citizens. When I first asked Ramaiyi how old she was, she told me she did not know her age and that I would have to ask her friend, because she only got her NIC and citizenship once she got married for the second time in the mid-1980s and thought about her age only when filing her pension paperwork. Later, during a trip we took to Hatton town, I was able to verify her age by looking at her NIC, which she only carried with her on the bus in the event of military or police checkpoints.

As the eldest child, Ramaiyi studied until the fifth grade, the highest level of education offered on the estates at the time. When she was eleven she began staying at home to help her mother take care of her siblings, and at fifteen she began plucking in the fields for *kai kācu* ("hand money"; i.e., off the books) to contribute to their household income. When she was twenty, she married a twenty-three-year-old man from Duncan estate (approximately eight kilometers away from Kirkwall by road) and had two children. In 1983 her husband traveled to Colombo and got caught in the July anti-Tamil riots, disappeared, and was presumed dead. With her daughter only two years old when he disappeared, she told me she had married her mother's brother's son from Kirkwall a few years later. He was already legally married and had a wife and children on Sāmimalai estate (about two kilometers away by road from Kirkwall). She told me that her relationship with his first wife was cordial, and she would, through family events, meet or see the children whom he had had with his first wife.

Early into my fieldwork and as I mentioned in chapter 4, Ramaiyi told me that she had an accident while working and had to stop plucking full-time; as we got to know each better, she opened up more about the life-changing incident during our sessions of recording her life history. While plucking on a rainy day, she had fallen from a considerable height in the fields with the weight of a fifteen-kilogram basket full of tea leaves on her head. The *kūḍai* (basket) band knocked out many of her front teeth. The dental wounds got severely infected; as a result, she was admitted to the nearby hospital for one month and had twenty-eight stitches in her mouth. Only forty-one years old at the time, she did not want to return to *koluntu vēlai* (plucking work) and decided instead to become a domestic worker in Colombo. This was seven years after most government-owned estates were privatized, and at that time the plantation on which Kirkwall is located suffered a labor shortage due to shifts in managerial practices.[16]

Working in the home of a Sinhala exporter of fruits and vegetables, she was a domestic for three years, earning enough money for her son's wedding in 2001. When his wife became pregnant with their first daughter, Ramaiyi returned to Kirkwall to care for her first grandchild. With two more grandchildren born between 2003 and 2007, she remained on the estate and took up her full-time responsibility as their caretaker while her daughter-in-law and son worked full-time on the estate. In 2007 she received her retirement funds from her Employees' Provident Fund (EPF) and Employees' Trust Fund (ETF), which she used to support her family—notably to supplement the lost income from additional time that her daughter-in-law had taken off past her given forty-two-day maternity leave, to pay for additional rituals to mark the auspiciousness of her grandchildren's births, and to buy the family a new television. During this period when she used her EPF and ETF funds, her family experienced a significant surge of household income. But those funds were relatively and quickly extinguished given the reality of the estate daily wage and cost of living that had elevated considerably due to the international economic crisis and Sri Lanka's return to civil war.

In our talks, Ramaiyi claimed that she had suffered troubles throughout her life and that her past losses had come to determine her beliefs and practices in the present. Becoming one of my closest interlocutors on Kirkwall and often acting maternally toward me during my times spent there, she would often tell me how much she looked forward to our conversations about the past. The genuine enjoyment she felt in giving accounts of herself and sharing her thoughts about the community in which she lived would come out in the animated ways she would speak. Echoing Valentine Daniel's sense of bardic heritage, she was incorporating storytelling as a form of communicating the suffering she had experienced in her life as a widow.[17] Her perceptions as well as those of other widows on Kirkwall complicate former anthropological conceptions of marriage and widowhood on the estates, and also demonstrate how explications of past suffering and grief can make those who describe these emotional transitions more valuable to their communities.

The most recent suffering Ramaiyi experienced was the sudden death of her second husband in May 2006. She remembered him fondly and mentioned him to me frequently; at least once a week during my first year of fieldwork, she would tell me how good a person her husband was to people on the estate and to her family and children. In May 2009, on the third anniversary of his death, she was particularly upset and described the night he suffered his fatal heart attack:

> That day, I had cut the chicken, gave him and everyone rice, chicken curry, and some vegetable curry. I put it in the center of our house, which is where we usually eat. I cleaned the house, took a head bath, and went to bed around nine thirty in the evening. A short while after lying down to sleep, he began making a noise in his sleep like a cough

[she makes a cackling noise]. When I came by his side, he was in a pool of sweat. I did not know what to do so I carried him on my back to the front door, and some others helped carry him to the steps to the main road, but he had already died.

[She began to cry.] *Enna cēyratu?* [Now what will we do?] He was a good man. He never hit, never yelled, or treated anyone badly. He never called children or anyone by their name. He always said, *"Vāratā? Pōratā?"*[18] [Are you coming? Are you going?] He had affection for everyone [*ellārukkum pācum*]. Usually a second husband would treat the children of your first husband badly. But he was not like that. He treated my children like they were his own, and because of that, I will never forget him.

Ramaiyi's account signals that bonds of kinship exist beyond previous anthropological conceptions of marriage and widowhood on the plantations. Oddvar Hollup mentions the higher frequencies of levirate and sororate marriages after widowhood among Paraiyar-caste Hill Country Tamil estate widows of younger ages.[19] But these instances would most likely result in children produced from the second marriage due to infertility or other issues in the first marriage. In Ramaiyi's case, she did not have children with her second husband, given that he was still married and had children with his first wife. Such shifting dynamics in widowhood transform preconceptions of caste-based and kinship-driven marital behaviors and how they correlate to a widow's sense of allegiance to her deceased husband.

Interestingly, Ramaiyi did not speak often or passionately about her first husband, who had disappeared in the 1983 Colombo riots. Another elderly retired woman and the wife of Ramaiyi's second husband's brother told me quietly that he in fact did not die but, rather, had run away with another woman in Colombo, which was why she never received information about his corpse or an official notice of his death. But it was a rumor I only heard from her, and I was never able to confirm its veracity from Ramaiyi or her children. This was partly because the presumed death (and more so absence) of her first husband was undocumented, unseen, and, most important, unconfirmed. His body literally did not show itself, and unstable social and economic circumstances forced Ramaiyi to move on in the best interests of her two fatherless children. He was also the only "deceased" ancestor that did not have a photograph framed and hanging in the main room of Ramaiyi's house. His photograph was kept in a box in the cupboard, and Ramaiyi only showed it to me in passing as she searched for another document.

Her second husband, on the other hand, was ever present materially and discursively. He had died in her arms, and she was able to vividly recollect his last breaths, the beads of sweat on his face, which foods he consumed before his death, and how heavy he was to lift onto her back in his unconscious state. Her memories and melancholia reflect that she had witnessed and confirmed firsthand the loss of his life in their home. Unlike her first husband, her second husband had left her in a condition of shock that was mutually shared and confirmed by her community in the lines. Although her second husband, like her first, was not present to tell his own life story—a fact she reminded me of at least once a week—she would constantly tell me how he *would have* spoken with me: "He would have been able to tell you the history of this estate nicely, when it was built, who built the temple, who were the field officers and accountants back then. I do not know that information. He knew it well." Her desire to defend his knowledge—his *arivu* or "skill" for knowing—in death reveals the love and respect she continues to have for him. Furthermore, her acknowledgment of his permanent physical absence and dignified roles as husband, father, and former *kankāni* also keeps active and validates her own status as a retired widow on the estate today.

Ramaiyi's transition into widowhood also brought on behavioral changes specifically connected to her working through the melancholia and loss she experienced. After his death, she struggled to fall asleep at night on the floor in the front room of her line room home, alongside her daughter and two granddaughters. To distract herself she had to watch television before falling asleep, a habit I witnessed during the several nights I stayed in her house, while sleeping in the twelve-by-seven-foot front room with her. Every night that I spent there I would drift in and out of sleep as she watched television on silent for nearly two hours before turning it off and immediately falling into a deep sleep. When I asked her about this habit, she told me she had first picked it up when she was a domestic in Colombo; her *durai* and *nōnā*[20] had put a television in the back room that she had slept in while there. She stopped watching when she came home but picked up the habit again once her husband died, because she did not like sitting still and needed to see the moving images to calm her mind.

For Ramaiyi, the melancholia introduced new habits into her everyday life and novel perspectives about what roles she could inhabit as a retired plucker and widow. When he was alive, her husband had played an integral role in the upbringing of her son's children. He would walk them to school and discipline them to study after school and obey their mother. He did this, she told me, because he was well educated; he had been a *kankāni*, so had held a certain degree of authority over residents in the lines. The goodness of her husband had also brought out a moral certitude in her about the value of the estate and its residents. When he died, she told me that she felt that such assurances had weakened: her family had experienced social and economic uncertainty in the recent years following his death while she saw other families around her prosper.[21]

Cāmi Varutal

One way Ramaiyi made a place for herself on Kirkwall was through communicating her faith and conversing with the divine. This capability is known colloquially among Hill Country Tamils on the plantations as *cāmi varum*, or the state of being with a higher being.[22] Throughout field research, I often witnessed Hill Country Tamil women and men in such a state on the plantations mostly during estate festivals, or *tiru vizhā*: in connection to Hindu religious festival practices of penitence and devotion such as *āavaṭi* (arches decorated and boosted on one's shoulders), *parava kāvaṭi* or *tūkkam* (where a man is hung from hooks in the skin of his back from beams and taken through the festival procession in a birdlike position), *thēkuti* (walking on burning coals), and *cāmiyāṭikaḷ* (those who begin dancing in a trancelike state upon "receiving the god"). Beyond these larger, outwardly performative ritual practices, Ramaiyi's more intimate and personal connection with *cāmi* further complicates how elderly women's experiences and their capacities to assert their knowledge transform their places within the community.

I first witnessed the *cāmi* come to Ramaiyi in her home on the evening of Civarāttiri in February 2009.[23] She and her family had invited me to spend the evening with them and go to the estate temple *pūcai* (a priest-based prayer ritual to deities and gods) later that evening. Before the temple ritual, Ramaiyi and her family held a small *pūcai* in their home. She started by taking the lit lamp (*viḷakku*) to worship at the small family altar (*cāmikaḷ*) in the corner of the main room.[24] She then blessed the framed photographs of their deceased ancestors. She took *vipūti* (holy ash) in her right hand and sprinkled it to the left, right, and center of the framed deity images, and then everyone in the room lined up to receive *vipūti* and blessings from her.

When Ramaiyi placed *vipūti* on my forehead, I noticed that her thumb lingered there a bit longer than it had on other family members' foreheads before me and that it had trembled briefly. She retreated her finger, and I knelt down to touch and pray at her feet and then retreated so that her nephew could receive her blessing. He stepped forward and as she placed *vipūti* on his forehead the trembling intensified. She then began writhing as though she had a pain in her stomach. Her breathing deepened and grew faster, developing into a rhythmic, staccato-like repetition of "Su . . . su . . . su." The entire time, she kept her thumb planted on the young boy's forehead. The boy did not flinch and kept his stance: his feet a little wider than shoulder width, locked knees, hands at his sides, and eyes lowered to avoid eye contact with her. Ramaiyi's daughter-in-law, daughter, and grandchildren retreated into the corner of the room looking intrigued and frightened, not taking their eyes off her. They motioned that I should join them in the corner, so I did. She continued breathing heavily and kept her thumb forcibly pressed into the boy's forehead, such that his body was now moving along with her in a side-to-side, writhing motion. After a minute, she lowered her hand to his neck with a similar motion and her right leg began violently shaking. She released her thumb and finally lowered to the ground and bent on her knee, clutching her stomach. She placed the lit lamp beside her and, with *vipūti* in her hand, shifted her weight from leg to leg and tossed the *vipūti* to the left, right, and center of the boy's neck. It became increasingly violent and at one point her daughter-in-law softly asked, "What is it, mother?" (*Enna, Ammā?*) After another minute, she lowered to the ground and her shaking slowed to a halt. She bent her head and upper half over her thighs and knees, remaining in this position for about ten seconds.

When she raised herself up to stand, she had slowed her breathing, and her eyes remained lowered. She then smoothed her hands on her sari at thighs' length and looked up. Her daughter-in-law told us to follow her into the front room and leave her alone. Ramaiyi joined us five minutes later, squatting on the floor opposite the television. Her smallest grandchild, Sobika, only fifteen months old, immediately went to join her, smiling and shifting her weight from one leg to the other while making the *su* sound and smiling. Everyone, including Ramaiyi, laughed. "Look at her" (*Pārunkalē*), she told me. "She is the center of this house," and she settled Sobika onto her lap. We continued watching television as if nothing had happened.

The incident came up in conversation a week later when I was talking to Ramaiyi about the estate's Māriamman festival and her faith. She told me that she was told that the *cāmi* first came to her when she was fourteen years old. She had practiced *kūttu*, a ritual where one pierces through both cheeks in divine penitence, at an annual festival for Kāliamman, consort of Shiva and the Hindu goddess of empowerment. After that point the *cāmi* continued to reappear. She told me that she has no memory of it after it happens, but that she knows it comes from her faith:

Cāmi does not come to everyone. It came for my mother, but not my daughter and not my daughter-in-law. It does not go to them [*Avanka-lukku pōkātu*]. I do not remember it when it comes, but it can happen anywhere. It is a good thing. It is god [*deivam*]. When you are with god, you will not even feel fire beneath your feet. Nothing will come to you [*Onnum varātu*]. It comes when it needs to. That day—that boy [her nephew] was not well. He had a fever—a heat in him. The *cāmi* came to me to get rid of it and in the morning he was better. If anything bad is coming, it will come. When you walk alone back from here in the dark, I think, "*Cāmi*, how will she go? Watch this, young girl" [*komari piḷḷai*][25] so that no boy approaches her. That is my faith [*nampikkai*]—for my family, for everyone here.

Ramaiyi's communication with god raises significant points about the centrality of Hill Country Tamil women's faith to addressing the everyday uncertainties of plantation life. Because elderly women do not contribute income to their households, they strongly emphasize their imparting of knowledge that actively contributes to generating more secure forms of living and recognition for their kith and kin. The presence of uncertainty remains shared in this diversity of practice—or, in Ramaiyi's terms, "the need" to address infelicitous conditions. Belief-based practices like *cāmi varatu* serve to purge negative energies, but its exclusive selection of individuals on the estates signals to differently inhabited and singular gendered experiences that elderly and retired women, like Ramaiyi, embody for active purposes.

Ramaiyi—like Dillon, Gunamalar, and other women struggling to make sense of their pasts in the ecosystem of hegemony, labor, and care on the tea plantations—actively work to make peace with their presents, despite histories of structural violence, economic hardship, pain, and loss. In many ways, her presence and our conversations convey what Angela Garcia frames as melancholy or "mourning without end."[26] But more compelling than the open wound itself is the life's work Ramaiyi was actively pursuing in an attempt to suture those wounds—namely, her unpaid intimate and household labor for her family, the use of her EPF and ETF funds to supplement their incomes, her larger role as a spiritual body and being to protect and guide community members through *cāmi varatu*, the stubborn grieving she expressed for her deceased second husband, and the care that she took to spend time with me during my research. But even through all those attempts, her wounds remained active and open.

The last time I saw Ramaiyi was in July 2016. A year before we met, she decided to go back to work. Her grandchildren were old enough to be in the house alone after school and so, no longer needed physically at home, she began working for a local tea smallholder. But one day, after her work shift, she was bathing on the premises with other women workers when she felt dizzy and fell, hitting her head on a sharp rock. She was rushed to a local hospital in a three-wheeler, but while there, the doctors could not determine what had caused her to feel dizzy and lose consciousness, so they transferred her to Kandy Hospital, about a two-and-a-half-hour bus ride from Kirkwall. She remained hospitalized in Kandy for a month, and when I looked at her medical record (which her family gave me to review during my visit to their home) I read in English that she had suffered a brain aneurysm due to hypertension. That July, as I walked to Kirkwall, I met her daughter-in-law on the footpath on her way to work in a plastic raincoat, her basket affixed to her forehead and wooden walking stick in hand. We hugged and kissed briefly, but then her eyes began brimming with tears as she asked me if I had seen Ramaiyi yet. I told her that I had not; she told me to go visit her and that she would see me after she got home that afternoon.

I walked up the footpath to Ramaiyi's line. I found her sitting on a chair in the middle of the path outside her home while her grandchildren played around her and her brother's daughter-in-law sat on the stoop outside her door chewing betel leaf. Her physical appearance had changed dramatically. She had lost weight due to sustained nutritional IV use because she could not swallow or eat properly during her hospital stay; she was wearing a catheter, but the bag was not affixed to the tube properly so she had stopped using it and was struggling with incontinence. During her stay the doctors took multiple scans and biopsies of her brain to rule out cancerous tumors, so they had to shave her head. We met two months after that had happened and her hair had just begun to grow back. But I could still see a somewhat freshly sutured incision and stitches on her scalp.

When she saw me, she could not get up from her chair and began to cry. I hugged her for a long time and as I held her hand I could not help but cry as well; as her family members watched me embrace her they cried, too. Later, while she was resting, they told me that they had thought she would die. Her son had stopped working and spent the entire month in Kandy by her side, and her daughter-in-law also would occasionally take off work to bring him food and visit her. When I left Sri Lanka a month after our meeting in 2016, I prepared myself for the possibility that our visit might be the last time I would see Ramaiyi alive. Knowing how grief operates, I tried desperately to suture my own wounds, which were fresh with sadness at seeing the condition in which she was actively struggling.

When I returned in 2017 she was still alive, only she was not staying on Kirkwall with her son and his family but with her daughter and her family on another estate. Using my cell phone, her family members and I called her; she was sad to have missed seeing me, for her daughter lived a good hour and a half away in a nearby hill station town. She was no longer working; rather, she remained in the house taking care of her daughter's children and cooking their extended family's meals. Concerned about her health, I asked how she was feeling, and she said that she had fully recovered. From the sound of her voice I could tell that she seemed to be in good health, but I remained unsettled. I could not see the evidence of her recovery for myself. I knew that when I would see her next, I would instinctively look for her scar, even if her head of silver hair was covering it and even if the incision had already faded from plain sight. I knew I would work to assure myself that she would be well. This work—the work that makes stark the limits of the ethnographic research and writing—is what led me to see her scars in the first place.

Finding Closure

August 2015. I attended Dillon's funeral service, during which, to a crowd of planters, Hill Country Tamil workers, friends, and family, his brother delivered his eulogy and shared a story from Dillon's early days as a young assistant superintendent on the tea estates. In his words, when Dillon had just started his position, a "creeper"—a diminutive, dehumanizing name that coffee and tea planters commonly used to refer to Hill Country young boys or adult male workers—was caught as he was about to steal a type of tall grass that was accustomed to being planted between the tea bushes. Dillon's boss, the superintendent, instructed him, "You better thrash him," in order to teach Dillon how to do his job and maintain control over his workers. According to his brother, Dillon did not want to carry out the act. But out of fear he went ahead and hit the worker. Then, according to his brother, the worker slapped him right back. Later, without the knowledge of the superintendent, Dillon helped the worker bring the grass back to his line room home. Soft laughter traveled through the room. His brother paused and looked away to walls of the room we were in and said, "He just didn't fit." Regardless of whether the story was true and irrespective of the potential distortions that come with the performance of eulogies that remember well those who have departed, the story aimed to provide closure and a way to remember his life for those who heard it.

It also made me think about how Dillon had in fact fit. He strove to perfect the language and landscape of plantation life. Like his "womb to the tomb" ideal, he did the work to keep up the myth of the tea plantation's lifelong industrial and paternalistic care for women. In undertaking that work, he was implicated in the erasure of Hill Country Tamil women's capacious stories of reproductive life. But despite his work and the objectives of the industry and state to create and control a productive workforce, the wounds of women's regenerative labor remain actively tended to and exposed. Like the way the scratched-out image of his mother remains visible in its absence, like the way a scar that is too faded for the naked eye to see is still sensed, regenerative labor is grounded in the memory and desire to keep something active and productive. Could it be that the communicative language designed to detract one's attention from the sight of the wound in fact magnifies its opening? Could it be that sliding a photograph to the bottom of a pile makes one never forget the original attempted erasure? I never asked Dillon's daughter or my friend what had happened between him and his mother, why her face had been scratched away, and by whom. Sometimes, in our grieving of loved ones, wounds are best left untouched because we know that, too often, what the dead leaves behind remains in and on our bodies. And it is too much to bear.

The currency of hegemony is strong but in flux. It demands that we not only push against its currents but also acknowledge where those currents have taken us and through which terrains. As anthropologist Kim TallBear urges, its force demands that we further "the claims of a people while refusing to be excised from that people by some imperialistic, naïve notion of a perfect representation."[27] "Excise" here is important. A surgical procedure, an excision removes the portion of the body that may be diseased or harmful so that the rest of the body can heal on its own. But for anthropologists, as TallBear warns, excisions in ethnography are "naïve" and violent; they erase the very histories of relatedness and experience that make individuals who they are. By keeping these wounds open and in their places, these stories from the plantation—the counter-sutures that move and act through care and investment—make space for stories of women's reproductive capacities to be told for what they are. In all their contradictions and implications, these stories do not replace the voices of their tellers or make them fit into some sort of perfect narrative, but strive to stand with them.

CHAPTER 6

Dignity and Shame

IN AUGUST 2009 THE BODIES OF TWO YOUNG GIRLS FROM A plantation were found dead face down in Torrington Canal on Bauddaloka Mawatha Road in Colombo. Next to the bank of the shallow canal were two sets of rubber thong sandals facing the water's edge. Sinhala, Tamil, and English news outlets reported that both girls, Sumathi and Jeevarani, had been employed as domestics in two adjacent households located near the junction since April 2009. Initial investigations ruled the deaths a double suicide.

The location and presentation of their bodies were jarring. The section of Torrington Canal where they were found was in a High Security Zone (HSZ) in Cinnamon Gardens, an affluent and elite suburb of Colombo's city center. Once known for its sprawling cinnamon plantations during British colonial rule, the suburb at the time was and still is home to prime real estate, fancy clubs, and maximum-security government offices. In a capital accustomed to military checkpoints, unannounced cordon and searches, and suicide (and even aerial) bombings during the civil war, how two Tamil youth had drowned themselves in less than three feet of sewage and trash in a High Security Zone on a prominent, high-traffic road was suspect to say the least.

News of the girls' deaths quickly traveled through the Hill Country by word of mouth, newspapers, and the evening news. Rumors were flying about what had happened, and English-based newspaper reports were biased, misleading, and often hugely inaccurate. In the first week following the discovery of their bodies, reports stated that the girls were eighteen and seventeen and that they had definitely committed suicide. Days later, the media reported that their ages were sixteen and fifteen. The girls' grieving parents, who were living on the same estate, were able to produce their birth certificates to confirm that their daughters were even younger: Sumathi was thirteen years old, and Jeevarani was fourteen. Their statement confirmed what Tamil politicians, development workers, and community leaders in the plantation sector had feared most—they were children, and they had been unlawfully employed as domestics to support their families back on the plantation.

Media and law enforcement investigating the case further fueled the sensationalism in their reporting. Media outlets appeared to have been given access to the crime scene, including the now-defunct human rights reporting website *War without Witness in Sri Lanka*, which showed images of the clothed backsides of both girls' corpses floating in the sewage- and trash-filled canal water. On August 28, 2009, one of Sri Lanka's largest English print newspapers, the *Daily Mirror*, published a two-page spread on the story in which the details of the case were further explicated. In the feature article, the officer in charge confirmed that there was no evidence supporting the possibility of foul play. He justified his statement with claims that evidence suggested that Sumathi and Jeevarani had in fact committed suicide, and he was quoted on the record in the following statement: "There is evidence that points to suicide. There was a letter, which had indicated homosexual behaviour. The victims slept on the same mat and there was evidence of sexual activity between the two."[1] While Tamil rights activists and politicians in the plantation sector were outraged, no one went on record to hold the newspaper or officer accountable for making such violating and public statements about the unverified sexual preferences and activities of minors, an act in direct violation of the Convention on the Rights of the Child. John, a human rights activist in the Hill Country, told me, "The media forgets that they are telling stories about children—false, uncorroborated ones, no less."[2] The handling of the incident by the media and police was appalling not because it provided too much information, but because its assumptions too easily stigmatized plantation workers and their socioeconomic marginality and because readers too easily accepted their narratives.

Though they initially ruled the deaths as a double suicide, investigations were reopened at the request of the girls' parents when they suspected foul play. According to a Colombo-based human rights group working on the case, the doctor who conducted the autopsies concluded that both girls had died from drowning, calling their deaths a double suicide. However, during the embalming process, signs of violence were found internally, and the girls' parents had observed indications of external trauma upon viewing their daughters' bodies after the autopsies. Furthermore, their parents confirmed speaking to their daughters on the phone only days before, and the girls gave no indication of trouble and told them that they were planning on coming home for the upcoming Deepavali celebrations in October.

For leaders in the Hill Country, the state of affairs at that time was clear: politicians and union leaders, in the throes of debating the pending wage agreement, were on the brink of collective action, and news of Sumathi and Jeevarani's deaths only bolstered their efforts. Union leaders staged protests in hill station towns in an effort to keep the story of their deaths in the news. The Hatton's International Children's Day program in October 2009 featured a drama staged by children about brokers coming into the lines and luring them away to work in Colombo. In the final act, the children wore black bands on their wrists to protest the unlawful hiring and tragic deaths of their peers. As one Hatton-based activist said in a meeting that I attended in early September 2009, "Our children are like a reserve stock [*iruppu*] because of this economic problem. More honorable wages and work are needed." The stakes were high—the public deaths of these two girls was one more instance where plantation leaders were forced to reconfigure the rights of Hill Country Tamil minorities not only against stubbornly held class- and caste-based hierarchies but also on behalf of a marginalized and precarious worker community.

One month after their deaths, I met with Mano Ganesan, who was a member of Parliament and president of the Democratic People's Front and Democratic Workers' Congress at the time. In a mix of Tamil and English, we spoke about the current economic and social status of Tamil plantation workers, and our conversation about the wage and its intractability inevitably turned to Sumathi and Jeevarani. In response to my question about how he felt about their deaths and the ongoing investigation, he said the following to me in frustration:

> Those who talk about the child soldiers do not worry about the child workers . . . I met the parents of the girls there [on their estate], and

emotionally I scolded the mother and father of those children. I said, "Why on earth are you sending those children—those young girls [and] boys—to get killed?" And they just came out and said, "What are the alternatives here?" And I had no answer. As a Sri Lankan Parliamentarian, as a trade union leader, as a politician in this country, I got ashamed . . . I do not know how many other Parliamentarians or trade unionists would have felt ashamed, or felt uncomfortable, but personally I hung my head because I had no answer. I had no direct responsibility. I am not a person who in any way is directly responsible for their poverty and living conditions, but as a politician and a Parliamentarian, I felt ashamed. Do you think, we, the Hill Country Tamils, want to be the womb of Colombo's domestics?[3]

His reporting of the parents' reaction and the question he then asked me were raw with anger and revealed the layers of shame operating around and affecting Hill Country Tamil women and their families as they work in Sri Lanka. On the one hand, political leaders scold and shame Hill Country Tamils for their labor decisions within informal economies, knowing well that plantation work itself is stigmatized across caste and class lines; on the other hand, leaders themselves are ashamed of the realities Hill Country Tamils experience in their pursuit of dignity within those same systems of caste and labor stigmatization. These layers of anger point out that shame is not singular and cannot work alone. Like the tea industry, its operations require multiple stakeholders and investments, and through those individuals and commitments, it works to mark, infuse, and encompass the social and labor relations of individuals and entire communities. Just as capital repeatedly extracts labor from working bodies, shame, too, thrives on being iterative. It is exchanged, as seen in the scolding of parents' grieving their dead children; but at the same time, it is constantly in motion and can (and often will) return to compel those who feel it to reckon with its consequences.

The injustices and risks evident in Sumathi and Jeevarani's deaths are not unsubstantiated and have been well documented in media and human rights discourse on migrant and intimate labor in Sri Lanka. These rights violations resulted in the Ministry for Foreign Employment's July 2013 issuing of the Family Background Report (FBR) circular, which made illegal the migration abroad of any woman with children under the age of five and required women with children over the age of five to provide a written guarantee that their children would be cared for in their absence. In this first iteration, the 2013 FBR gravely concerned migrant worker and women's rights activists in Sri Lanka. Asha Abeyesekera and Ramani Jayasundere argue that the FBR was a result of the state's own moral panics about women's work and the health of the family, and that it disregarded previous assurances of gender equality in the Constitution as well as the 2008 National Labour Migration Policy.[4] These moral panics, they claimed, also "resulted in blaming poor migrant women as the receptacle of all social ills."[5] In this first FBR iteration, shame used rights-based discourse and the law to operate *for* the state as a strategy to manage the productivity of workingwomen's labors, but also to make workingwomen potential scapegoats across intersections of sexuality, motherhood, and marriage.

While the state was undoubtedly anxious to recover postwar, the 2015 revision to the 2013 circular demonstrated that the Sri Lankan state's interest in women's work went beyond protecting human rights. In this version, a clause specific to women living on the estates reads as follows: "In the plantation sector, the residence and civil status of women living in estates should be endorsed by the Superintendent of the relevant estate. If the Superintendent is not agreeable to such endorsement, the relevant women should not be recommended."[6] The explicit inclusion of the plantation sector clause reveals again the operating of shame—this time, in the Sri Lankan state's discriminating regulation of Hill Country Tamil women's mobility as well as their reproductive and labor rights. It restricts—if not implicitly designates—within which labor sectors Hill Country Tamil women should be working. Further concerning, the regulation and verification of a woman's civil status and residence falls extralegally into the hands of a plantation superintendent, who is an employer of a private entity supported by government subsidies for economic and social development.

As I describe in chapter 2, for many Hill Country Tamil women, plantation work lacks dignity because of its low wages and lower social prestige attributed to the work performed. In 2016 I interviewed Arun, a senior decision maker within the Planters' Association of Ceylon, in his Colombo office. In our conversation, he claimed that the low turnout among women workers made perfect sense: "Women [workers] do not like to be instructed to come to the muster shed [for weighing their tea leaves]. They do not like to line up like a parade. It is embarrassing. It is degrading. No one wants that kind of treatment—that feeling of being lower, watched, and scolded to work."[7] With more and more women on the plantations desiring to migrate abroad for work due to its higher wages and prestige, the state's restriction of Hill Country Tamil women's bodies through the 2015 FBR is all the more poignant in its attempt to control their work within two overlapping but competing sectors of plantation and migrant domestic labor.

The Politics of Labor Shaming

This chapter explores the shame, prestige, and self-worth cultivated in the social worlds of work on Sri Lanka's tea plantations. Through the account of three Hill Country Tamil families whose histories are built on informal and intimate migrant labor, I explore what work means to them, how it shapes their sense of self and kin relations, and how communities on and off the estate measure and evaluate their labor. Griffith, Preibisch, and Contreras argue that "reproductive labor and productive labor add value to one another and, in the process, serve as sources of happiness, dignity, and social legitimacy to women and men working in jobs that many consider onerous, dirty, smelly, undignified, and poorly remunerated."[8] Their intervention departs from Marshall Sahlins's "negative reciprocity," which argues that in systems of accumulation by dispossession there could be no way that those on the receiving end of dispossession could reap positive value.[9]

The negative effects of child and domestic labor stories of loss on rights-based policy and discourse produce a politics of labor shaming around migrant work alongside experiences of social value and prestige. This politics—promoted by the state and implicitly felt across middle- and upper-class communities in Sri Lanka—consists of strategies deployed and designed to blame and shame women for the stigmatized or low-wage labor and reproductive choices they make and to occlude the potential and actual value that their work contributes to their lives and families. The politics of labor shaming operates in three ways. First, Hill Country Tamils face systemic caste, class, and ethnic discrimination across education, health, and social sectors, and these conditions of sociality effectively reduce their opportunities to work in better-paying, upwardly mobile areas. The work they perform is often shamed and stigmatized by broader Sri Lankan civil society for being poorly compensated, intimate, and associated with menial and informal forms of payment and tasks. This became most clear to me, throughout fieldwork, when middle-class and elite non–Hill Country Tamils in Sri Lanka would learn about where I was doing research and with whom and then immediately ask me if I knew any women on the estates who could be a domestic or caretaker in Colombo for them or an acquaintance. Second, the government invests in the plantations through state subsidies and ministerial programming such that the state is ultimately invested in keeping Hill Country Tamils working on the fields, despite their desires for higher incomes and upward mobility. Third, through rights-based discourse and approaches to intimate labor, workers are shamed for participating in forms of work where their rights (and in many cases, their bodily safety and assurances) are unprotected. But they feel compelled to work elsewhere and find informal and flexible labor in response to the stigmas and inequalities attached to plantation work, and do so knowing that intimate labor is embedded with structural inequalities that render them more invisible and put them in harm's way. Across these three areas, the politics of shame circulates and flows uninterrupted, and yet Hill Country Tamil women continue to work and survive within it to sustain their families.

The politics of labor shaming also builds on the scholarship of feminist labor anthropologists Michele Gamburd, Caitrin Lynch, and Sandya Hewamanne, all of whom examine Sinhala-speaking women's work in Sri Lanka's garment and migrant industries. Intersections of gendered expectations, moral judgment, and state policies affect women's self- and kin perceptions of stigmatized and morally suspect labor. Building on Lynch's "good girls of modernity" and Gamburd's account of sensationalized "horror stories," I demonstrate how the politics of shaming works to hide the structural inequalities that shape minority Hill Country Tamil waged labor under the language of blame. Hill Country Tamil women must negotiate communal and state judgments of their labor and their commitments to being "good" women from their community relations and the state but also risk becoming flattened subjects of a simple but effective story of risk and poverty.[10] The stories that follow reveal the more complex dimensions of migrant labor that rights-based discourse often misses by presenting the affective and material investments that stem from women's life choices. Tracing both the added and negative values of prestige helps disrupt the politics of labor shaming in Sri Lanka and complicates more binary understandings of the waged labor that women and their families perform.

A Community on the Move

To transform the conditions and perceptions of poverty attached to a life sustained by only estate work, Hill Country Tamil parents recognize the untapped financial and long-term incentives to be gained by having their sons and daughters work in Colombo or abroad. Women like Sadha, whom I had met on the road before she left for Colombo as a housemaid, use the capacity to move and shift between formal and informal labor sectors to care for their families back home in the form of household remittances. In my research, it was uncommon to find a Tamil family on the tea plantations without any nuclear kin working (or having worked) in Colombo or abroad. Depending on one's education and gender, migrant occupations ranged from domestic work for women and children with low levels of education, garment and office work for female O/L and A/L graduates, shop work for boys and young men with low levels of education, and manual unskilled and semiskilled labor for young to middle-aged men. The range of employment opportunities was appealing not only for its diversified portfolios but also because these jobs provide higher levels of income than estate jobs and casual agricultural labor in the South-Central plantation areas.

The financial appeal, however, is not without internal dynamics of inequality and risk. Caste and class discrimination among Hill Country Tamils is real and practiced, and it is also affected by social and kin-based networks of labor exchange, educational experience, and socioeconomic mobility. The type of work one performs not only depends on specific levels of education one has to have but also on gendered divisions of labor across caste and the family's economic status and ability to financially invest in employment searches within formal and informal labor economies. Domestic work has been a seasoned yet informal mode of employment for lower-caste, Hill Country Tamil women since British rule and ideologically stems from colonial traditions of subservience and indentured labor. White superintendent *durais* may very well have departed from the plantation landscape, but in their places are upper- and middle-class urban household heads in Colombo and the Middle East as Hill Country Tamils' employers. Because of long-term institutional and informal discrimination against lower castes within the community and among Tamil speakers in Sri Lanka more broadly, I did not hear of or speak to middle- to upper-caste domestic workers during my fieldwork. Most middle- to upper-caste women living on the plantations would, because of their higher levels of education and familial wealth in the form of liquid cash, material assets, and social networks, seek office or retail employment in nearby hill stations like Hatton, Dickoya, Bogawantalawa, and Maskeliya. In contrast, I found that domestic work in Colombo or foreign domestic work among Hill Country Tamil women who self-identified as Paraiyar was more commonplace.

Likewise, upper- to middle-caste Hill Country Tamil men I spoke to, ranging from the young to the middle-aged, either worked under formal contracts with small to large Sri Lankan Tamil, Muslim, and Sinhala businesses in Colombo or, more respectably, in semiskilled to skilled labor in India and countries in the Middle East such as Qatar, United Arab Emirates, Iraq, and Saudi Arabia through the Sri Lanka Bureau of Foreign Employment (SLBFE). In contrast, lower-caste men among the same age range would, if able to migrate outside the estate sector for work, take noncontractual jobs in Colombo such as hotel cleaning, shop work, and private agricultural or manufacturing businesses through Hill Country Tamil informal employment brokers or recruiter networks on the plantations. In conversations with these men, they told me that they would like to work in the Middle East but did not have the desired education levels, required skills, or capital to finance the application processes and required documents such as passports, marriage licenses, and birth certificates. These caste- and class-based differentials suggest that while movement is a mutually agreed-on method for Hill Country Tamils seeking to work off the plantations, it is, as with most venues for advancement and opportunity, rife with historical and institutionalized practices of caste- and class-based discrimination.

Given the nature of the work, statistical information on informal domestic and contractual shop labor within the estate sector is difficult to verify. Comprising mainly women and children, this unorganized workforce informally solicits employment through estate brokers, sub-agents, kinship networks, and word of mouth in Colombo, Kandy, and other urban locales. Employer-employee relationships and experiences, unless otherwise procured from the employer or employee, are often undocumented and without contracts or documents detailing job security in the form of prior salary confirmations, assurances of safe accommodation, and clearly delineated job responsibilities. Being as such, this work carries more potential risk of harm to the employee's physical and emotional security. Without documentation, work hazards such as sexual harassment and assault, payment withholdings, poor accommodations, and physical and emotional abuse readily occur, and workers have little, if any, formal assurances for their personal safety and job security despite earning incomes higher than what is offered for estate work. Most concerning, the conditions of risk for women and children in Sri Lanka who, working within culturally specific gender and age dynamics, are higher, and if dominated in abusive labor situations, are less likely to seek the formal modes of assistance that would be available or sought out in greater civil society and within international norms.[11]

Sri Lanka ratified the International Labour Organization's Convention on Domestic Workers No. 189 in June of 2011, but international labor law is difficult to apply to the often invisible, informal, and undocumented intimate work in Sri Lanka. On the one hand, Hill Country Tamils work in service-based economies that have little to no means of redress and face more potential for bodily and emotional harm. On the other hand, they know and see regularly the actual financial and status-based rewards to be gained through remittances, and they weigh their life decisions against the above risks and benefits.

The desire to seek foreign employment, particularly in Southeast Asia and the Middle East, exists within the plantation sector as well as across Sri Lanka's urban and rural sectors, which face comparable conditions of economic insecurity and social immobility. Increasing levels of Sri Lankans working abroad regimented and institutionalized domestic labor employment in Sri Lanka with the 1985 establishment of the SLBFE, which addresses the needs of foreign employees, implements employment policies with partner nation-states, and promotes foreign employment within Sri Lanka.[12] According to the organization's 2014 *Annual*

Statistical Report of Foreign Employment, 125,493 women migrant workers traveled abroad for work in 2005, roughly 54 percent of the total migrant workforce, and in 2009, that percentage dropped to 46 percent (113,678 women); by 2014, the number of housemaids further declined to 88,661 out of 300,413 total migrant workers (roughly 29.5 percent).[13] The drop in numbers was most likely due to increased state regulations on migrant work, like the 2013 FBR, but also due to ongoing debates on the gendered risks and moral questions involving migrant domestic work. In 2009, 52 percent (or 16,600 women) of the country's total foreign migrant workers were housemaids from Central Province (comprising the districts of Kandy, Matale, and Nuwara Eliya); specifically, in Nuwara Eliya district, whose majority population is Hill Country Tamil, 69 percent of the district's foreign migrant workers (3,113 women) traveled abroad for housemaid work in that same year.[14] In 2014, both the provincial level and district specific percentages declined, to just 4.25 percent (12,794 women) and 30 percent (348 women), respectively.[15]

The statistical declines of housemaids working abroad countrywide and within the plantation areas testify to the double impacts Hill Country Tamils face as a result of the state's interest in regulating working-women. Desiring to make housemaid work harder to qualify for, the state builds up selective infrastructures of surveillance, such as the monitoring of foreign remittances, airport arrivals, and mandatory job trainings. These forms of tracking support the flow of capital in between Sri Lanka and the Middle East through foreign remittances, but they also negatively affect Hill Country Tamil women who do not have the bureaucratic or, in the case of the FBR, equal legal access to those foreign employment opportunities. This dynamic makes domestic intimate labor in Colombo more accessible, and women's working worlds uneven terrains of prestige, possibility, and economic support.

The Prestige of Colombo

In this context, intimate labor in Colombo is a distinct feature of Hill Country Tamil labor heritage on the plantations and continues to stigmatize the community within Sri Lankan civil society's caste and class hierarchies. These stigmas reveal themselves in actual and conceivable consequences, including caste- and class-based discrimination and inequalities across experiences of educational and economic mobility, employment opportunity, and access to health care and government services. Since their construction, the plantations were never bound economic institutions or enclaves but rather fluid sites of informal and formal labor and socioeconomic transaction.[16] Migration and movement were and remain key features of plantation life despite former characterizations of the estates as spaces of capital bound strictly by cultural practices and gendered hierarchies.[17]

Scholars studying caste dynamics on the estates specifically connect shifts in gender, age, and caste-based roles to migrant workers' returns to their home estates. As Balasundaram, Chandrabose, and Sivapragasam note, "Colombo boys"—Hill Country Tamil young boys and men who live on the estates but work in Colombo—shift the responsibilities taken up during such life and community ritual events, including duties formerly designated along caste lines.[18] Anthropologists have yet to critically examine the impact of women's migrant labor to Colombo from the estates. Beyond the category of "Colombo boys," women workers also confront and navigate split subjectivities about the actual work they perform in Colombo and the monetary and social prestige their work brings to their line room homes and families. The circulation of shame and prestige talk within workers' kin and social relations contribute significantly to the building of plantation, intimate, and resident worlds of work and Hill Country Tamils' evaluations of their shared labor heritage. Managing and responding to shame and prestige requires a delicate balancing of intimacy, trust, risk taking, and stranger sociality—an undertaking unique to Sri Lanka's tea plantation economy and the weakening of its landscapes and productive workforce.

The unevenness of terraforming and kinship investment also creates social ruptures that reconfigure former hierarchies of caste, class, and gender. Leaving the estate not only ensures the return of monetary remittances and capital to line room households, but also introduces the possibility that the chance (*vāīyppu*) to earn an income off the estate might improve the living conditions and standards of life for one's family remaining there in the long run. Opportunities in Colombo also have status-based benefits. Beyond my more intimate conversations with Hill Country Tamil migrant workers based in Colombo, I often observed conversations between close friends, acquaintances, and community members in town, on buses, and in public spaces like hospitals or shops. In those instances, when work in Colombo (*Kozhumbu vēlai*) or abroad (*veliyūr vēlai*) was mentioned, both phrases, in Tamil, did not often produce further questions about what work was actually being performed or if the conditions were safe or respectable. The phrases themselves were indices of success, orienting those who heard them to the known financial and social values of the migrant work without focusing on the work's specific context.

For Sri Lanka's Tamil speakers particularly, Sharika Thiranagama describes how Colombo, as a global city, affords a distinct mutability directly tied to minorities' unmet claims to political rights and belonging.[19] Colombo as a dignity-enabling site of imagination helps to explain why Hill Country Tamils find the city and its possibilities more appealing than the social and economic work conditions on the estates. But, as gender scholars of work note, migrant labor often assumes a double valence: away from home, workers perform labor such as cleaning and housemaid work that is highly stigmatized within their caste, ethnic, and class communities; but because the wages are relatively higher, the stigma is relatively lower, ignored, or unmentioned due to the accompanying economic and material transactions of prestige.[20] Furthermore, entry into Colombo's informal labor networks is not without social and economic challenges, despite the historical presence of Hill Country Tamil migrant labor in Colombo. Beyond the communal effects of migrant labor on the weakening of estate caste consciousness, a host of behavioral shifts on the estates take place at the intersections of gender and kin relations, rights-based policies, and industrial discourse. These shifts not only demand a deeper examination of the prestige and shame of Colombo work but also shed light on the uneven relationship among coolie labor heritage, political and labor rights movements, and globally shared ideals of industrial sustainability.

Incommensurable Worlds

While informal migrant labor ebbs and flows on the estates, it nevertheless remains a lifelong fixture in families' collective pursuits. I met Manivannan in 2009, when I first began to follow his entry into Colombo's informal labor sector. He was twenty-six years old then and had been working in and around Colombo since he was seventeen. After his O/Ls, he dropped out of school and went to work for a candy shop in one of Colombo's suburbs. The job paid well at Rs. 18,000 (roughly $167), a net monthly salary far above any plantation daily wage at the time. He and four other boys, all young Tamils from the estates, slept in one room on mattresses, and their employer paid their shared rent. The work, he told me then, was hard (*kashttam*), but he was young, his body was fit, and he worked well. His employer gave him two weeks' leave each year—one week for Deepavali in October/November and another week for Sinhala and Tamil New Year in mid-April. His mother and father were once workers on the estate but were now casual day laborers earning between Rs. 300 and Rs. 500 per day for tea smallholders and other private landholders in the area. With his higher salary, his parents were able to renovate and expand their line room, buy material goods such as a television and furniture, and provide gifts, *moi*, and basic needs items like clothing and food for his extended family, which included five young girls under the age of fifteen in 2009.

In 2011, Manivannan married a Hill Country Tamil girl he had met in Colombo while he was working in a new restaurant as a cook and she was working in Katunayake's free trade zones (FTZs) as a garment worker. She was nineteen at the time and had also dropped out of school after her O/Ls to work and support her mother, whose husband had left her with three children when her youngest daughter was five years old. I asked his wife how they had met given the sex segregation of their respective labor sectors. She told me that he and other young men would often visit girls working in the FTZs. Soon after they began dating, they registered their marriage without a large ceremony, and she moved into his parents' home on Kirkwall along with her mother and her youngest sister. That same year, Manivannan returned to Colombo to a new job as a cook in a restaurant. His wife initially did not work on the estate, but in 2013 she began plucking on Kirkwall.

I visited Manivannan's home one afternoon in July 2015. His wife had finished work an hour earlier and was washing her hair because he would be coming home from Colombo by bus later that evening. I noticed that she was wearing a *taiyattai*, the Tamil term used to describe a pendant affixed to a thread and worn for protection or good fortune. I asked her why she was wearing it. She told me that Manivannan and she had started trying to have children in 2011 after their registration, but that it had been four years and they still had not succeeded. They went to government hospitals as well as private medical and fertility clinics in Hatton, Dickoya, and Nawalapitiya but with no luck. Out of options, her father-in-law suggested they visit a local Hindu priest attached to a nearby Māriamman temple. He performed a ceremonial prayer and offering for her fertility, and told her to wear the *taiyattai* and that all would be resolved. After she finished washing her hair, we sat in the kitchen and her mother-in-law came home from work at the smallholder nearby, her tea-leaf basket still fastened to her forehead. Manivannan's wife remarked on how she looked different when she had worked in Colombo. Her body had been fuller; her skin had not been dull. Plucking, she said, had changed her. She showed me the tips of fingers, the skin under her nails, and the insides of her palms. The creases of her skin had become permanently stained black (*kārum*) from plucking tea leaves day after day.

Later that evening, Manivannan arrived after a long bus journey with his mother-in-law, a domestic also working in Colombo. I sat with them in the main room of their line room amid bulging duffel bags and parcels securely wrapped in string and brown paper, all gifts and items they had bought for their family members. His parents and extended relations from the line were gathered around him while he spoke. The journey had been long and tiring. Since 2014, the last time I had seen him, his appearance had changed. He had put on weight, lost some hair, and his eyes and skin looked tired. I asked him about his new job, and he immediately responded that it was very difficult. He shared a room at the back of the restaurant with seven other young men on bunk beds, all Tamils from the Hill Country. They would wake up at 4:00 a.m. and begin cooking breakfast buns, savory pastries, and snacks at 5:00 a.m. At 9:00 a.m. they would break for tea and breakfast and rest until 2:00 p.m. Then they would continue cooking for dinner from 2:00 p.m. until 8:00 p.m. All the standing had made his legs and heels ache, and he showed me his swollen calves and the cracked skin on his heels. His mother ran to the kitchen to get coconut oil, poured some into her hands, and began massaging his calves and feet. He winced a bit in pain, but she told him it would feel better in the morning. He told me he would like stay here with his family on the plantation, but that the salaries were not as good for young men like him. In just six years, his Colombo salary of Rs. 18,000 had grown to Rs. 45,000 per month (roughly $337), and despite the fact that inflation and the cost of living had also risen steadily in those six years, his salary still increased at rates faster and higher than the collective wage or smallholder wages in the estate sector had. With that money, he and his wife could pursue fertility treatments to have a child, and he could also provide for his parents who were getting old and would soon need to retire. That month, he was supposed to leave after just four days at home, but he, along with his mother-in-law, extended their stays to one week so that he could rest. In 2016 and 2017, when I returned to Kirkwall, Manivannan was still working at the same restaurant and extending his time at home due to exhaustion. His wife was still plucking without a child but had removed the *taiyattai*, telling me it was all lies (*pōy*) and that she had planned to visit a new fertility clinic in Hatton town that had just opened its doors. Her mother was still a domestic worker in Colombo at fifty years old, and his parents were still working to pay off the debts they had incurred for her fourteen-year-old sister's recent age attainment celebration.

Their family's story of labor and reproduction brings out the ways in which the informality of labor not only builds effective forms of economic capital within individual households but also strains workers' reproductive desires for the future. For many families like Manivannan's, migrant work in the cities is a necessary supplement to RPC estate wages. In other words, the plantation wage is not able to reproduce a workforce on its own, and the families with full-time estate laborers such as Manivannan's wife are forced to rely on economic household inputs from other, off-estate forms of employment. But it is important to note that what keeps most Hill Country Tamil families on the estates is the line room that they call home but do not own and the communities of family and neighbors that they trust and rely on. With migrant remittances, Manivannan and others working in Colombo, as seen in chapter 3, are able to enhance their homes and build internal networks of prestige on the estates. His entry into Colombo gave his family standing within Kirkwall's line room community—though, given his unfilled desire to start a family, this was not without sacrifice. Hill Country Tamils in Sri Lanka strongly value having children and reproductive capacity—that is, the bearing of biological children and sustaining of human life across generations—despite family planning practices and narratives of "two or three is enough" among estate doctors and midwives in an effort to curtail large families and conditions of poverty.

In 2014, when I first met Manivannan's wife, his father's elder sister, who lives in the line room next to his home, remarked, "*Pāvum* [Poor one], he wants a child so badly. He loves children and has a strong affection [*pācum*] for them. What to do?" To not have children and be married on the plantations was a stigma that Manivannan and his wife had to bear. Since their marriage, he had been home with his wife for only a few days every three or four months and yet, in all the medical files they shared with me, no doctor or medical professional had mentioned or investigated evidence of the effects of migrant labor on their reproductive capacity as a couple.

Alongside those noticeable gaps, however, the prestige produced by Manivannan's work, while incommensurate with his actual embodied experiences of labor and life in Colombo, was real, and it could be located in the most intimate of gestures during his visits home, such as his mother's massaging of his feet and calves with oil. These gestures were value-producing not only because they communicated forms of love and care among kin but also because they were outwardly visible and performative for others. Bernard Bate, in his discussion of the "hierarchical intimacy" of praise, or *bhakti*, wrote, "The ritual practice, though intimate, is performed for others to see; it is meant to be observed and evaluated by onlookers. As such, it is an aesthetic practice in the sense both that it is a practice that can be evaluated positively or negatively and that it has emotional content."[21] Available for evaluation, the positive and negative values Manivannan's informal labor produces and his status as a "Colombo boy" turned husband, family caretaker, and aspiring father cannot simply be taken as monetary contributions to his and his family's total prestige and standing. Rather, they signal that a life of informal work on the estates is a constant and delicate balancing act and series of evaluations between the social insecurities and hardships of a world of work unseen and the sacrifices and investments one can communicate and leave behind upon one's return.

Returning Home

One month before the end of the war, I celebrated the Tamil and Sinhala New Year on Kirkwall. New Year's is a particularly important celebration on the plantations because workers are given longer periods of time off work, during which many migrant workers from Colombo travel home to be with their families. Kumar, a married man in his early thirties with three young boys, was working at the time for a smaller, Sinhala-owned packing business in Pannipitiya, a suburb of Colombo, On April 14 he came home for the New Year festivities and brought along with him seven Colombo Tamil and Sinhala male friend co-workers. Staying in a nearby hotel, his friends from Colombo came to his home on the first day of the weekend celebrations. When unknown people enter the estate's residential lines, their presence does not go unnoticed—there is an awareness among Hill Country Tamils directly linked to the state of emergency and their shared history of targeted violence and militarized surveillance. I was sitting in the line room home adjacent to Kumar's, visiting his relation through marriage, Pachchayamma. Soon after the men arrived, we heard Tamil music blaring from the other side of the wall their homes shared. One of Pachchayamma's granddaughters went next door and came back reporting that they were watching an old Rajni Kanth Video CD on their player and that the men were all dancing.

After some time Pachchayamma's daughter, Ramya, who was twenty-six years old and unmarried at the time, got up and started to sweep the main room of their line, moving in and out of the room from the kitchen area in the back. "I do not like if these Colombo Tamils were to see our house and kitchen like this," she told me. Later she told me that last year, Kumar brought nearly twenty people for New Year's and that it was a *karaiccal* (nuisance) because they were loud and drinking a lot. Ramya then changed out of her clothes. Debating over wearing a dress or skirt, she finally settled on denim jeans and a graphic print T-shirt, and her mother chastised her for caring so much about these unknown visitors. Intrigued by their arrival, I stepped halfway onto the front threshold of Pachchayamma's home to get a better look, and startled Kumar's father who was walking in at that same moment. The younger brother of Pachchayamma's first husband, he was approaching seventy and walked slowly into her house, claiming that it was too noisy for him and that he was irritated with the way his son and daughter-in-law were acting. He was also carrying my slippers with him, pointing to the six pairs of sandals and slippers outside Kumar's door on the veranda. "You should keep them inside here for now so that they do not get stolen," he told me with a smile. With the commotion and precedent of bad behavior from last New Year's, Kumar's surrounding kin had learned their lessons and were adjusting their habits accordingly.

Soon after we moved into the kitchen to start preparing the evening New Year's meal, Kumar's wife, Rati, having changed from her work clothes, came in wearing a fancy skirt and new blouse. Talking quickly and with slight impatience, she asked Pachchayamma for a carrot and potato. Pachchayamma started to voice her irritation but gave them to her grudgingly. She took the vegetables and ran back to her home, presumably to resume cooking for her guests. Twenty minutes later, Kumar walked into the house with a burned-out light bulb, demanding that they give him a replacement. Pachchayamma's son gave him one that he found tucked away in a box of wires and batteries from their main cupboard. Within minutes he came back and claimed the bulb was not working. When her son told him there were no others, he stormed out, saying, "Nothing works! You don't have anything!" and returned to his guests. After he left for the second time, Pachchayamma voiced her frustrations to me: "Before they used to help [us] so much. Now they will not help. Once I gave them Rs. 3,000 [twenty-eight dollars] when they needed it. They are like that. If you just sit, think, and wait, there will be a fight [*sandai*] with them. He even took our glass plates before and did not even ask. He just came in talking like a *rāṅki* [arrogant fool]. *Manacukkulla vētanai* [My mind has been soured]. We should not give them anything from now on."

The presence of Colombo through returning migrant workers and visitors triggers a series of effects among estate residents. The reputedly arrogant behavior of Kumar and his wife was out of line with customary codes of conduct in the lines. It brought out in Pachchayamma, her family, and Kumar's father feelings of slight and resentment and reflects how formerly governed social relations such as respect for the elderly and gift giving among kin shift and make way for reevaluations of migrant workers and their communal obligations. Significant also is Pachchayamma's recounting of previous transactions between Kumar and her family. Her family was over Rs. 25,000 in debt to various moneylenders at the time, and they were pawning most of their valuables to make ends meet. Kumar and Rati's disruptive behavior only reminded her of the money her family lacked and of the assistance they would not reciprocate. Because they had shown off having visitors from Colombo and treated their own relations at home badly in the moment, Pachchayam-ma's vow not to honor the obligation of giving kin money in the future reveals her attempt to control her own economic situation and social standing. The very public handling of their newfound wealth directly affected the kinship relations between both households and demon-strates how work in Colombo has the potential to transform the value systems that govern group life and economic decision-making among estate residents.

In 2014, I returned to Kirkwall to find that Rati had left to work as a domestic for a family in Saudi Arabia in 2010. Kumar was now at home, working as a casual laborer on and off the estate. His father had passed away, and his mother, who had spent most of her life as a domestic, had moved back home from her job in Colombo to help him care for his three boys. Over the next three years, I would return to Kirkwall to find Kumar along with his mother and boys, the eldest of whom had dropped out of school at age seventeen to work in a shop in Colombo. Upon arriving on Kirkwall in August 2016, Kumar immediately ushered me into his line room home, a gesture that still irritated Pachchayamma and others in her house. And when I looked around their home I understood why his relations and neighbors were upset. Their front greeting room was teem-ing with new leather furniture, sealed in plastic to protect it from mold and damage as well as a large television, a stereo, and a landline phone. Inside the anterior main room sat a new Singer sewing machine and a refrigerator, the first I had seen in the line rooms on Kirkwall since beginning my fieldwork in 2009. He brought me inside the kitchen where he showed me the chimney they had installed for better ventilation, as well as new electric grinders and a larger electric rice cooker they had purchased over the years.

I asked him how Rati was doing in Saudi Arabia. He explained that she was working hard and lamented that I had just missed her, as she had come home in June of that year and would have wanted to see me. I agreed and asked if we could call her, to which he said that he would but that his phone line had been cut because he had not paid the bill in two months. He asked to use my cell phone to call her, and I gave it to him. There was no answer; as it was ringing, Pachchayamma's daughter-in-law walked in, saw him on my cell phone, and scolded angrily, "Why are you using her phone when you can put money on your own line?" Cutting the call mid-ring on my cell phone, he thrust his finger in her face and angrily told her to keep quiet. He then he ran into the front room and returned with his hands full of used prepaid, scratch-off Rs. 100 reload phone card slips, amounting to at least Rs. 5,000. He held his hands in front of my face to show me and shouted, "Do you see how much money I have spent calling her?" He then brought down a bulging black suitcase from the top of their armoire, which was filled with Rati's personal items from her time working abroad. He showed me an expired passport and work visas and remarked how she had been the first in their family to hold such forms of documentation. He then held up a black *abaya*, which she was required to wear in public according to the clothing customs for women in Saudi Arabia. After moving the fabric around to find the sleeves, he put it on his own body, and the hemmed edges barely came to his knees because he was significantly taller than his wife. He eagerly asked me if I had ever seen one and told me that she had to wear the customary dress whenever she went out to the market or with her employers in public. After taking off the *abaya*, he held it to his nose and paused to inhale. "You see? It still smells like her," he said as he thrust the garment in my face. I inhaled into the cloth, and sure enough, it smelled faintly of a woman's perfume. "It does," I told him, and his ten-year-old son looked at me, took it from his father's hands to smell it for himself. After inhaling into the black fabric, he looked into my eyes and smiled. Without saying a word, Pachchayamma's daughter walked out of his line room and went back to her home next door.

We finally reached Rati on the phone later that evening. It was seven thirty in the morning in Saudi Arabia, and she had been up since two because her employer's family had come home from a party and had wanted her to prepare food. Her voice over the phone had changed since we had last been together in person. She sounded tired and told me that she was sad she could not see me and that she would return in 2018 when her contract finished. I asked her about her work and her employers. The house, she said, was not a problem, for which reason she was lucky. I listened and watched as her family members passed my cell phone around the room so everyone could speak to her. She asked her two younger boys what they had eaten and if they were studying and behaving well, to all of which they replied positively. Kumar then spoke to her briefly before the rupees on my phone ran out, only to assure her that he would pay the landline bill so that they could call her more often.

Migrant labor can heighten financial inequalities and degrees of trust and jealousy among neighbors and kin on the plantations. But it can also strengthen, however subtly, other forms of exchange, intimacy, and desire among and within families. The interchange of migrant work keeps families afloat financially, but the relationships and material goods they cultivate through that labor do much more than financially improve their means. As Kumar made a point of showing me with his fistfuls of phone cards, his relations with the kin around him were strained. But despite their resentment, however justified, nothing could take away Rati's prolonged absence from her family and the affection everyone had for her. She was and remains a mother of three boys, a close family member and neighbor, and the primary breadwinner of their household. Her absence—as manifest in Kumar's sensorial longing for her presence—had momentarily disrupted neighborly and kin tensions. But both resentments of new wealth *and* happiness upon her return would eventually resurface. And the precarity and prestige of worlds of work beyond the estates would contrive to shape the resilience and unevenness of lifelong relationships.

Intimate (In)humanities

With Sri Lanka's plantation sector experiencing record losses and the lowest worker turnouts since privatization, Hill Country Tamil women, children, and men, now more than ever, do not want to make their living working on the fields. As a member of the Planters' Association explained, industrial agricultural work lacks dignity and is incommensurate with workers' aspirations due to low wages and lower levels of prestige attributed to the labor they are required to perform.

Migrant labor is also a communally shared objective. When pursued and mapped out in the individual lives of newly formed and growing families, it demonstrates how contradictions of intimacy, shame, and prestige bring into sharp relief the sometimes buried and often overlooked political and structural constraints that Hill Country Tamils face as aspirational minority subjects in postwar Sri Lanka. As they struggle to secure a place in the nation for themselves and their families, the informality and intimacy of their labor, while reinforcing social inequalities that supposedly kept their ancestors in their place, at the same time fuels their desires to delink from the current shaming and stigmas associated with the labor they perform. These tensions are embodied in Manivannan's swollen calves, Pachchayamma's resentment and jealousy, and Kumar's inhaling of Rati's perfume on her *abaya*. They are costs that speak to the intimacy with which informal labor continually infuses line room life and Hill Country Tamils' own measuring and evaluations of self-standing, waged labor, and ever-shifting labor possibilities.

Alongside attributions of prestige and worth, politicians and policy discourse espouse the rhetoric of shame and anxiety around trends of housemaid and Colombo work. Trade unionists, politicians, NGO personnel, and activists monophonically label informal and migrant labor as risks that actively threaten the rights and security of Hill Country Tamils as an ethnic and once disenfranchised community. The prevalence of Colombo *vēlai* irritates Hill Country Tamil politicians and community leaders who worry about the social and political future of their constituents and struggle to defy their constant depreciation. As one Hill Country Tamil activist said in a meeting about the plantation wage after Sumathi and Jeevarani's deaths, "This *vītu vēlai* [housework] trend is horrible. Colombo is becoming a Colombo *tōttam* [estate]. We must take this struggle seriously and cannot further deny that the people are desperate." Bolstering their views are news reports and very real consequences and evidence of child labor and sexual abuse, which suggest that the move to Colombo is, at the very least, a risky one and a symptom of the plantation sector's chronic poverty and inequalities.

As a feminist scholar, I struggle to recognize the pathologizing undercurrents of these views and remain cognizant of the contexts of caste, class, and patriarchal hierarchies in which these utterances are made. How should we, as engaged scholars committed to standing alongside workers who invest in their futures, make sense of informal and intimate migrant work's incommensurability of prestige and shame? What do workers' feelings about the labor they perform and about what their income provides have to say about the state of solidarity among Hill Country Tamils on the plantations, their larger representatives, and the Sri Lankans and countries who benefit from their labor?

The mutuality of aspiration and risk that intimate and informal labor demands complicates formerly sticking representations of the Hill Country Tamil plantation community. Striving for a dignified story of labor that has the least amount of associated risks and harm to the self, Hill Country Tamils seek to break from visceral strains of poverty and socioeconomic immobility, but in doing so perform the types of work that do not provide acceptable levels of dignity and safety. As I was told by the mother of one man who had recently applied for his identification card after a lifetime of statelessness in 2009 before the war ended, "This ID is like giving life to our family. Now he can go to work in Colombo. Then the children can go to school, and we will have no money problems. Even to go to Hatton, he is afraid. Now he can do anything." Such splits within self and collective representations suggest that the sense of belonging that Hill Country Tamils and emerging generations in particular experience on the plantations and within the Sri Lankan polity is not only in flux but also contingent on their capacities to make claims to forms of dignity previously not experienced by their parents and ancestors.

But intimate desires do not always suit the instrumentalist ethics of rights-based discourse around labor assurances and entitlements. The features which informal and intimate migrant workers often take pride in and which reap them material and social rewards are in fact the very objects of the politics of labor shaming that operates across state policies and politicians' speeches in the name of human rights. This all became clear with the introduction of the plantation clause in the 2015 FBR amendment and the collapse of rights-based solidarity initiatives across labor sectors to represent the intersectional and fluid needs of Sri Lanka's plantation workers who have always been intimately and strategically woven into narratives of state building and economic production. Labor solidarity movements for informal and intimate laborers are only now emerging, but even so they face significant structural and legal challenges of sustainability and acceptance in their advocacy for the rights and dignity of workers across caste, class, ethnicity, and heritage experiences.

Sumathi and Jeevarani's story of violence and violation is a flattened narrative of labor that human rights discourse, modalities of state surveillance, and the politics of labor shaming wish to see and remember in worlds of work on the estates. But these stories alone do not capture the untold and speculative realities of what workers intimately feel and desire and how their labor activates and transforms their present relations and futures. With 62.7 percent of all employment in Sri Lanka from the informal labor sector, richer understandings of the stories of migrant work not only dignify the decisions and desires of Hill Country Tamils in the context of their labor heritage but also include their stories in larger, shared narratives of mutuality and minority aspirations in postwar Sri Lanka.[22] For Colombo's Hill Country Tamil workers who have neither laws nor protections to regulate their labor and who face pervasive caste, class, and socioeconomic inequalities across generations, this shared labor heritage is not new to the national landscape. Rather, it is the story of how perceptions of what they once were in Sri Lanka dynamically inform their senses of self and their desires for a better, more dignified future.

An activist in Sri Lanka once told me, "History is neither the rule nor the law but a series of struggles. And it is up to us to be on the right side of the struggle."[23] If the right side of the struggle is acknowledging how the politics of labor shaming operates in moments of lawlessness and uncertainty, then this recognition seems to be a small methodological step toward a space within rights-based discourse that is not as comfortable to inhabit but perhaps is more commensurate with workers' uneven labor experiences in Sri Lanka. Recognizing this shame acknowledges that one needs to know the life conditions and daily strategies that minority workers on the estates take on to feel secure in their bodies and labor in order to make a place for themselves and for those under their care. For Sri Lanka, a postcolonial state whose past and present have been marred by illegitimacy and fear, acknowledging the politics of labor shaming brings forward more nuanced approaches to standing alongside Hill Country Tamil workingwomen and their families as they do the work of generating for the future.

CHAPTER 7

Contingent Solidarities

IN AUGUST 2009 I ATTENDED A TWO-DAY RETREAT WITH THE
Plantation Social Sector Forum (PSSF), a development network of plantation trade unions, NGOs, and community-based organizations (CBOs).
The network emerged from participatory dialogues among select members at the 2003 Asian Social Forum. From 2003 to 2009 it gained
momentum through national lobbying efforts around Sri Lanka's MDG-
driven Ten-Year Action Plan and international movements such as International Tea Day, a day of tea worker recognition held annually on
December 15.[1]

The two-day retreat was attended by thirteen network
representatives—eleven men and three women, including myself. We discussed topics like estate housing, citizenship, women's, and labor rights
issues; the purpose of the retreat was to finalize PSSF's programming
efforts. Priya, a young female CBO leader from Nuwara Eliya district and
one of two leaders of the Women's Wing and Gender Unit, was next to
present on the pressing women's issues in the sector. Each participant was
given twenty minutes to speak, and Priya knew the time was too brief
for her to get through what she wanted to say. She began speaking quickly
in Tamil, barely pausing for a breath for ten minutes as she outlined the
wide range of issues affecting women on the plantations: the lack of
awareness around the UN's CEDAW Convention, the expendability and
maltreatment of widows, the lack of female overseers, instances of respi-
ratory disease among pluckers, young girls committing suicide due to
domestic violence and love problems, increasing rates of divorce, and
familial tensions over transnational migrant labor and remittance management. The weight of what she had curated in just those ten minutes

was overwhelming and presented an urgently sewn web of risks and relations into which Tamil women were meaningfully struggling to live. The format of the retreat, where each speaker was given an allotted time, mirrored the way grant seekers make their pitch—a plea for those listening to not turn a deaf ear to their realities and to believe they are worthy of the required time and energy. She finished her list and then began linking each issue to a specific proposal of more pragmatic, culturally appropriate approaches to achieving women's empowerment.

Suddenly, one of the older male participants interrupted her to ask the session organizer, Patrick, if the group could move on to more "pressing issues" such as the CA and the Ten-Year National Action Plan. Patrick hesitated slightly and the other men in the room followed suit and looked around at one another for consensus. But then Patrick startlingly slammed the table with his fist, yelled in Tamil at first, and then emphatically in a mix of English and Tamil, "*Inta uravu vēṇḍum!*" (We need this relationship!). He continued, "We *need* this! We, as *men*, must *admit* this— they have *no* space! We must give the space! Now, at this moment, the women have no chance! It is all hypocrisy! We can talk on air, but on the ground, we must admit we have not given them the space!"

His comments silenced and shamed the participants in the room, including me. The man who had interrupted Priya had cut her off and taken her space, despite time being set aside to have her speak. If this solidarity network could not even give its women members the space to discuss constituent issues, then the group, as a collective force, was effectively not ready to stand alongside women workers. It was a lucid and rupturing moment that had been brought on and made public by the very conditions of solidarity and cohesion the network had fostered.

In *Feminism and Nationalism in the Third World*, Kumari Jayawardena writes that men were seen as the "main movers of history" whereas women "worked within the boundaries laid down by men."[2] The project of disruption, she argues, "in itself is important, asserting that women have played a role that has been consistently ignored, and correcting the picture of men as the only historical actors."[3] Patrick's outburst, in this sense, was shocking coming from a man. But like so many other moments of discontent and uneasiness in the estate sector, it came and went. The meeting continued to proceed uneventfully; the discussion turned to the CA and the Ten-Year National Action Plan; and at the end of the retreat, closing remarks were made, meals were eaten, and a group photograph was taken to send to international donors.

In this final chapter, I explore emergent rights-based and labor-organizing spaces for Hill Country Tamil women workers in Sri Lanka's national and transnational development sector. I examine two initiatives, both of which reveal the challenges of reorienting Hill Country Tamil women's labor futures and rights. The first program is an NGO-led transnational human rights–based program involving young women from the tea plantations. I trace the successes and failures represented in its development archive. In doing so, I ask what it might mean to deconstruct the discursive binaries of success and failure in transnational gender development programming and delve into the more relational, grounded stakes that these programs have for their participants. I then shift to Sri Lanka's first women-led trade union, the Working Women's Front (WWF). This trade union serves women workers across formal, informal and unorganized sectors. Its members employ feminist and transnational methodologies to carry out their outreach and programming, and they take on the task of organizing the unorganized and reserve labor forces on the estates such as the young and elderly. With most plantation trade unions historically patriarchal in both structure and practice, WWF, as a feminist labor-organizing movement, breaks away from hegemonic patterns of labor politicization in Sri Lanka and embodies the politics and praxis that trade unions ought to embrace locally and transnationally.

Structured by their commitments to international rights-based and transnational feminist discourse and praxis, both programs rely on what I call contingent solidarities. At first glance, contingency and solidarity are antithetical. Smita Rahman writes that contingency is "grounded in the instability and disruption of time and attentive to moments of fragmentation and contestation in a world of difference."[4] To be contingent on is to encounter the unpredictable in relation to the possible; it requires a scooping up of what is available in order to make sense of and search for evidence or something that will mutually support our move toward what we want (i.e., the state of being "contingent upon"). Contingency is a coming together of individuals in their acknowledgment of a shared purpose (i.e., "a contingent"). Solidarity, the coming together and commitment to stand alongside, in this way, requires contingency. It requires productively contentious disruptions that compel people to come together, make them doubt, and keep them invested in the ideal of cohesion. At the same time, that very contingency—in its unpredictability to be there and provide support when needed—can shake the core of solidarity and its calls for movement. For both gender-based programs I trace here—one grounded in transnational rights-based discourse and the other in feminist labor organizing—I am interested in pulling out the tensions that emerge when individuals invested in creating effective changes in workingwomen's lives come together and what actual and potential fragmentations they encounter in that shared space. I am also interested in identifying what resources these transnational and rights-based feminist movements need to continue and move forward with mutual support. As both programs center on and involve Hill Country Tamil women workers on the tea plantations, these contingent solidarities are grounded within Sri Lanka's larger politics of postwar development and the structural challenge of fully acknowledging women's labor rights.

National Coalitions, Transnational Solidarities

The growth of rights-based development in the plantation sector correlates to specific political and developmental shifts taking place in the immediate aftermath of the civil war. Within the first six months postwar, Hill Country Tamil plantation workers and residents were being consistently and effectively excluded from reaping significant government benefits or any of the social and political recognition promised at the end of the war within the upsurge of economic development. Locally, the network of which Priya and Patrick were a part lost relative momentum after 2010 when their international funding ended. The tripartite organization was forced to reduce the scope of its efforts, though today it maintains limited programming around rights-based issues and events such as International Tea Day.

Between 2010 and 2014, I was in the United States teaching and writing, when I heard about two development outcomes from another member of the network who had received a significant US State Department grant to take part in a three-way cultural exchange among women in the United States, Chile, and Sri Lanka. The purpose of the exchange was to create a dialogue around diverse, shared issues of women's rights and social change. On a technical level, it was designed to connect different women-focused NGOs through local and international dialogues and transnational visits among young women between the ages of seventeen and eighteen from three different countries. During the dialogues, which were carried out online via video conference calls, one of the twenty girls from each site would give a brief presentation to the larger group about their respective history, their culture, and the particular issues faced by girls and women in their communities. The participants would then hold what was called a "critical dialogue," in which they were charged with talking about the significance of the program and if and how intercultural forms of exchange could enhance young women's knowledge about systems and institutions of educational, rights-enabling venues for women within their own countries and forms of gendered violence that prevent women from fully enjoying their rights in local contexts. Following the international dialogues, four girls from each site then would be elected to travel to their partner sites in a three-part intercultural exchange tour between January and May 2013. In Washington, DC, I met with the US-based program organizers in the planning meetings in September 2012, and in April 2013 two girls, Jayaluxmi and Nagarani, traveled with a staff member to the United States to attend the program, during which I served as a translator and participant observer.

The coordination of the program and its traveling components was, to say the least, a human-technological feat and form of contingent solidarity in action. Heavy rains in the Hill Country, weak Internet connections in Chile, and missing audiovisual equipment in the United States continually disrupted and restarted the three-way video Skype calls. Visas were initially questioned due to participants' language capabilities but were quickly honored after felicitous emails to consular contacts reassuring all parties that the participants would have translators. One program participant, a woman teacher from the Hill Country who had applied to attend and had been an active participant in the yearlong program, had an unexpected death in her family just days before the group's departure, and after all the flights were booked and visas obtained she was not able to travel. Nevertheless, in the face of these obstacles and unpredictable circumstances, participants and organizers persisted in their responses and the program stayed on schedule. Project coordinators in all three countries generated quarterly and mid-evaluation reports, meticulously documenting each and every event with photographs, press releases, and Facebook updates; the girls, too, contributed written narratives about their lives and audio recordings of interviews with women from their own communities, which were then transcribed and translated for wider dissemination.

Analyzing the love letters of young couples in Nepal, Laura Ahearn describes the confluence of literacy, education, and gender commitments that guide how young subjects perform national expectations and practices of development in the form of intimate and affective relations.[5] Similar dynamics of expectation and intimacy held for the transnational relationships among the young girls participating in this program. Writing and communicating about the gender rights issues of girls required a certain type of girl subject who would be open to the discomforts and newness of different languages, cultures, and experiences. The openness was created for the purpose of being performed in writing but also in person. Accompanying Jayaluxmi and Nagarani while they were in the United States, I found that they were genuinely excited to connect. They were open and affectionate toward the women they were meeting for the first or second time after months of video interface communication and readings of their translated life narratives from Spanish to English and English to Tamil. They, alongside the other girl participants, discussed the legacies of slavery on Freedom Trail sites in upstate New York and reflected on the unventilated sweatshops of the Tenement Museum in New York City. As ambassadors and participants, Jayaluxmi and Nagarani embodied and performed the ideal development encounter, exceeding the program's expectations.

Girl Subjects

The "girl" and "girl-child" are not new to transnational and rights-based gender development.[6] The time I spent with Jayaluxmi and Nagarani during the United States cross-cultural exchange trip moved me to look more closely into the recent history of gender development in a transnational context, and more specifically into programs funded by organizations based in the United States and Europe dedicated to the empowerment and development of "girls" living in decolonized countries such as Sri Lanka and countries across South and Southeast Asia, Africa, South

America, and the Caribbean. Since 1979, international human rights law in the form of UN's Convention on the Elimination of All Forms of Discrimination Against Women has protected women, and ten years following its adoption the Convention on the Rights of the Child was adopted in 1989.[7] Following the CRC's adoption, the category of "girl-child" began finding traction in human rights and development discourse. The UN declared 1990 the year of the "girl-child," and in that same year, at the fifth meeting of the South Asian Association for Regional Cooperation (SAARC) Technical Committee on Women in Development held in Delhi, that organization declared the upcoming decade that of the "girl-child" in a commitment for all South Asian member states to adopt a national plan of action for protecting the rights of young girls.[8] Throughout the 1990s, the girl-child remained a key focus issue in international human rights discourse and policy making, as seen in the 1994 International Conference on Population and Development in Cairo, the 1995 Fourth World Conference on Women in Beijing, and the February 1997 UN Resolution 51/76 ("The Girl Child"), which specifically called on all states to honor the rights of the girl child with respect to equal treatment and support for their physical and mental health, educational opportunities, nutrition, and protections against sexual violence and exploitation.[9] By 2000, the human rights and development of girls had been included in the 2000 UN MDGs under goal 3 ("Promote Gender Equality and Empower Women"), and her place was reaffirmed in the 2016 UN Sustainable Development Goals under goal 5 ("Achieve Gender Equality and Empower All Women and Girls").

In this recent history of the girl-child in international human rights discourse, many of the commitments to and success of developing "girls" are contingent on the timing and management of representing girls as liminal, gendered subjects filtered through the nation. During the 1989 SAARC Delhi meeting, for instance, specific agenda items included commitments to "project [a] positive image of the Girl Child," and a photo exhibition on the girl-child was held during the SAARC Summit featuring commemorative stamps, postcards, and coins designed by member states. Following market-based trends of international development, the circulation of girl-child images extended beyond the rights-based circles of national policy making and solidarity building and into the corporate and private sector as well. Programs such as Nike Girl Effect capitalize on the potential of the girl in the Global South as reproductively and relationally liminal—looking up to the horizon of gendered expectations but not yet constrained by them, and all the while reliant on being saved by the empowered consumer located in the Global North. But this image is what Cynthia Caron and Shelby Margolin call a "Žižekian fantasy"—a collapse and distortion of the Real such that girls in need of empowerment are thought of as stripped of their gendered relations and commitments, ready to actualize their potential.[10] She becomes a dehistoricized and decontextualized subject of development who is oriented to an open future. This form of bare potential makes her one of the more appropriate, more effective subjects within the international development apparatus.

Beyond Nike Girl Effect, other transnational gender-based empowerment programs extract and repackage the intimate narratives of encountering gender experience, rights, and development in ways that tap more into the intimacies and storytelling that Ahearn describes. The crowdfunded film *Girl Rising*, for instance, features front and center the globally dispersed narratives of girls who have experienced gendered and sexual forms of violence, civil war, and natural disaster across formerly colonized nations. In the film project, internationally and industry-recognized women in their home countries collaboratively organize and write their stories, which are then re-narrated in a docudrama format by the voices of celebrities who are mostly based in the United States. It is not surprising that despite its praises from within the United States and among liberal feminists, the film also attracts legitimate critiques that fall well within longer histories of feminist calls to avoid the hegemonic narratives of "rescuing" and Othering Third World women.[11] Beyond these critiques, the structural directives that guide the design and implementation of this gender-based empowerment project adds another layer to understanding how calls to "rescue" Third World women persist unchallenged. As stated on the film's website, one of the project's goals is to "tell true-life stories of girls and those that support them. These stories raise awareness and inspire individuals who want to stand up for girls in their lives and around the world, but might not know how."[12] The orientation of the program's language is key. It reveals that the program exists less to give space for its girl subjects to speak, and more to amplify the voices of those who want to feel good while supporting them. Directing the message to supporters rather than to the girls featured, the film's use and treatment of the girl subject places projects of gender development back in the "emergency room." As "surgeons of hegemony," programs like Girl Rising and Nike Girl Effect struggle to make cohesive, suture, and close the gaps of knowledge and representation in transnational development that remain unclosed under conditions of structural inequality and intersectional violence.[13] What remains are programs that take the credit for presenting narratives that are easy to digest and that conclude optimistically with girl subjects as representational "stand-ins." In the spaces they cultivate, development stakeholders strive to be recognized for "standing up" for women. In doing so they distort what it means to stand alongside and listen to what women are saying.

Ethical Endeavors

The program ended in July 2012 and, after reviewing the positive annual reports, I anticipated returning to Sri Lanka in August 2014 to carry out follow-up research with Jayaluxmi, Nagarani, and the other girl, now women participants. I wanted to know how their involvement in the program—which had been unprecedented in scale and focus in the plantation sector—had affected their perspectives on growing up on the estates. But when I arrived, I learned that what I had outlined would not be possible—a not entirely unanticipated situation. Of the twenty girls that had participated, only three had remained in sustained contact with the NGO. Ten of the teenage girls had completed their A/Ls, three had gotten married within a year of the program's completion, and seven were working in semiskilled to skilled jobs such as garment labor, childcare, and vocational training. Only Jayaluxmi was able to meet with me in person; after the program ended, a male schoolteacher had strongly advised Nagarani to cut off all ties with the program following her trip to the United States. With only Jayaluxmi present to give her account, I found myself taking on a process that anthropologist Joanne Rappaport calls "co-theorizing": as a researcher, I was searching with Jayaluxmi for the situated knowledge that we could both identify as common ground. From there, perhaps we could move forward with a clearer understanding of how the program that had meant so much to her had ended with lingering questions about its broader legacy and impacts.[14]

Born in 1995, Jayaluxmi was the last of three children of two estate workers in Galaha. Her father died suddenly when she was ten years old, and after his death, she went to live with her mother's brother and his family of five on another plantation with her maternal grandmother and mother. Her family's monthly household income for eight was Rs. 15,000 when we spoke in 2014. Her mother, who had injured her leg while working on the estate, could no longer work and had been carrying out informal jobs cooking and cleaning around the estate areas. In her case study, which I found in the program's archives, Jayaluxmi wrote, "I aspire to become a lawyer, and I also wish to encourage women who are in subordinate positions in the community to study and create awareness among them. Moreover, I wish to be a consultant in preventing child and women abuses."[15] When we met again in 2014, she explained that the program had given her the opportunity to "honor herself" (*suya gowram*); now, when she sees anyone disrespecting women in her presence, she feels not only compelled but also confident enough to confront them. I asked if she had always been confident, and she said she had not. She would walk by the younger Hill Country Tamil assistant manager on her estate for a year while he would berate older women workers for being slightly late for the tea-leaf weight call on the road. In those moments, she could never muster the confidence to say anything and would look away. But she surprised herself one day after she returned from the United States in May 2013 when she stopped and asked him, "Is that how you speak to a woman who is older than you?" and he was taken aback. While she agreed with me that he was probably still speaking disrespectfully to the older workers, she said, at least, in her presence, he is respectful and careful with his words. Now, she told me, when he sees her walking down the path to the bus, he asks her about what she learned in the United States, and she would tell him about the program. As she explained these small changes, I began to see how the productivity of transnational connections for Hill Country Tamil girls like Jayaluxmi has the potential to brush up against and push past what plantation cartographies of women's work cut out and map for them. Jayaluxmi, by articulating her connection to the program, had provided herself an opportunity to rupture long-held gendered subjectivities of silence and subordination, which the tea industry continues to reproduce.

Where Jayaluxmi expressed doubt was in the program's lasting effects on the larger group of her friends. In our conversations, she remained fixated on one particular friend and her story—that of Vishanthi, a promising student and program participant. Despite Vishanthi's potential to embody the program's mission and objectives, the social realities she had experienced could not accommodate the positive effects of solidarity that the program had in mind for its girl participants. Her story would also reveal the workings of contingency and the limits of transnational and feminist solidarity in the context of gender development on Sri Lanka's plantations.

I was first introduced to Vishanthi through one of her required case study contributions in the archive. Through the reflections and writings of the girls who participated in the program, I had been attempting to piece together what rights-based and transnational solidarity looked and felt like for the Tamil young girls who had "experienced" it. Each girl participant was required to go out into her community and conduct research about issues that girls and women faced using oral and life histories. As grassroots researchers, the girls used pseudonyms and wrote up individual case studies that were then translated and disseminated for all sixty girls to read across the three countries. Vishanthi's case study was the story a five-year-old girl named "Rosa." Below is a redacted translation of the Tamil account that Vishanthi submitted, which my research assistant and I translated from Tamil to English in late 2014:

> Rosa is five years old and studying in Montessori. Her mother left her alone at home and went to work as a domestic in a foreign country for eight months. She was left with her mother's brother, who was thirty-three, and his wife was also working as a domestic in a foreign country for economic reasons. Her father was not working on the estate but was a casual day laborer working here and there to earn money, which is why she was sent to stay with her mother's brother.
>
> Her uncle was a hard drinker, and when he did not have money to drink, he would sell their things to buy any bottle of liquor so that he could drink. One day at noon, she came home after school and unfortunately no one was outside. She found her uncle sleeping in the bed after having drunk a lot. She had to stay at home alone as it was not like other days when there were other children to play with outside. Her uncle awoke and began to rape her. He spoiled her life and at the age of five, her body felt like it was being crushed, and she was

near death. For three days, he spoiled her without anyone knowing. Finally someone checked for her and knocked on the door only to open it and find her spoiled. She was taken to the hospital and her body was cared for and treated. The police caught Rosa's uncle and after an inquiry he was remanded and imprisoned for three months. From Rosa's life story, we can know the importance of development and change—namely, that from three to twelve years of age, the safety of young girls should be entrusted to good people and should be looked after carefully. This girl continues to bear the burden of household poverty and inhumanity in her. Even though she has now been sent to be with her mother working overseas, how can this girl, only a young child, continue to live bearing this burden?

Like Le Guin's "killer story," Rosa's story made a difference, but in doing so called out the very inhumanity that made it one to record and store. Vishanthi had captured the intersectionality of acute and often forgotten gender violence that young girls and women face in Sri Lanka's plantation sector to this day. As one of twenty similar case study accounts that the program participants produced and collected from women in their communities, it made space for the emergence of untapped silences in which women often remain during experiences of sexual assault and violence. After I read the story of Rosa in Tamil for the first time, I brought it to the project officer of the program with hopes of speaking to Vishanthi about her experiences. He told me with sadness that that it would not be possible. He said that Vishanthi had been a talented and brilliant young woman with promise and motivation. In fact, she had been the first selected, along with Jayaluxmi, among the twenty girls from the estates to travel to America for the exchange trip. She was an active participant in the program despite a life of social and economic hardship. To earn money, her mother had been working in Saudi Arabia as a domestic, and Vishanthi's father was not present as a strong parental role model in her life. She had battled bouts of depression and attempted suicide twice before joining the program, which had been at the urging of her teacher at the school she was attending at the time. A year away from taking her A/Ls, she and Jayaluxmi, embodied what the program stood for. They were the ideal liminal girl subjects—looking to a future of actively mapped possibilities and turning their backs on the conditions that had made them ideal candidates for gender development to begin with.

After the project officers selected Vishanthi to go on the exchange trip to the United States, they met with her father and received his permission to apply for her Sri Lankan passport so that she could travel with the other participants. She received her passport and three days later, without notice, she was said to have eloped with a young boy on the estate and left home; within the first three months of their marriage, it was rumored that he had physically abused her and that she had to have an abortion.

In the 2013 quarterly reports the program submitted to donors, the last documentation of Vishanthi's participation in the program was in January of that year. The NGO staff had called a meeting with students and the participating school teachers to select and announce a new girl ambassador in her place "because she no longer expected to attend school due to a personal reason."[16] Nagarani was selected to replace her, and the program proceeded as planned. Vishanthi remained out of touch with the program, and her case studies remain the only record of her participation. The last that I heard about her was that her mother had been killed in Kuwait as a domestic worker in June 2014; according to NGO workers with whom I was in contact, the cause of her death was unknown and her body was being brought back to Sri Lanka amid suspicions of foul play.

Vishanthi's "killer story" left me frustrated and uneasy. I could not help but wonder what the program's reports had missed by not recording her own struggles, what specifically compelled her to record Rosa's story, and how her own experiences had given her the space to see or perhaps not see the underlying injustices in which she was enmeshed as a girl-child on the estates. What is left in the archive suggests that gender development, in its objectified forms, material accompaniments, and technological sensibilities, does not often *want* to remember such types of discomforting experiences. The violence and traumatic events that Vishanthi had experienced in her life did not amount to the type of situated knowledge that a local NGO would be permitted to record and reflect on in a quarterly newsletter or outcome section of an annual donor report. Since this knowledge never made it back to the ears of donor organizations, it is also not likely that donors felt the need to formally recognize and reflect on them. For instance, might donors value or learn something new from Vishanthi's sense of outspokenness and advocacy for women as she became a woman herself? Her partial absence from the archive shows us that the ruptures and risks of gender empowerment do not fit neatly into the categories of programmatic success or failure. Remaining outside these categories, they remind us that participants are often unable to live up to those ideals as they encounter the social and stigmatized realities in which they are enmeshed. But their locations on the peripheries and capacities to disrupt uncover the challenges, uneven realities, and transformative potential of rights-based engagement. In Sri Lanka's plantation sector, this type of development, when compared to the tangible development and unmet promises of politicians ahead of elections, more appropriately responds to the acute effects of the patriarchy and labor injustice that women experience on the estates.

As ethical endeavors, rights-based gender programs echo Lauren Berlant's practices of "cruel optimism": they create "a cluster of promises we want someone or something to make to us and make possible for us."[17] These promises require that the rights-desiring girl participant act. Some girls, like Jayaluxmi, meet those promises and retain the objectives that "stay behind" in what Behrends, Park, and Rottenburg call the "travelling models of development."[18] But when it is not possible—when the actual risks that a girl faces get in the way of her meeting those promises and possibilities—it is the girl who is often silenced, and it is the girl whose actions are discredited, *not* the development object or promises made by the model. So the model of development persists and prevails, suggesting that the silencing and discrediting of women subjects keep their praxis viable, desirable, and intact. These stories sharply call out that contingent solidarities in plantation development do not presume an end to the work but the creation of spaces for coming together itself. Rights-based development, like the humans that carry out its "work," is not immune to the intersectional forces of violence and patriarchal politics that enable gender hypocrisy to silence dialogue and admissions of error.

The NGOs on the plantations that perform this labor face unique social and economic constraints within Sri Lanka's postwar international development landscape. State strictures on reporting and registrations, funding competition, and the political patronage and patriarchal domination of the tea industry make it difficult for those committed to social justice to locate long-term allies and resources to carry out their work. Even when those resources and allies are secured, women continue to struggle to hold onto the space to voice their issues. Solidarity work needs ethical moments like Patrick's outburst and Vishanthi's departure to hold the architects of gender injustice accountable and to discomfort those standing by who are willing to listen. These moments rupture the normativity of development because they focus on what is not recorded in the official accounts of development. Instead, they foreground their participants' histories, words, and experiences. Such endeavors can present a more attuned understanding of what sustaining solidarity and giving space to women on the estates requires in order to remain an equitable form of gender justice praxis in Sri Lanka.

Organizing Women Workers, Reorienting Labor Power

A fundamental piece of the girls' human rights program was its orientation toward future generations. With Hill Country Tamil youth looking to alternative forms of income and career opportunities, the program aimed, albeit with little quantitative success, to ensure that girls would advocate for their rights, which included their rights as future workers. Part of the problem, according to the program, are representations of workingwomen on the estates as immobile, burdened, or lacking agency under a patriarchal system of plantation labor, culture, and economy. Calling these gendered relations and commitments "burdens," scholars and leaders alike argue that women's work in the household goes undervalued or uncompensated within the context of the industry's socio-ecological structure.

These narratives suggest that men work fewer hours than women but have fewer household responsibilities, and that the only women who can assume leadership roles in the unions and in civil society are those who do not have or can distance themselves from their household and familial responsibilities. As stated by a prominent Hill Country Tamil woman leader from the Red Flag Union, "There are women who have qualities that make them leaders. Many of these [women] were nurtured in supportive family environments but many developed coping strategies that helped their leadership abilities to be expressed and used. Their capability has been nurtured by skills and knowledge through praxis. Here, the women have moved beyond their socially prescribed role of nurturer and 'caregiver' in the family."[19] What women do and their reproductive force on the estates and in their homes and communities are often read as mere representations of the labor inequalities and social roles that stand in for them—those of caregiver, wife, and daughter. Union leaders present these roles as more or less incompatible with qualities of leadership and agency unless supported as exceptions to the culture in which they are enmeshed and evaluated.

I found a different orientation and strategy toward membership and labor organizing in WWF, a trade union led only by women that was first inaugurated and registered in 2011. In 1997, following the structure of other NGOs in the plantation sector, the Institute of Social Development, a local NGO based in Kandy, founded a women's wing, which eventually became known as WWF. Before obtaining its union status in 2011, the wing mainly promoted the awareness of rights among working-women in the plantation sector and attached labor economies. Following its registration, WWF developed its own set of goals with the following objective: "to mobilize and strengthen the capacity of working women of organized, unorganized, and informal sectors to enjoy decent working conditions with equal rights."[20] Acknowledging the uneven but also diverse landscape of labor for women on the estates, WWF expands what a union can and should do in three key ways. First, they foreground attention to reproduction, place-making, and kinship across all their outreach and membership activities. Second, they conduct regular good-governance trainings for community-based organizations and hold youth-training workshops for school dropouts, the unemployed, the elderly, and the self-employed to promote vocational literacy and rights-based education on labor and gender rights. Third, as the only exclusively women-led trade union in Sri Lanka to date, WWF distances itself from political affiliations, challenging a feature of most other politically affiliated and aligned unions with prominent women leaders, such as the Red Flag Union, the Ceylon Workers' Congress, and the Democratic Workers' Front.

In August 2015, I sat down to interview WWF General Secretary K. Yogeshwari, who has been working on behalf of women since 1994, first as a CBO mobilizer and later as a project coordinator at ISD. She explained that the decision to transform the Front into a union had been difficult. "In all unions in Sri Lanka, you have three basic levels in the structure: top-level leaders, representatives (district and local level), and the workers at the bottom. What we were seeing was that women were working in the office but under men, and there were no women leading. We agreed to it but only if workingwomen could be in top-level positions and [serve as] representatives. Only if we feel and agree that men can be leaders without compromising the gender rights of women, then it will happen. Until then, women only can continue to lead."[21]

Plaguing Sri Lanka's union politics on the estates is the lack of trust in politicized union structures to adequately see and understand the women workers they claim to represent.[22] On this front, WWF is unique in Sri Lanka's labor union history because its organizes women who work across multiple sectors—on the estates, in the garment industry, domestic work (abroad and domestic), clerical jobs, and shop work. Its approach to gender and work accommodates the shifting realities and contradictions that women face on the estates today and seeks to detach from former approaches to labor organizing that have lost their appeal and utility among workingwomen, as seen in low degrees of union participation and meaningful engagement from women across the Hill Country.[23] Most important, WWF provides support to a woman's family, provided that the woman herself is a member (though she need not be actively working), and workingwomen themselves run the union. In other plantation unions, many leaders no longer work as pluckers or field workers and are somewhat detached from the embodied labor realities of the estates. As of 2017, WWF had 1,272 registered members, and at least a quarter of that base comprise a reserve labor force—non-working or unemployed young, elderly, and self-employed women living on the plantations. While the union represents many ethno-linguistic communities, most registered members are Hill Country Tamil women in Central Province, though they have also reached out to non-Hill Country Tamil women workers in Northern and Uva Province.

In 2014 I spoke with Kala, a young WWF mobilizer, and she described to me one of the first labor cases WWF successfully fought. The case involved Gunasundari, a plantation worker whose husband of fifteen years had appeared to have abandoned her three years after he left to be a migrant worker in Qatar. Gunasundari noticed that she was not receiving financial support as he had promised and that he had stopped calling. After his disappearance, WWF mobilizers began helping her in late 2012 and secured legal services to enable her to approach the Sri Lanka Foreign Employment Bureau, police, and local-level government offices and courts to demand that he pay the money he had promised (Rs. 12,000 a month). Learning that he was in fact alive and had left her, she was eventually able to file for a divorce. Using her reproductive labor and social roles as a wife and mother to justify her demands for financial support and a divorce from her migrant worker husband, WWF stood alongside Gunasundari and gave her the space to shift her social relations and economic choices by securing the government services she should have had access to in the first place.

More meaningful was the means by which she secured the divorce—a self-penned 2014 letter to the courts that Kala showed me in our conversation and that ended with the following lines, as translated from Tamil to English by WWF: "In these fifteen years, I have not done anything wrong. I am living a very sad married life and I want a divorce because hereafter I do not wish to live with him." The language clearly and simply communicates her beliefs about her conduct and role in the marriage, her desire to move out of a current state of unhappiness, and her wish to secure a future beyond that state. Her case reveals how foregrounding rather than avoiding the complexity of workingwomen's lives can bring about more expansive ways of understanding the realities they and their kin face. It also reminds us that women, despite being solely characterized as performing "triple burdens" and occupying a subordinate place on the plantations, are also socially embedded actors who carve out spaces of gendered embodiment in their homes, communities, and work to produce risky futures for their families. While their aspirations do not always get met, nor are they always desirable to their kin or their leaders, they are here nonetheless, making explicit that women want to be seen as agents of change rather than objects of subordination.

Organizing the Unorganized

Addressing workingwomen's desires does not necessarily fall within the purview of Sri Lanka's traditional trade unions. WWF's uniqueness within the landscape of union organizing in Sri Lanka lies in its ambition to organize informal and unorganized women workers. As a union, WWF stretches the bounds of what a union can and should do in the field. In August 2016 I escorted Pramila, a WWF mobilizer, on her field visit to an estate outside Kandy town. While taking the bus to "the field" as she called it, I asked her what she did during such visits, which she carried out three days a week in her position. While sitting on the bus, she showed me her hand-drawn map of the field site. On that map she had marked which lines rooms and houses she had visited and the names of each estate that fell within her mobilizing area. Each day, she would focus on a different area and see who was home. Sometimes, she would be able to call in advance and make appointments with members who had specific questions or concerns. Other times, she would stop by unannounced. If women workers or job seekers whom she had not yet encountered were present, she would ask them about their work experiences and encourage them to join the union for support.

We arrived at 8:30 a.m. and set out by foot, first visiting the home of a self-employed woman working in catering and making savory snacks and meals for special functions and gatherings. We then made our way again by foot to speak with Shasta, a young woman who was also self-employed and doing sewing and embroidery work. Over tea, we sat and looked at her work; she brought out her certifications, manuals from trainings she had completed in Colombo and Kandy, and photographs from recent exhibitions in which she had sold her items. Thinking of the youth workshop I had attended the year before (as described in chapter 1) and the aspirations and challenges facing those who believe self-employment to be more dignified than plantation labor, I asked her why *suya vēlai* (self-employment) worked for her. She replied:

> This work gives me dignity. My rights are with me and no one else. Whatever I want to do, I do, and whatever I want to make, I make. If I want the style of a particular sari to be just as such, I make that style. On the estate, there is no dignity. The *kankāni* will tell you to pluck eighteen kilos [of tea] and there is no way that you can pluck that much so you do not profit. You can't take leave, there are no facilities to use the bathroom. In my work, if I want to the go to the bathroom, I go to the bathroom. I know exactly how much profit I am making for each piece

I make because I know how much the material was and how many hours I spent making it. I determine the price.

Shasta's point about the uneven valuation of women's time and labor across the plantation industry echoed that of the Planters' Association member who told me that he could understand why women plantation workers were finding the industry's labor practices degrading. At the same time, the myth that self-employment offers a long-lasting and less-detached means to achieving economic security is not uncommon in Sri Lanka. While Shasta rightly voices her aspirations of dignity and identifies the structural and gendered inequity that exists in the tea plantation sector, she also lacks organized support to navigate the systems of local government, financial, and private-sector stakeholders that operate within the self-employment labor regime in order to avoid crippling debt from predatory loans and microfinance schemes. As anthropologist and activist Ahilan Kadirgamar writes, "There remains the challenge of finding credible alternatives [to microfinance and self-employment] for the generation of incomes and social welfare in the rural and urban arenas."[24] It is important that concerns about self-employment and microfinance in the postwar context do not include Hill Country Tamils' debt experiences on the estates, as it is often wrongly assumed that women and men there are only plantations workers.

WWF responds to these often-ignored realities. It acknowledges the increasing trends of informal sector employment on the estates and recognizes that self-employment is happening. But in doing so, it provides a non-shaming, community-based approach to income generation by recognizing the aspirations of women like Shasta. Lastly, it provides women in the informal sector legal advocacy and rights-based awareness trainings that identify the pitfalls of self-employment and microfinance. Cautious but pragmatic, the union takes on a task that has yet to be taken by other unions in the estate sector since unorganized work remains ungoverned by national and international rights-based legislation. WWF recognizes that until more credible alternatives emerge, home-based work, self-employment, and local informal domestic work should be union concerns and that these unorganized sectors ought to be in conversation with the formally organized and informal sectors of women's work. Creating this link allows women workers to strategize shared ways to hold local government, international donors, and micro-finance stakeholders accountable for their actions.

Central to the effectiveness of labor-organizing efforts are the connections unions make with workingwomen so that, in the event of a labor rights violation or indignity in the workplace, the act can be either rectified or the offender brought to justice. Timing was key in the WWF case involving Sinnamma, a forty-five-year-old mother of two children I met on another field visit with Pramila. A long-term foreign migrant domestic worker, Sinnamma began working in the Middle East in 2006. When we met ten years later, she was between migrant worker jobs and had taken up work as a plucker on a tea estate outside Galaha. From 2006 to 2012, she worked in Qatar and then came home for a three-year gap to work on the estates. In 2015, she returned to the Middle East, but this time to Saudi Arabia to work for another family. However, five months into her job, the husband of the family for whom she was working began touching her inappropriately and making unwelcome comments. Eventually, she told me, he began sexually assaulting her. She called her brother who was working on the estate in Sri Lanka and told him she needed to leave because the house was not good. He did not know what to do, but he happened to know a colleague of Pramila's in WWF. He registered as a member so that they could legally advocate for Sinnamma. Pramila's colleague called the SLBFE main office in Colombo, and as a result Sinnamma was relocated to another house three hours away within forty-eight hours. As she described leaving the house, she told me with a vacant look in her eyes, which were swelling with tears, "I left around 5:00 or 6:00 in the evening. The husband packed my bags and did not say anything to me when I left. The next house I went to was a good house. They gave me clothes and there were fewer children to look after. But even after that, I was afraid to sleep in that bed." Soon after her transfer, however, still traumatized, she had to return to Sri Lanka and again took up work on the estates to support her children.

In the aftermath of the more public and shaming cases of sexual violence that Sri Lanka's migrant domestic workers experience, it is not surprising that the SLBFE acted so quickly to remove Sinnamma from her position. But more significant were the innovative methodologies and transnational strategies that WWF employed in organizing both at the source of women's labor and at their labor destinations beyond Sri Lanka. Investing not only in women workers but also in their kin, WWF mobilizers, already members of the community, become kith and kin whom women workers can depend on and trust. This flexible wielding of influence suits the diverse working conditions that Hill Country Tamil women experience and puts forth new and productive alternatives for organizing the unorganized in Sri Lanka.

Contingent Solidarities

From tracing girl subjects to making visible the realities of unorganized and informal workers on the estates, sustaining solidarity with Hill Country Tamil women is not without challenges. The shift in international funding from rights-based programming to transitional justice in the postwar context has significantly reduced the funds available for human and labor rights development on the estates. Under these conditions, unions like the WWF and NGOs committed to building awareness around human rights in the estate sector face the inevitable test to self-sustain their programming and networks without donor support. Akin to what anthropologist Scott Freeman calls the "tyranny of projects," gender- and rights-based development is subject to temporalities that demand its subjects label, measure, and evaluate their empowerment—acts that directly obscure the fluidity and complexity of their experiences; in the process, the language of rights also demands that participants make their rights divisible and public to the world.[25] The girls' rights program that Jayaluxmi and Vishanthi took part in was just one slice of a particular time period in their lives, and its omissions in the record call to question the ethics of framing the rights of the girls and women who had the chance of participating in the moment. Regeneration of the social and financial capital that funds the measurement of positive effects on girl participants' is not guaranteed and often disappears at the end of a funding cycle. Equally important, the eyes and ears of the development stakeholders, as enclosed and invested in the traveling model of gender development, do not necessarily stick around to see how the stories of these girls—soon to be women—unfold.

The question of contingent solidarity then becomes one of visibility and reception. When transnational development organizations and Sri

Lanka's industrial and labor stakeholders choose to see workingwomen, and more specifically Tamil women working in Sri Lanka's Hill Country, what do they choose to see? Do they see women as objects, subordinated and burdened? Or do they see women how they want to be seen—on their terms? The former has been the norm as images of subordinated Hill Country Tamil women have proven to be easier to digest and accept. Such images also more easily fit the fixed narrative of "once a coolie, always a coolie," and they do not move into and alongside the Tamil working-women they claim to represent.

In a 2016 lecture, Tamil feminist and social historian V. Geetha argued that the consolidation of nation-states in colonial Asia was contingent on the violent resolution of the class situation, which specifically mani-fested in Ceylon in the 1948 disenfranchisement of Hill Country Tamils, most of whom were lower-caste and -class plantation laborers.[26] Their statelessness and labor exploitation were and have always been central to the birth of the Ceylon nation and the crux of Hill Country Tamils' long-standing dispossession in contemporary Sri Lanka. Following this violent rupture, Ceylon's labor issue, Geetha contends, retreated into a category of "ethnicity"; conflict worsened and exploitative labor as a form of life was not necessarily forgotten but became comfortably accepted. The rest is remembered as Sri Lanka's "history."[27] Acknowledging the nation's unresolved treatment of Hill Country Tamils' labor, Geetha raises an important question I want to consider for the case of organizing minority workingwomen in Sri Lanka today: if labor cannot make claims to belonging within the nation, despite being so clearly linked to its beginnings, then what are the chances that women's reproductive and productive labor can make claims on political forms of place making and belonging?

I do not have an easy answer to her question. But the fragments of the transnational girls' rights program I recorded and the unconventional emergence and approaches of the WWF challenge the former organizing principles of gender and reproductive labor. Like Patrick's 2009 outburst, these moments interfere with normative constructs of women's work in Sri Lanka and suggest that girls and women ought to question the stan-dards by which they are judged. Organizing the unorganized and sup-porting women who work beyond the estates, plantation trade unions have been effectively castrated by their roles as political patrons of the nation. Regardless of whether their leaders have chosen to do so or not, current plantation unions remain deeply invested in projects of patriarchy and political patronage and in doing so are constrained to value women and their work as antecedents to more pressing concerns.

Beyond sustaining unconventional forms of union mobilization, additional challenges for effective gender development and labor organizing remain at both the local and national government levels. Tamil women workers must negotiate with policy makers, businesses, and government sectors to ensure that their desires, bodies, and reproductive labor will be recognized on their terms: for the values that their work brings to the accumulation of capital in their lives, not the profit and accumulation of others. But in doing so, these stakeholders desire that workingwomen remain orderly and organized as their reproductive labor and work build and expand the nation's economy. These negotiations have no guarantees for ending well, as the Sri Lankan nation, its politically motivated trade unions, donor-driven development programs, and private-sector interests do not seem to be able to hold workingwomen's trust.

They can, however, advocate for productive reimaginings of Sri Lanka's national histories of labor to more commensurately give workingwomen due recognition for building the social and economic foundations of the nation. By committing to this type of solidarity, they have the potential to create spaces that are more honest and suitable for women to challenge formerly valid and accepted ways of knowing their unique places and modes of belonging in the multiple worlds of work on the estates. They can push against the traveling model of gender-based development and neoliberal, donor-driven projects that only exist to monitor and evaluate. They can build up locally organized, cooperative-based, gender-focused programs that attend to the life cycle of work and intersectional realities workingwomen on the estates face. Most important, transnational feminist labor organizing specifically can disrupt dominant power structures of patriarchy and paternalism that continue to subordinate women in order to make room for more substantive and long-lasting forms of organizing and support. These spaces also demand the attention of the Sri Lankan state and the solidarity of activists, development workers, and industrial stakeholders across Sri Lanka. Feminist forms of labor solidarity across rural, urban, and estate sectors allow workingwomen throughout Sri Lanka to identify the shared social conditions that contribute to gender hierarchies, economic inequality, and worker alienation. Identifying these factors enables an ethical mapping of actor linkages among stakeholders across the government, private, and public sectors to identify specifically who allows forms of gender injustice to operate and persist.

This type of solidarity also taps forms of knowledge not always utilized—namely the knowledge produced and held by workingwomen themselves. As evident in the work of WWF, women workers know and understand well labor and gender injustices they face, and they can clearly identify what needs to be remedied. Transnational donor organizations can put UN-based principles of sustainability and gender equality into practice by foregrounding monitoring and evaluation mechanisms grounded in qualitative research and analysis that focuses on outcomes beyond numbers and binaries of success and failure; they can emphasize longitudinal plans to evaluate what skills and relationships sustain networks of support that allow girls to grow into the women they want to become and push against caste, ethnic, and gender discrimination in their communities of labor and social exchange. Beyond Sri Lanka, these organizations can connect with transnational gender labor movements to strategize best practices and unconventional forms of collaboration to design investments that challenge traditional donor objectives and union relations.

International development, human rights, and unionization are not perfect instruments of social change; by focusing on their imperfections and failures, we easily overlook their roles in framing ethical endeavors of supporting women workers in the Hill Country. But as integral features of the tea industry, each reaches deeply and complexly into women's worlds of work on the estates and therefore cannot be detached from a revised ethics of gender justice on the plantations. The goal then should be to challenge these components to more consciously think about what the sector and lives of its workingwomen would look like if they acknowledged how women want be valued and provide spaces for them to voice their desires for dignity. Even if discomforted by the outcomes, such interventions, as the new norm to which to aspire, would more attentively incorporate the past, present, and future terrains of women's work in Sri Lanka.

Conclusion

THIS BOOK EXAMINES HOW GENDER, WORK, AND VALUE-MAKING shape Hill Country Tamil women's lives and how the historical marginalization and structural inequalities they experience informs Sri Lanka's national and economic development. I provide evidence of (1) how Hill Country Tamil women workers pursue their desires in light of those injustices, (2) how they view their efforts to seek dignified lives and how they wish other Sri Lankans and those in the world at large to see them, and (3) what social, economic, and political resources they have and what they lack in pursuing those ends. While cultural anthropologists have presented the lives of Hill Country Tamil plantation workers through primarily male-focused, structural, economic, and rights-based lenses, I have approached these ecosystems of work and life by engaging humanistic and often discomforting forms of knowledge from a diverse range of actors. A decolonial and feminist research praxis can more closely link to what Hill Country Tamil workers and their families desire for themselves as well as to an ethics of representation, collaboration, and knowledge exchange about their lives. Pursuing one's aspirations and desires for dignity, I argue, constitutes an unending process of unbecoming—one that began with the ancestors of today's Hill Country Tamils desiring to delink from their heritage of coolie labor, and one that continues today in the aspirations of youth who want to work anywhere but on the tea plantations on which their ancestors, parents, and kin labored.

In July 2017, signals of that unbecoming resurfaced when I visited with the Hill Country Tamil artist Hanusha Somasundersam in Hatton.

C.1. *Stain II*, 2016. Ink on tea cups by Hanusha Somasunderam. Photograph taken and provided by Art Space Sri Lanka and Saskia Fernando Gallery in Colombo.

We met to talk about her work early on a Saturday morning at her home, and there she introduced me to her mother, father, grandmother, and infant son. Her mother and grandmother took her son into the back bedroom so she and I could speak without being disturbed. She brought out her laptop and portfolios and showed me an image of her work, *Stain II* (figure C.1), a mixed-media piece consisting of ink drawings on six plain, white porcelain cups. Inside each cup was a different scene from tea plantation life:

> A "beef coolie" (*petti-kāran*) carrying his box—his face transformed into that of a mule with horns coming out of his head. A sign of his work, the dent in his skin around the frontal base of his skull.
> A pregnant woman plucker who goes to the mountain to pluck and gives birth to two infants in separate buckets.
> Two babies sitting on the ground—one faceless, the other crying tears— their arms outstretched for their working mother.
> The bars of a crèche window with saris hanging from the ceilings to cradle sleeping children while their mothers work.

A two-room line room, almost too small to recognize but including a small square in the corner of the back room where the firewood stove would be kept on for cooking and heating.

In the bottom of the last cup is a woman worker, her head covered, with tea leaves falling from her hands. Around her, the twelve months of the year on pay slips lining the cup's rim, indicating her continual work across the seasons—in the sun, in the rain.

Hanusha was born on a tea plantation outside Hatton to a Hill Country Tamil garment factory worker whose parents had worked on the estate for their entire lives until retirement. After giving birth to her and her twin brother, her mother continued to work in order to support her family, and she sent both of her infants to the estate crèche, where attendants cared for them while she and her parents worked. From the crèche, Hanusha went straight into school because she and her family did not have access to Montessori or preschool programs on the estate. Her grandparents and parents' wages supported Hanusha, allowing her to complete her A/Ls and go on to study art and design at Jaffna University in the North. There, she told me, she experienced caste and ethnic discrimination, but managed to find a group of fellow students with whom she connected over their shared love of art and of communicating their respective communities' experiences. While finalizing her thesis project in Jaffna, she struggled to find the right material and story to tell. Her professor, she told me, said to her, "Look at *your* area. Look at the materials you have. Use what you see."

Today, Hanusha has exhibited her art internationally, in Colombo's elite gallery spaces and in a 2016 exhibition hosted by the Centre for Policy Alternatives and the Vibhavi Academy of Fine Arts in commemoration of the March 24 International Day for the Right to the Truth concerning Gross Human Rights Violations and for the Dignity of Victims. With the income she earned as an artist, her family was able to rent a house in town off the estate, and she had recently begun a job as an art teacher in a local school. As we drank tea her mother had prepared for us, I noticed that the six cups in *Stain II* had small tea bag labels and strings affixed to their handles, but that she had purposely removed the brand names from the labels. In their places, she had listed five single words or phrases to accompany each cup. On the label attached to the cup featuring the pregnant woman giving birth were the following words: "Pregnant woman. Labour. Risk. Income. Why." As we sat holding our own cups, she said, "Our tea—this Ceylon tea—everyone around the world knows. But when they drink our tea, they do not know who made it, and yet here she is. The taste of Ceylon tea is not human."

I looked back at the image on her laptop screen and studied the images of labor and life that she had inked and then sealed with glaze onto the white porcelain. "If only everyone could drink tea from your cups," I remarked as I looked up and met her eyes. She smiled. "Yes," she said, "if only."

Why Work?

After I left her house, I kept thinking about the word string she had typed on the tea bag label, and their arrangement brought me back to a particular afternoon on Kirkwall in August 2015. It was two weeks before the parliamentary elections, and I was visiting in the early evening hours shortly after the women were finishing a full day's work. Three young girls ran to me as I approached the main quadrangle of line rooms and the temple, yelling, "Akka, you came too late! The minister was here and gave a speech." "Which one?" I asked. "Diga, Diga, Diga!" they screamed, smiling. Diga is nickname of Palani Digambaram, a leader of the NUW, at the time a minister in Parliament, and one of three deputy leaders of the Tamil Progressive Alliance. On June 3, 2015—just over eight weeks before the parliamentary elections—the three Hill Country Tamil unions joined together to form the TPA under the UNP's coalition, the United National Front for Good Governance. I had first encountered Digambaram in 2009 when, not yet a minister of Parliament, he was contesting the 2009 Nuwara Eliya Provincial Council elections. He had attended the Christian Workers' Fellowship union meeting, during which Rani had voiced the aspirations of Hill Country Tamil youth and the declining labor force of Hill Country Tamil workers.

As I walked up to the line rooms above the temple, I saw Mahilmani, a twenty-four-year-old plucker and recent newlywed drying her hair on the threshold of her home, and she invited me in for tea. As she took small pieces of wood for the kitchen fire from the ground below the hearth, I caught sight of a small book of matches next to the stove featuring the faces and ballot numbers of three TPA candidates. I asked her if she would be voting for Diga. "Yes," she replied. "He seems like a good person," as she placed some wood on the fire. But then she said, with sarcasm and a smile, as she lit one of the matches from the book, "See, Akka? He even gives us fire to cook with!" We laughed. "How do you know he is a good person?" I asked. "He is not like other politicians," she responded. "He doesn't look or act like a *pannikkaarar* [rich person]. He is a boy that came from the lines."

I asked Mahilmani what he had said to the crowd that had gathered to hear him speak in front of the closed Kirkwall temple. She and other women workers had been let off work early to attend the event, and she had recorded part of it on her phone. Over tea we listened to her recording. In the speech he promised to push for a higher daily wage and to uplift the plantation community. Toward the end of the recording he yelled in Tamil, "Do not send your children to work on these plantations! Do not raise plantation workers! Raise your children to be educated so that they do not have to do what you are doing!"

After listening to the speech, Chandralukshmi, a female plucker and mother of three who had come in halfway into the recording, nodded and agreed: "He is right! I have no desire for this work. But I have to work. My husband is in Colombo. My children need to study. We have to pay their school fees and live well. I am forty years old now, and my life is over. Now, everything I do is for my children." His call to action aligned with what had already been a long-shared understanding among Hill Country Tamil women who work to support their families on the plantations. It also gestured to building an alternative political platform for Tamil plantations residents beyond the geographic bounds of the tea plantation as a site of their future labor.

Two weeks after Digambaram's speech on Kirkwall, the TPA alliance won six seats in Parliament across four provinces. But the ongoing work investments that Mahilmani, Chandraluxmi, Sellamma, and other women workers on Kirkwall make in their everyday lives made me wonder: What are the effects of transitional justice for once disenfranchised Hill Country Tamils who continue to work and reside in conditions of economic marginality and landlessness on Sri Lanka's tea plantations? If politicians are urging women workers to raise children to be better off than their parents, where does that call leave presently employed Hill Country Tamil women workers, and how do these calls make women feel about their current life experiences and sacrifices?

In 2016 I wrote to a member of the TPA to ask him where the Alliance had found solidarity within the new Sirisena government and where TPA's position on plantation workers and the larger industry stood. He responded in an email as follows: "The TPA is a partner entity of the united national front . . . within the government. But this is not permanent as nothing is permanent in politics. As a political entity we will decide on our solidarity partners at all necessary moments. . . . The industry is going through a bad period. They are concerned about productivity. We are concerned about the socioeconomic well-being of the workers. These two concerns should meet at a point. We are not irresponsible. We are for a strong plantation industry. We must capture this moment to bring the change."[1]

Throughout 2017, Sri Lanka celebrated 150 years of the tea industry despite managing an ongoing financial crisis. Had this capturable moment already passed or is it still possible? If Ilancheliyan's anti-caste movement of the 1950s and 1960s, the 2009 protests around the deaths of child laborers Sumathy and Jeevarani, and the outrage over the internally displaced from the 2014 Meeriyabedda landslide were not capturable moments, then when would the dignity of Hill Country Tamils' become a priority for Sri Lanka's larger political reform agenda?

Transitional Justice for Tenants

One such passing moment came to me on June 6, 2009, two and half weeks after Prabhakaran's death. I was attending a regular dialogue meeting among Hill Country Tamil activists, unionists, and community leaders in Hatton town. The dialogue focused on the "war situation," or *yutta nilai*, and where Hill Country Tamils could fit within emerging conversations around the minority question and political solutions postwar. The first speaker, Jeyaraman, claimed that plantation workers were always "behind" the political scene. The position of Hill Country Tamils in the background of Sri Lankan national politics, he said, needed to change. He then proceeded to list ten political events that had affected Hill Country Tamil political participation in Sri Lanka.[2] Hearing the public listing of historical exclusion riled the participants, one of whom chimed in saying, "In what kind of country are people placed in brackets within the law? Are we citizens [kuṭimakkal] or tenants [kuṭiyāl]? Our history is being forgotten. No birth certificates, forced repatriation. How do we keep a place in Sri Lankan politics when there is no national dignity or honor? We still remain tenants."

In February 2010, a majority of internally displaced persons (IDPs) had been resettled on lands in the North and East, but the majority of displaced individuals and families who remained in the North's IDP camps until 2011 were Hill Country Tamils from Sri Lanka's tea plantations. Displaced two or three times from recurring ethnic riots spanning from 1958 to 1983, Hill Country Tamils relocated to the North and East and settled to work as landless laborers with modest monthly government food ration assistance and little access to the equal rights of their Sri Lankan Tamil employers and neighbors. Like most Sri Lankan Tamils in the North and East, many Hill Country Tamil youth joined or were forcibly conscripted into various separatist movements and, like their Sri Lankan Tamil neighbors, were caught up in the No Fire Zones during the final stages of war, were killed, or disappeared.

In 2015, Kilinochchi district, once the LTTE's stronghold during the 2002 ceasefire agreement, was home to 34,620 Hill Country Tamils— roughly 25 percent of the district's entire population. They reside in a concentration of thirty-six Grama Niladhari Divisions, within which they constitute 51 percent of the resident population.[3] Beyond Kilinochchi, throughout the North and East in war-torn locales such as Mannar, Mullaitivu, Batticaloa, and Vavuniya, Hill Country Tamils continue to live and labor without equal citizenship rights, including access to land and housing ownership, basic sanitation and health needs, educational opportunity, and dignified working conditions. But within and despite such conditions, these dispersed communities, displaced from their plantation homes and places of origin, continue to live. They have built homes and cultivated the land; they have married and intermarried; and women, men, and children—like their Hill Country Tamil counterparts who remain on the tea plantations—work to invest in their gender and kinship relations and ways of being that exceed what the Sri Lankan state is able to afford them. In May 2017, Hill Country Tamil community members in the Northern and Eastern Provinces established the North-East

Hill Country Tamils' People Forum, a movement to advocate for the specific rights and infrastructural support of Hill Country Tamils in the North and East. Under internationally funded transitional justice mandates (which many in Sri Lanka have lost faith in), Forum leaders felt it necessary to meet with the UN special rapporteur on minority issues and submit constitutional reform recommendations for power-sharing and political representation of Hill Country Tamils living in noncontiguous territories within the country.[4]

Still, meaningful, structural change on the tea plantations is a marginal priority within postwar transitional justice efforts. In October 2018, responding to yet another set of failed CA negotiations, the children of plantation workers, all migrant and informal workers in Colombo's shops, restaurants and hotels, wore black; in crowds that swelled from one thousand to twenty thousand in just three days, they filled Colombo's public spaces to demand a living wage for their parents and grandparents. But we ought to note the optics of their demands, for the women plucking the tea leaves that make Sri Lanka a household and global name were largely absent, because the nation refuses to see them.

What will it take to realize that Sri Lanka's tea plantations can no longer remain exclusive and productive sites of imperial nostalgia for a heritage of coolie labor and dispossession? What will it take to revise the language of instrumentality through which political leaders, development actors, and industrial stakeholders understand and represent Hill Country Tamils' labor and lives, and foreground the reality that their lives and work are critical to the future of the Sri Lankan nation? Would such an undoing be capable, in the long run, of transforming Hill Country Tamils' gender, labor, and land relations beyond the plantation's calculations?

This project requires a praxis of solidarity, one that commits to seeing Sri Lanka's tea plantations as activated sites of conscience that go beyond the current industrial and legal frameworks in order to incorporate Hill Country Tamils as active stakeholders in their futures. Multiple actors in and beyond Sri Lanka must make long-term investments to embrace an anti-casteist strategies that foreground what workers desire and the situated knowledge they can contribute if recognized as equal stakeholders in the country's future. Development actors, politicians, donors, lawmakers, community leaders, workers, and families alike should come together to acknowledge that they, too, share and contribute to the contradictory and fraught place that Hill Country Tamils occupy in Sri Lanka's larger heritage of labor.

Being comfortable with Hill Country Tamils' ongoing dispossession directly detracts from the rights of minority women and their families who work across intersecting formal and informal economies of labor integral to Sri Lanka's survival. In the place of comfort, a praxis of refusing the plantation's resilience is in order. Its resilience maintains rather than dismantles economic dispossession and reinforces the wealth of those who refuse and look away from their own exploitative actions. Refusing it, while uncomfortable for many, would be a productive alternative for the Sri Lankan nation, which needs to detach from the violence of accumulation that made the tea industry successful. For, as James Baldwin writes in *The Evidence of Things Not Seen*, "a people who trust their history do not find themselves immobilized in it."[5]

. . .

One of the last collections Hanusha and I looked at together in Hatton during the summer of 2017 was her 2016 *Backbone* series. It consisted of four mixed-media ink drawings on tea bags and paper. The last piece, *Untitled II* (figure C.2), features a woman resembling those in the ancient frescoes atop Sigiriya. A UNESCO World Heritage site outside Dambulla town in Central Province's Matale District, Sigiriya is famous for its historical, archaeological, and ecological significance and one of Sri Lanka's main tourist and local attractions. With one hand, the woman holds her pregnant, naked stomach; in her other hand, a single, delicate, "two leaves and a bud" balance upright in her slender fingers. Fixed to her forehead and resting on her back is a wooden basket. The labels on the tea bags have been painted over in white limestone and removed. The bags themselves are stained brown with black tea.

The story of women in tea is not over. But for now, its unbecoming pauses with Hanusha's description of her piece, *Untitled II*, and her demand as an artist, teacher, daughter, wife, and mother:

C.2. *Untitled II Backbone*, 2016. Tea bags and ink on paper by Hanusha Somasunderam. Photograph taken and provided by Art Space Sri Lanka and Saskia Fernando Gallery in Colombo.

This woman working on the plantations is the backbone of her home.
This woman is the backbone of the nation.
The women of Sigiriya stand high on a mountain.
These women also stand high on mountains.
The women in Sigiriya have delicate fingers that hold slender leaves.
The women here also have delicate fingers but hold tea leaves.
The women in Sigiriya are women.
These women are women, too.
To see the ladies of Sigiriya, everyone in Sri Lanka goes to that mountain.

They make that place a tourist place.

This place, too, is a tourist place.

But the Sigiriya ladies in the paintings do not have life.

Our women have life.

I am asking those who come here to look at them.

To look back.

To see.

Hanusha voices a call for the world to see Hill Country Tamil work-ingwomen how they want to be seen: for what they have contributed and what they have brought into this world and sustained. She asks those who are willing to give her ancestors and Hill Country Tamil working-women due recognition for bearing a type of violence that breathes and is activated by a plantation language and landscape that has long been known, cherished, and consumed in Sri Lanka.

But she also voices a demand for Sri Lanka, the industry, and its consumers to see the value of women's work, not as mere accumulation by dispossession but as testament to the durability of life itself. She makes these demands because it is entirely too easy to not see Hill Country Tamil women plucking tea leaves on the rolling hills of Sri Lanka's plantations close up. It is entirely too desirable to consume tea without thinking of their perpetually stained hands, crumbled up pay slips, and line rooms buried in mud.

We need to ask what conditions allow this optics of complacency to operate. What might shift within the ethics of gender justice if the industry's stakeholders and those who love tea would be willing to stand alongside Hill Country Tamil children and turn the streets of Colombo black with their demands? We must be willing to unsilence and expose past records of violence. We must contrive to keep the past exposed and be discomforted by standardizations of labor injustice in order to push for more equitable ways to live and work. This would be the story of Ceylon tea to tell.

Notes

Preface

1 Rajapaksa, "President's Speech to Parliament."
2 Ganesan, "Kathai Muththusamy."
3 Ahmed. *Living a Feminist Life*, 2.
4 Pallister and Chamberlain, "Sri Lanka War Toll near 6,500, UN Report Says."

Introduction

1 I have changed the names of all mentioned persons and places beside public figures or incidents unless the individuals asked to have their names remain in the text. I have also removed any unique identifiers to protect the privacy of my interlocutors and places where I conducted research.
2 Unless otherwise indicated, all quoted speech from my research has been translated from Tamil to English.
3 *Amma* is the Tamil word for "mother."
4 *Sha* is a colloquial expression that roughly translates to an exclamatory "wow" in English. *Akka* is the Tamil word for "older sister."
5 Annamalai, *Cre-Ā Tamil-English Dictionary*, s.v. "durai."
6 Māriamman, the Tamil Hindu goddess of smallpox and other diseases, is commonly worshipped by Hill Country Tamils.
7 Sumathy, "Gendered Fictions," 46.
8 Roti is a common staple among Tamil plantation workers for breakfast and evening meals. Subsidized flour (*mauvu*) was, and on some estates continues to be, sold to workers and deducted from their monthly salaries. Roti is easy to transport, and many women bring it with them to eat during work breaks in the fields since they often do not have time to eat before morning shifts.
9 Chewing *vettilai* is a common pastime among plantation laborers. Women, both those retired and currently working, explained to me that

chewing keeps them warm while working but also helps pass the time and keeps them stimulated during long hours.

10 All Sri Lankan rupee amounts are indicated by the currency abbreviation used in Sri Lanka, Rs; in instances referring to the rupee used during the British colonial period, Rs. may be used as well, as this was the common abbreviation found in the archival sources I used. US dollar equivalencies for any rupee amounts between years 2008 and 2018 were computed using historical exchange rates. See Board of Governors of the Federal Reserve System, "Sri Lanka / U.S. Foreign Exchange Rate."

11 Tinker, *New System of Slavery*, 43.

12 Breman, *Taming the Coolie Beast*.

13 Kelly, "Coolie as a Labour Commodity," 264–65.

14 Breman and Daniel, "Making of a Coolie," 269.

15 Breman and Daniel, 269.

16 Breman and Daniel, 279.

17 Wesumperuma. *Indian Immigrant Plantations Workers in Sri Lanka*; Moldrich, *Bitter Berry Bondage*; Peebles, *Plantation Tamils of Ceylon*.

18 Chatterjee, "Abolition by Denial."

19 Beyond the South Asian context, Gwyn Campbell's edited volume *Abolition and Its Aftermath* provides a comprehensive and cross-imperial history of labor terminologies from slavery to indenture.

20 Peebles, *Plantation Tamils of Ceylon*, 53–54.

21 Bass, *Everyday Ethnicity in Sri Lanka*, 56.

22 Viswanath, *Pariah Problem*, 3.

23 See Carter and Torabully, *Coolitude*; Bahadur, *Coolie Woman*; and Bates and Major, "Becoming 'Coolies.'"

24 Arasu, "Karuppi (The Dark Woman)."

25 Major and Bates, "Abstract."

26 Daniel, "The Coolie."

27 Daniel, *Charred Lullabies*.

28 Nithiyanandan, *Cooly Thamizh*.

29 Peebles, *Plantation Tamils of Ceylon*, 9.

30 Samarasinghe, in "Puppets on a String," and Daniel, in *Charred Lullabies*, used the term Estate Tamil, while Peebles, in *Plantation Tamils of Ceylon*, used Plantation Tamil. In the 1990s and 2000s both terms had scholarly currency in ethnographic and historiographic contexts.

31 See Balasunderam, Chandrabose, and Sivapragasam, "Caste Discrimination among Indian Tamil Plantation Workers in Sri Lanka"; Bass, *Everyday Ethnicity in Sri Lanka*; and Neubert, "Power, Everyday Control, and Emerging Resistance in Sri Lanka's Plantations."

32 Institute of Social Development, *Report of the Experts Committee on Constitutional Reforms*, 3–4.

33 I refer to Sri Lanka as Ceylon when discussing historical events that took place before the country's name change in 1972 to the Democratic Socialist Republic of Sri Lanka.

34 See Moldrich, *Bitter Berry Bondage*.

35 According to the Planters' Association of Ceylon (PAC), "Out of a resident plantation population of 987,074 people, only 163,068 persons (16%) are registered workers." Rajadurai, *Productivity-Based Revenue Sharing Wage Model*, 10.

36 For a comprehensive account of the socio-legal effects of statelessness on the Hill Country Tamils, see Kanapathipillai, *Citizenship and Statelessness*; and Sriramachandran, "Life Is Where We Are Not."

37 See Kanapathipillai, *Citizenship and Statelessness*; Sriramachandran, "Life Is Where We Are Not"; and Bass, *Everyday Ethnicity in Sri Lanka*.

38 The CDMK was modeled closely after the Indian Drāvida Munnētra Kazhagam, which aimed to establish a separate Dravidian state in South India. Led by A. Ilanchezhian, CDMK began in 1950, shortly after the disenfranchisement of Indian-Origin residents. Focusing on the rights of Hill Country Tamils in Ceylon, Ilanchezhian faced opposition from other rising, predominantly upper-caste, plantation trade unions such the Ceylon Workers' Congress (CWC) and Democratic Workers' Congress (DWC), and during their tenure as a movement the government of Ceylon called for their island-wide "ban" citing their "using [of] guerilla and revolutionary tactics as means to usurp power." Muthulingam, *History of the Ceylon DMK*, 102.

39 In the early years of Tamil militancy, Eelam People's Revolutionary Liberation Front (EPRLF), People's Liberation Organisation of Tamil Eelam (PLOTE), Eelam Revolutionary Organisation of Students (EROS), and, later, Tamil Eelam Liberation Organization (TELO) included the rights of Hill Country Tamils in their political platforms; however, the LTTE mostly killed off or diminished these groups during the 1980s. Hill Country Tamils in those movements later joined the LTTE but were not given leadership positions, instead restricted to ground cadre roles. See Muthulingam, "Hill Country Tamils in the North-East and Their Political Aspirations," 74–81.

40 In May 2011 the government lifted some, but not all, PTA provisions. See Human Rights Watch, "Sri Lanka."

41 For reports on the 1977 and 1983 anti-Tamil riots in the Hill Country, see Satyodaya Centre for Social Encounter, *Voice of the Voiceless* 14 (September 1983): 4–9; and *Voice of the Voiceless* 15 (December 1983): 6–12.

42 Fernando, "Uneasy Encounters."

43 See Caspersz et al., *Privatization of the Plantations*; and Manikam, *Tea Plantations in Crisis*.

44 During this period, RPC-led housing purchase and renovation schemes through the Plantation Human Development Trust (PHDT) focused more on renovations than the obtaining of land titles and deeds.

45 *Household Income and Expenditure Survey, 2009/10*, 1.

46 Campaign for Fair and Free Elections, "February 2009 Parliamentary Elections Report."

47 Chandrabose, *Implementation of Outgrowing System in Selected Tea Plantation Sector in Sri Lanka*, 21.

48 An exception to this rule came with the TPA's victory and increased Hill Country Tamil political representation in transitional justice programs and Parliament.

49 Rajadurai, *Productivity-Based Revenue Sharing Wage Model*, 10.

50 For a larger discussion on Hill Country Tamils as an Indian diaspora, see Bass, *Everyday Ethnicity in Sri Lanka*, 22–47.

51 Daniel, *Fluid Signs*.

52 See Daniel, *Fluid Signs*; Daniel, "Lost Ūr"; Mines, *Fierce Gods*; and Mines, "Waiting for Vellalakanthan."

Chapter 1: Productive Alternatives

1 Gunetilleke, Kuruppu, and Goonasekera, *Estate Workers' Dilemma*, 6.

2 Daniel, *Charred Lullabies*; Bass, *Everyday Ethnicity in Sri Lanka*; Balasundaram, "Structural Violence of Sterilization"; Jayawardena and Kurian, *Class, Patriarchy, and Ethnicity on Sri Lankan Plantations*; Kanapathipillai, *Citizenship and Statelessness*; Little, *Labouring to Learn*.

3 R. Kurian, *Women Workers in the Sri Lanka Plantation Sector*; Phillips "Kinship, Marriage, and Gender Experiences of Tamil Women in Sri Lanka's Tea Plantations"; Samarasinghe, "Puppets on a String."

4 Walter Mignolo as cited in Bhambra, "Postcolonial and Decolonial Dialogues," 118.

5 Balasundaram, Chandrabose, and Sivapragasam, "Caste Discrimination among Indian Tamil Plantation Workers in Sri Lanka," 82–83.

6 Bass, *Everyday Ethnicity in Sri Lanka*, 30–33; Balasundaram, Chandrabose, and Sivapragasam, "Caste Discrimination among Indian Tamil Plantation Workers in Sri Lanka"; Hollup, *Bonded Labour*, 221.

7 One exception to this case is the DMK. The movement was anti-caste but in 1971, with the Janatha Vimukthi Peramuna (JVP) insurrection in 1970–71, Ilanchezhian joined more Trotskyist-leaning labor activists and unionists like Bala Tampoe and Rohana Wijeweera, and eventually calls for Tamil self-determination came to dominate Tamil political movements. See Muthulingam, *History of the Ceylon DMK*.

8 Samarasinghe, "Puppets on a String."

9 Phillips "Rethinking Culture and Development"; see also Phillips, "Kinship, Marriage, and Gender Experiences of Tamil Women in Sri Lanka's Tea Plantations."

10 Balasundaram, Chandrabose, and Sivapragasam, "Caste Discrimination among Indian Tamil Plantation Workers in Sri Lanka."

11 Hollup, *Bonded Labour.*

12 Red Flag Women's Movement, *Women's Leadership*; Jayawardena and Kurian, *Class, Patriarchy, and Ethnicity on Sri Lankan Plantations.*

13 Berlant, *Desire/Love*, 19–20.

14 Le Guin, "Carrier Bag Theory of Fiction," 151–52

15 Le Guin, 152.

16 Here I refer to recent discussions around the evidence of citation bias in favor of a predominantly white, cisgender male authorship in cultural anthropology. Useful resources on this ongoing discussion can be found in Footnotes Editor, "Guest Post."

17 Thiranagama, *In My Mother's House*; Cox, *Shapeshifters.*

18 Curtis, *Pleasures and Perils*; Ralph, *Renegade Dreams.*

19 Hodgson, *Gender, Justice, and the Problem of Culture*; Sen, *Everyday Sustainability*; Dhillon, *Prairie Rising.*

20 See Ameeriar, *Downwardly Global*; Williams, *Pursuit of Happiness.*

21 Fischer, *Good Life*, 15.

22 Max Scheler discusses the combination of two forces—life-urge (*lebens-drang*) and spirit (*geist*). This combining keeps a human being whole, as the life-urge, or desire to experience dignity and a "good life," creates and maintains an inextricable link between what a person does and what a person is. See Frings, *Lifetime.*

23 Heidegger, "Question Concerning Technology," 11.

24 Heidegger, 13.

25 Berlant, *Desire/Love*, 19.

26 Powis, "That's Enough about Tim Ingold!"

27 Here I find Paul Kockelman's three meanings of the term *enclosure* useful: (1) aestheticization, (2) *bios* or biography, and (3) articulation. See Kockelman, "Enclosure and Disclosure."

28 See Visweswaran, *Fictions of Feminist Ethnography*; Chatterjee, *Time for Tea*; Seizer, *Stigmas of the Tamil Stage*; Hewamanne, *Stitching Identities in a Free Trade Zone*; Hewamanne, "Suicide Narratives and In-Between Identities"; Vora, *Impossible Citizens*; Amrute, *Encoding Race, Encoding Class*; Ameeriar, *Downwardly Global*; Ahmad, *Everyday Conversions.*

29 TallBear invokes Neferti Tadiar's concept of *sampalataya* (Tagalog for "act of faith"). Tadiar, according to TallBear, "explains the concern as referring in part to being 'already caught up in the claims that others act out,' which is different from speaking on behalf of." In doing so, TallBear claims, "one speaks as an individual 'in concert with,' not silenced by

one's inability to fully represent one's people." See TallBear, "Standing with and Speaking as Faith"; and Tadiar, "Noranian Imaginary," 73.

30 I conducted unstructured, semi-structured, informal, and group interviews, as well as oral histories, depending on the context and persons engaged.

31 Emerson, Fretz, and Shaw define "jottings" as a "brief written record of events and impressions captured in key words and phrases." See *Writing Ethnographic Fieldnotes*, 29.

32 Anderson, "Photographic Methods."

33 Ellingson, *Embodiment in Qualitative Research*, 16–19.

34 Smith, *Decolonizing Methodologies*, 201.

Chapter 2: Unfixing Language and Landscape

1 *Iṅgē vā!* translates as "Come here!" The *vā* (second-person informal / impolite imperative), rather than the colloquial *vāṅga* (second-person formal / polite imperative), indexes informality and often disrespect. *Sinna durai* is Tamil for a plantation's assistant superintendent.

2 Ferguson, *"Inge va!"* 27.

3 In *The Planters' Colloquial Tamil Guide in Roman and Tamil Characters*, Joseph claims that his publication presents a better method: "There are some books published on the system of Ollendorff, but this Work has been written with the greatest care as a better and easier method of learning to read and speak colloquial Tamil . . . together with those natural objects that a person should know" (56–57).

4 Manesca, *Oral System of Teaching Living Languages*, iv.

5 Manesca, vii.

6 Scott, *Weapons of the Weak*; Besky, *Darjeeling Distinction*.

7 Carter and Torabully, *Coolitude*, 117.

8 Forrest, *Hundred Years of Ceylon Tea*, 113–14.

9 Solomon, "Sri Lanka Is Ready for Its Close-Up."

10 Jayaraman, *Caste Continuities in Ceylon*.

11 Hollup, *Bonded Labour*.

12 Bass, *Everyday Ethnicity in Sri Lanka*.

13 Peebles, *Plantation Tamils of Ceylon*.

14 Hollup claimed that plantation residents lived in isolation from other ethnic groups and were geographically bounded by the fields on which they toiled. See "Impact of Land Reforms, Rural Images, and Nationalist Ideology on Plantation Tamils," 78. Hollup, Gnanamuttu, and Kanapathipillai contend that even more intimate spaces of family life are institutionalized. See Gnanamuttu, *Education and the Indian Plantation Worker in Sri Lanka*; Little, *Labouring to Learn*; and Kanapathipillai, *Citizenship and Statelessness in Sri Lanka*. As already discussed above, works live in line rooms, which they do not own but rather inhabit only if

a family member is working regularly on the plantation. In this traditionalist portrait, the estates provide their own schools (from crèche facilities to grade school level) within the plantation in order to educate children in close proximity to their mothers working in the fields. See Little, 49–51. This blending of work and leisure within an institutionalized space nicely fits the category of what Goffman terms the "encompassing tendency," which defines the "total institution" as such. See Goffman, *Asylums*, 4.

15   The "enclave" myth has been challenged, beginning with Meyer and then Balasundaram and Bass discussing migration and changes in labor and community leadership practices on the plantations. See Meyer, "Enclave' Plantations, 'Hemmed-In Villages and Dualistic Representations in Colonial Ceylon"; Balasunderam, "Structural Violence of Sterilization"; and Bass, *Everyday Ethnicity in Sri Lanka*. Given the high productivity and success of the tea industry, concerted efforts were made to sustain the plantation as a capitalist and institutionalized space after independence. In my conversations with activists and development workers, nationalization was mentioned as the moment that determined the inapplicability of Goffman's term to the plantation system. Veeran, an activist in Kandy, wrote to me in an email on May 7, 2012, on the issue of the plantation as "total institution": "Currently 75% of youths work outside of plantation sector. Therefore the total institution is no longer valid in relation to Sri Lankan plantation labour. Above all, currently the state is responsible [for looking] after the social welfare of the community. Except [for] primary health care, all other needs are to be provided by the government."

16   Mintz, *Caribbean Transformations*, 132.

17   Ferguson, *"Inge va!"* 3.

18   Ferguson, 6.

19   Ferguson, 3.

20   I want to thank Sasikumar Balasundaram for our conversation about these three transliterated words and his translation of *pēsamaliru*. Email message to author, May 12, 2017.

21   Ferguson, *"Inge va!"* 23.

22   From a linguistic perspective, *Vāy potthu!* appears to lack J. L. Austin called "illocutionary force"—the coinciding of the speaker's objective to produce what is said (i.e., to "shut up" the person). Even if the planter did make the laborer shut up right then and there, the fact that it would have to be scripted (and, it is assumed, repeated) as a hypothetical exchange leaves the reader questioning the utterance's effects as a "perlocutionary act"—a speech act that persuades, scares, or convinces. For it seems that if this command would have to be learned and memorized to say over and over again, the speech act itself may not have been that effective in the long run. See Austin, *How to Do Things with Words*.

23 Ferguson, *"Inge va!"* 3–4.
24 Duncan, *Private Life of a Ceylon Coffee Planter*, 23–24.
25 Steuart, *Every Day Life on a Ceylon Cocoa Estate*, 43–44.
26 Cave, *Golden Tips*, 185–86. A *cumbly* was a lambswool blanket covering worn by Tamil workers to protect them from the natural elements during plucking and other manual agricultural labor tasks.
27 Cave, 189–90.
28 Perera, *Sri Lanka Export Development Board Industrial Capability Report*, 3.
29 Sri Lanka Tea Board, "Why 'Ceylon' Tea?"
30 Planters' Association of Ceylon, "Planters' Association Chairman Says Productivity Increase Imperative for Industry's Survival."
31 Stoler, *Duress*, 25.
32 Each of these categories had one participant listing it as a career aspiration.
33 Gnanamuttu. *Education and the Indian Plantation Worker in Sri Lanka.*
34 Little, *Labouring to Learn*, 103–9.
35 Gnanamuttu, *Education and the Indian Plantation Worker in Sri Lanka*, 16.
36 Little, *Labouring to Learn*, 121.
37 Karim, *Microfinance and Its Discontents*; Kadirgamar, "Failure of Post-War Reconstruction in Jaffna."
38 Breman and Daniel, "Making of a Coolie."
39 International Coalition of Sites of Conscience, "About Us."
40 Breman and Daniel, "Making of a Coolie," 269.
41 Wickramasinghe, *Metallic Modern*, 138.

Chapter 3: Living the Wage

1 Clark-Decès, *Right Spouse*, 7; Trawick, *Notes on Love in a Tamil Family*, 129; Thiranagama, *In My Mother's House*, 184.
2 Jayaraman, *Caste Continuities in Ceylon*; Hollup, *Bonded Labour*; Balasundaram, Chandrabose, and Sivapragasam, "Caste Discrimination among Indian Tamil Plantation Workers in Sri Lanka"; Bass, *Everyday Ethnicity in Sri Lanka.*
3 Kurian, *Women Workers in the Sri Lanka Plantation Sector*; Samarasinghe, "Puppets on a String"; Phillips, "Kinship, Marriage, and Gender Experiences of Tamil Women in Sri Lanka's Tea Plantations."
4 Thiranagama, *In My Mother's House*, 184.
5 The Legislative Council was established in 1833 by recommendation of the Colebrooke-Cameron Commission and considered the first legal form of representative government in Ceylon. However, its official members were required to be British (unofficial members included some Ceylonese elites).
6 *Handbook of the Ceylon National Congress*, 421.

7   "Report on an Enquiry into the Wages and the Cost of Living of Estate Labourers," 3.

8   Under the Coinage Act of 1835, the Indian rupee came to replace the British pound, and the rupee was decimalized to cents and roughly exchanged at the rate of two shillings per one rupee (or ten rupees per pound). Between 1876 and 1923, the instances I encountered in the archives discussing coolie wages paid were paid in rupees, cents, and annas (one anna = two cents). See Davis, *Foreign Exchange Tables*, 46–47; for evidence of usage of money terms such as rupee, anna, cent, pound, and shilling in the coffee estate industry, see Clark, *Hand-Book of Tamil for the Use of Coffee Planters*, 99–100.

9   The transliteration of the Tamil word *santōcam* is "contentment," "satisfaction," or "happiness." Most likely this word would have been taken directly from interviews with Tamil workers and means monies spent on gifts, celebrations, and relations.

10 "Report on an Enquiry into the Wages and the Cost of Living of Estate Labourers," 10.

11 "Report," 10.

12 "Report," 3.

13 "Report," 10.

14 According to the 1921 census data in section 19 of the report, the Tamil population on the estates was surveyed as follows: 175,910 males over fourteen years, 155,492 females over fourteen years, 45,943 children between the ages of ten and fourteen, 37,121 children between the ages six and ten, and 79,478 children under the age of six. See "Report," 8.

15 "Report," 9.

16 Nadesan, "Plantation Workers," 6.

17 Gunwardena and Biyanwila, "Trade Unions in Sri Lanka."

18 Maliyagoda, "Plantation Workers' Collective Agreements," 9–10.

19 It is on this basic wage that Employees' Provident Fund (EPF) and Employees' Trust Fund (ETF) benefits are paid.

20 This supplement is only for workers whose attendance level is above 75 percent and over the number of days per month for which the management offers work. Days on which a worker leaves early, takes a half day, or arrives late do not count toward this incentive.

21 The basic daily wage (*adipadai sampalam*) does not include the daily attendance incentive and price wage supplement (inclusion of the latter is referred to as the total daily wage, or *motta sampalam*).

22 During such campaigns, workers perform only as they are required to but no more. The primary purpose is to hurt company profits while still technically working.

23 Somarathna, "Estate Workers Get Wage Hike."

24 International Labour Organization, "Right to Organise and Collective Bargaining Convention."

25 International Labour Organization, "ILO Ratification Index for Sri Lanka."

26 Even this statistic was disputed by key leaders within the vocal non-signatory unions; they claimed that the numbers for the three signatory unions were even lower. At local protests and union discussions that I participated in during 2009, these leaders cited the refusal and inability of CWC, LJEWU, and JPTUC to provide other unions with up-to-date subscription records for membership verification.

27 This is not the daily wage rate but the *cumulative* wage rate, in which Rs. 135 is not guaranteed pay. The daily wage increased from Rs. 290 to Rs. 380 in this last agreement.

28 Jabbar, "Cost of Living Has Risen 200 Percent in Eight Months."

29 Wijesiriwardena, "Sri Lankan Plantation Workers Speak to the WSWS."

30 Bass, *Everyday Ethnicity in Sri Lanka*, 113–14.

31 The CILC did not last, and Thondaman, an emerging CILC leader, renamed the organization the Ceylon Workers' Congress in 1945. Soon after, Sivapākkiam left CWC to work in the government sector but stayed in touch with plantation unions and development groups to coordinate labor-related movements and activities.

32 Personal interview with Sivapākkiam Kumaravel, May 11, 2012.

33 See Janaka Biyanwila, *Labour Movement in the Global South*; Bass, *Everyday Ethnicity in Sri Lanka*.

34 One lakh is equivalent to Rs. 100,000.

35 Siva's actual daily wage (*kai kacu*) was Rs. 1,000, but the bus ride itself cost Rs. 100 roundtrip—still amounting to better wage than he would have received on the estate.

36 The Sri Lanka's Department of Census and Statistics definition of the poverty line is absolute rather than relative, fixed at "a welfare level of a person who meets a certain minimal nutritional intake, which is measured by calculating the per-capita expenditure for a person to meet that intake." It is important to see the limits of this calculation, a point to which I will return at the end of this chapter. See *Announcement of the Official Poverty Line*, 2.

37 *Household Income and Expenditure Survey*, 2016, 33.

38 The poverty headcount index is the percentage of the population below the official poverty line.

39 *Household Income and Expenditure Survey*, 2016, 41

40 *Household Income and Expenditure Survey*, 2016, 38.

41 See Bear et al., "Gens."

42 Kadirgamar, "Myth of Self-Employment."

43 Karim, *Microfinance and Its Discontents*; Sen, *Everyday Sustainability*.

44 Griffith, Preibisch, and Contreras, "Value of Reproductive Labor," 234.

Chapter 4: Building Home

1   Butler and Athanasiou, *Dispossession*, 20.
2   Daniel, *Fluid Signs*, 63.
3   Daniel, 65.
4   Kockelman, *Chicken and the Quetzal*, 6.
5   Mines, *Fierce Gods*, 56–57.
6   Thiranagama, *In My Mother's House*, 152.
7   Basso, "Speaking with Names," 102.
8   Dunn, *No Path Home*, 21.
9   Sumathy, "Gendered Fictions," 46.
10   Roberts, *To Be Cared For*, 51.
11   Daniel, *Fluid Signs*; Daniel, "Lost Ūr"; Mines, *Fierce Gods*; Mines, "Waiting for Vellalakanthan"; Thiranagama, *In My Mother's House*; Bass, *Everyday Ethnicity in Sri Lanka*.
12   Thiranagama, *In My Mother's House*, 152.
13   Daniel, "Lost Ūr," 325.
14   Daniel, 325.
15   Daniel defines one's *conta ūr* as that home "whose soil is compatible with [one's] own caste." In this way, it is interesting that this definition does not match Sunil's claim, given that he is not of the caste of a majority of Kirkwall's workers. See Daniel, *Fluid Signs*, 67.
16   Anthropologists have documented the practice of erecting and maintaining shrines to plantation deities on the estates in the context of religious ritual and belief. See Jayaraman, *Caste Continuities in Ceylon*; Hollup, *Bonded Labour*; Daniel, *Charred Lullabies*; Bass, *Everyday Ethnicity in Sri Lanka*. More recently, Wickramasinghe argued that such shrines were erected and "located next to the factory itself to satisfy the spiritual needs of the workforce," but also that "the management probably encouraged these beliefs as they allowed workers to accept the inevitability of work-related incidents." See *Metallic Modern*, 143.
17   Stoler, *Duress*, 8.
18   Mines, "Waiting for Vellalakanthan," 200.
19   Mines, *Fierce Gods*, 48–49.
20   Elyachar, "Before (and after) Neoliberalism," 83.
21   Besky, *Darjeeling Distinction*; Li, *Land's End*; Rubinov, "Migrant Assemblages"; Willford, *Tamils and the Haunting of Justice*.
22   Besky, *Darjeeling Distinction*, 178–79; Besky, "Fixity," 619–20.
23   Willford, *Tamils and the Haunting for Justice*, 194–95.
24   Rubinov, "Migrant Assemblages," 208.
25   Hauser, "Land, Labor and Things," 50.
26   Li, *Land's End*, 59–66.
27   Rajapaksa, *Mahinda Chinthana*.

28   Ministry of Nation Building and Estate Infrastructure Development, *National Plan of Action for the Social Development of the Plantation Community.*

29   Ministry of Nation Building and Estate Infrastructure Development.

30   Ministry of Nation Building and Estate Infrastructure Development, ix.

31   Ministry of Nation Building and Estate Infrastructure Development, 28.

32   Rajapaksa, *Mahinda Chinthana*, 41.

33   Ministry of Plantation Industries, "Land Titling and Ownership of Housing."

34   This society was first registered as an organization under the 1972 Co-op Act No. 5 to support the socioeconomic needs of estate workers, but only after privatization in the 1990s did it begin addressing housing assistance. In 1993 the EWHCS began providing assistance for housing, including the provision of housing loans, insurance, building plan assistance, and building materials. Through the EWHCS, Ramaiyi, Chandran, and other registered workers on Kirkwall received the construction materials for renovating their unowned line room homes.

35   As of July 2016, the government agreed to hand over the lands to the EWHCS and relinquish land ownership and all lease agreements in support of the housing program. This move, however, ensures that the EWHCS will maintain true ownership of the land through co-op shares that full-time workers must buy into with their RPC labor and wages.

36   As of now, two versions of the ministry exist: the Ministry of Hill Country New Village, Infrastructure, and Community Development (per official Cabinet decisions) and the Ministry of Up-Country New Villages, Estate Infrastructure, and Community Development.

37   I obtained a copy of the Cabinet Decision (2016.12.06) on Provision of Land Ownership in an email from a colleague working closely as an advisor of the Tamil Progressive Alliance (TPA).

38   Personal interview with A. R. Nanthakumar, August 20, 2017.

39   Advocacy in these areas is ongoing; more recently, the issue has become entangled with housing problems in the North and East, specifically with the fitting of steel prefabricated houses from the French company ArcelorMittal. As of mid-2017, TNA's M. A. Sumanthiran had filed a fundamental rights case citing the instability of such prefab houses. Closely thereafter, PHDT and select politicians representing the plantation sector stated that ten thousand prefab houses would be granted to the plantation community.

40   UN-Habitat, "Construction of Permanent Houses for Estate Workers Underway in Nuwara Eliya District."

41   "PM Modi Inaugurates Dickoya Hospital, Addresses Tamil Community in Sri Lanka."

42   Srinivasan, "Long Journey of a Forgotten People."

43 The exclusion from government services but inclusion in state govern-mentality most poignantly revealed itself when, during the final months of the civil war in early 2009, resident communities reported to me that local police were entering the line rooms and removing television satellites to prevent the transmission of war coverage from television channels in Tamil Nadu, South India.

44 See Institute of Social Development. *Background Note.*

45 Daniel, "Lost Ūr," 325–26.

46 Daniel, 336.

47 It should be noted that the number of lives lost differs widely, with National Building Research Organization (NBRO) claiming the much higher figure of thirty-seven. See National Building Research Organisa-tion, *Impact Evaluation of Landslide Induced Displacement and Relocation.*

48 World Health Organization, "Meeriyabedda Landslide."

49 Nagaraj, "Plantation Labour Buried by the Neoliberal Company-State."

50 National Building Research Organisation, *Impact Evaluation of Landslide Induced Displacement and Relocation.*

51 Povinelli, "Rhetorics of Recognition in Geontopower."

52 See Gamburd and McGilvray, "Introduction"; Choi, "Anticipatory States"; Webb, *Tropical Pioneers*, 149–51. In the last twelve years, Sri Lanka has seen an increase in natural disasters, most prominently with the 2004 Indian Ocean tsunami, the May 2013 Cyclone Mahasen, and the May 2016 Cyclone Roanu, the last of which resulted in a landslide in South-Central Sri Lanka's Aranayake district, the burying of three villages, and the displacement of 2,000 persons. See UN-OCHA Regional Office for Asia and the Pacific. *Sri Lanka*; International Federation of Red Cross and Red Crescent Societies, "Coping with Loss after Sri Lanka's Aranayake Landslide Disaster."

53 Arendt, *Human Condition*, 7.

54 Arendt, 8–9.

55 Centre for Policy Alternatives, "This House Is Not a Home."

Chapter 5: "From the Womb to the Tomb"

1 The English word *operation* is uttered and known among Hill Country Tamils in its English form and refers to a tubal ligation. A tubal ligation is a permanent form of birth control for women with fallopian tubes. In the procedure, an incision is made under the belly button and the woman's fallopian tubes are cut, blocked with clips or by cauterization.

2 Gramsci, *Selections from the Prison Notebooks*, 246.

3 Gidwani, *Capital, Interrupted*, xiv.

4 Barrett, "Ideology, Politics, Hegemony," 249.

5 The survey defines the following contraception methods as modern: male and female sterilization, the pill, IUDs, injectables, Norplant, and

lactational amenorrhea method. See Department of Census and Statistics and Ministry of Healthcare and Nutrition. *Sri Lanka Demographic and Health Survey*, 258, 74.

6   Plantation Human Development Trust, "Welcome."

7   Plantation Human Development Trust.

8   Caspersz et al., *Privatisation of the Plantations*, 20.

9   Vamadevan, "Sri Lankan Estate Sector Deprived of Full Budgetary Allocations."

10 Periyasamy, "History, Health Care, and Challenges of Health of Estate Community."

11 Ministry of Health, "Family Health Bureau."

12 Bass, "Paper Tigers on the Prowl," 39–40; See also Chapin, *Childhood in a Sri Lankan Village*.

13 Personal interview with Tanya, September 28, 2009.

14 Periyasamy, "History, Health Care, and Challenges of Health of Estate Community."

15 Balaunderam, "Structural Violence of Sterilization," 49.

16 Manikam, *Tea Plantations in Crisis*; Shanmugaratnam, *Privatisation of Tea Plantations*.

17 Daniel, *Charred Lullabies*, 30.

18 In Tamil, the -*ā* suffix at the end of a question denotes a speaker's affection for their addressee.

19 Hollup, *Bonded Labour*, 265–66.

20 The Sinhala term of respect for a woman.

21 This plummeting in economic security following her husband's death resulted from the absence of his work as a casual day laborer off the estate in private gardens, hotels, and nearby shops. Although the family received his remaining retirement benefits after his death, the amount was minimal given the size of their growing, intergenerational family.

22 Moffatt, *Untouchable Community in South India*; Dumont, *South Indian Subcaste*; Nabokov, *Religion against the Self*. Bass confirms the colloquial use of this phrase in observing a particular Māriamman estate festival in the Hatton area. See *Everyday Ethnicity in Sri Lanka*, 131. Likewise, Hancock in her ethnography on ritual practices among Tamil women in Chennai uses *amman vantatu*, meaning "the deity, Amman, has come." See *Womanhood in the Making*, 144.

23 Civarāttiri is the Hindu festival held every year usually between mid-February and mid-March in reverence of Lord Shiva.

24 In her family's altar hung framed photographs of various Hindu gods, including Shiva, Parvati, Ganesha, and Murugan.

25 *Komari piḷḷai* is a Tamil colloquial term of an unmarried girl.

26 Garcia, *Pastoral Clinic*.

27 TallBear, "Standing with and Speaking as Faith."

Chapter 6: Dignity and Shame

1   Rizvi, "How Did Jeevarani and Sumathi Die?"
2   Personal interview with John, October 13, 2009.
3   Personal interview with Mano Ganesan, September 29, 2009.
4   Abeyasekera and Jayasundere, "Migrant Mothers, Family Breakdown, and the Modern State," 20–21.
5   Abeyasekera and Jayasundere, 21.
6   Quoted in Abeyasekera and Jayasundere, 3.
7   Personal interview with Arun, August 29, 2016.
8   Griffith, Preibisch, and Contreras, "Value of Reproductive Labor," 224.
9   Negative reciprocity refers to the economic relation of getting the most out of the least—which for Sahlins, at the extreme, was accumulation by dispossession. See *Stone Age Economics*, 195. See also Griffith, Preibisch, and Contreras, 224.
10 Gamburd, *Kitchen Spoon's Handle*; Constable, *Maid to Order*; Lynch, *Juki Girls, Good Girls*; Hewamanne, "Negotiating Sexual Meanings."
11 In November 2000, Sri Lanka ratified ILO Convention No. 138 on the Minimum Age for Admission to Employment and Work, specifying that to be fourteen years.
12 Gamburd, *Kitchen Spoon's Handle*; Kelegama, "Introduction."
13 Sri Lanka Bureau of Foreign Employment, *Annual Statistical Report of Foreign Employment, 2014*, 3.
14 Sri Lanka Bureau of Foreign Employment, *Annual Statistical Report of Foreign Employment, 2009–2010*, 38.
15 Sri Lanka Bureau of Foreign Employment, *Annual Statistical Report of Foreign Employment, 2014*, 10.
16 Meyer, "'Enclave' Plantations, 'Hemmed-In' Villages and Dualistic Representations in Colonial Ceylon"; Bass *Everyday Ethnicity in Sri Lanka*; Jegathesan, "Deficient Realities."
17 Peebles, *Plantation Tamils of Ceylon*; Jayaraman, *Caste Continuities*; Hollup, *Bonded Labour*; Samarasinghe, "Puppets on a String"; Phillips, "Rethinking Culture and Development"; Phillips, "Kinship, Marriage, and Gender Experiences of Tamil Women in Sri Lanka's Tea Plantations"; Jayawardena and Kurian, *Class, Patriarchy, and Ethnicity*.
18 Balasundaram, Chandrabose, and Sivapragasam, "Caste Discrimination among Indian Tamil Plantation Workers in Sri Lanka," 93.
19 Thiranagama, *In My Mother's House*, 255–56.
20 Gamburd, *Kitchen Spoon's Handle*; Gamburd, "Milk Teeth and Jet Planes"; Hewamanne, *Stitching Identities in a Free Trade Zone*; Hewamanne, "Negotiating Sexual Meanings"; Constable, *Born out of Place*; Brown, "From *Guru Gama* to *Punchi Italia*."
21 Bate, *Tamil Oratory and the Dravidian Aesthetic*, 120.
22 *Household Income and Expenditure Survey, 2009/10*, 7.

23   My activist friend of mine said this to me in context of a September 2009
      workshop in Colombo to commemorate the anniversary of the murder of
      Rajani Thiranagama, the Sri Lankan Tamil human rights activist mur-
      dered by the LTTE in September 1989.

Chapter 7: Contingent Solidarities

1   For a detailed history of the Plantation Social Sector Forum and interna-
      tional funding of plantation-sector NGOs during the 1980s and 1990s, see
      de Fontgalland, *Impact of Globalization on the Plantation Sector in Sri Lanka*;
      Fernando, "Uneasy Encounters."
2   Jayawardena, *Feminism and Nationalism in the Third World*, 260–61.
3   Jayawardena, 261.
4   Rahman, *Time, Memory, and the Politics of Contingency*, 6.
5   Ahearn, *Invitations to Love*, 149–52.
6   Croll, "From the Girl Child to Girls' Rights"; Moeller, "Proving 'The Girl
      Effect'"; Caron and Margolin, "Rescuing Girls, Investing in Girls."
7   UN Committee on the Rights of the Child, CRC/C/SAU/CO/2.
8   The member states of SAARC at the time were Afghanistan, Bangladesh,
      Bhutan, India, the Maldives, Nepal, Pakistan, and Sri Lanka. See SAARC
      Secretariat, *Gender Initiatives in SAARC*, 11–21.
9   UN General Assembly, "The Girl Child."
10   Caron and Margolin, "Rescuing Girls, Investing in Girls," 882.
11   Baker, "Film 'Girl Rising' Has Good Intentions."
12   "What Is Girl Rising?"
13   Barrett, "Ideology, Politics, Hegemony," 249.
14   Rappaport, "Anthropological Collaborations in Colombia," 27.
15   Institute of Social Development, "Student Participant Profiles
16   Institute of Social Development, "Quarterly Report, 2013."
17   Berlant, *Cruel Optimism*, 24.
18   Behrends, Park, and Rottenburg, *Travelling Models*.
19   Red Flag Women's Movement, *Women's Leadership*, xiii.
20   Working Women's Front, "Vision and Missions Statement."
21   Personal interview with K. Yogeshwari, August 28, 2015.
22   This lack of trust goes extends to women across South Asia, as seen in the
      more than six thousand women plantation workers of Kerala's Pempilai
      Orimai (Women's Unity) group who chased male union leaders away from
      their protests, brought Kerala's plantation industry to a standstill, and
      secured a 20 percent wage bonus in October 2015.
23   See Kandasamy, *Struggles Continues*; Phillips, "Kinship, Marriage, and
      Gender Experiences of Tamil Women in Sri Lanka's Tea Plantations";
      Bass, *Everyday Ethnicity in Sri Lanka*.
24   Kadirgamar, "Myth of Self-Employment."
25   Freeman, "Cutting Earth."

26 Geetha, "History of Tamil Nationalism and Secularism."
27 Geetha.

Conclusion

1 Personal email communication with a member of the TPA, May 13, 2016.
2 The 1948 Citizenship Act, 1964 Srimavo Shastri Pact, 1976 Vadukottai Resolution, 1983 July riots, 1985 Thimpu Declaration, the military intervention of Indian Peace-Keeping Forces in 1987, the 2000 Draft Constitution, the 2002 ceasefire agreement, and the 2005 victory of the ruling party at the time, the United People's Freedom Alliance.
3 Institute of Social Development, *Inclusion of Hill Country Tamil Community Residing in the Kilinochchi District into the Ongoing Transitional Justice Process*, 1–3.
4 Thambiah, "Hill Country Tamils Face the Butt of Discrimination."
5 Baldwin, *Evidence of Things Not Seen*, 82.

Bibliography

Abeyasekera, Asha L., and Ramani Jayasundere. "Migrant Mothers, Family Breakdown, and the Modern State: An Analysis of State Policies Regulating Women Migrating Overseas for Domestic Work in Sri Lanka." *South Asianist* 4, no. 1 (2015): 1–24.

Ahearn, Laura M. *Invitations to Love: Literacy, Love Letters, and Social Change in Nepal.* Ann Arbor: University of Michigan, 2001.

Ahmad, Attiya. *Everyday Conversions: Islam, Domestic Work, and South Asian Migrant Women in Kuwait.* Durham, NC: Duke University Press, 2017.

Ahmed, Sara. *Living a Feminist Life.* Durham, NC: Duke University Press, 2017.

Ameeriar, Lalaie. *Downwardly Global: Women, Work, and Citizenship in the Pakistani Diaspora.* Durham, NC: Duke University Press, 2017.

Amrute, Sareeta. *Encoding Race, Encoding Class: Indian IT Workers in Berlin.* Durham, NC: Duke University Press, 2016.

Anderson, Ryan. "Photographic Methods." *Savage Minds: Notes and Queries in Anthropology,* June 5, 2011. http://savageminds.org/2011/06/05/photographic -methods.

Announcement of the Official Poverty Line. Colombo: Department of Census and Statistics, 2004.

Arasu, Ponni. "Karuppi (The Dark Woman)." Filmed May 5, 2013 in Toronto, Canada. YouTube, 28:41. www.youtube.com/watch?v=r1fMg_wS-ME.

Arendt, Hannah. *The Human Condition.* Chicago: University of Chicago Press. 1958.

Austin, J. L. *How to Do Things with Words.* 2nd ed. Edited by J. O. Urmson and Marina Sbisà. Cambridge, MA: Harvard University Press, 1962.

Bahadur, Gaiutra. *Coolie Woman: The Odyssey of Indenture.* Chicago: University of Chicago Press, 2014.

Baker, Natalie. "Film 'Girl Rising' Has Good Intentions—but Ends Up as Cinematic Chivalry." *Bitch Media Magazine,* March 21, 2013. www .bitchmedia.org/post/film-girl-rising-cinematic-chivalry-review-feminist.

Balasundaram, Sasikumar. "The Structural Violence of Sterilization: Politics of Sterilization in the Plantation Tamil Communities of Sri Lanka." MA thesis. University of South Carolina, 2009.

Balasundaram, Sasikumar, A. S. Chandrabose, and P. P. Sivapragasam. "Caste Discrimination among Indian Tamil Plantation Workers in Sri Lanka." in *Casteless or Caste-Blind: Dynamics of Concealed Caste Discrimination Social Exclusion and Protest in Sri Lanka*, edited by Kalinga Tudor Silva, P. P. Sivapragasam, and Paramsothy Thanges, 78–96. Colombo: Kumaran Book House, 2009.

Baldwin, James. *The Evidence of Things Not Seen*. New York: Owl Books, 1985.

Barrett, Michèle. "Ideology, Politics, Hegemony." In *Mapping Ideology*, edited by Slavoj Žižek, 235–64. London: Verso, 1994.

Bass, Daniel. *Everyday Ethnicity in Sri Lanka: Up-Country Tamil Identity Politics*. New York: Routledge, 2013.

———. "Paper Tigers on the Prowl: Rumors, Violence, and Agency in the Up-Country of Sri Lanka." *Anthropological Quarterly* 81, no. 1 (2008): 269–95.

Basso, Keith H. "'Speaking with Names': Language and Landscape among the Western Apache." *Cultural Anthropology* 3, no. 2 (1988): 99–130.

Bate, Bernard. *Tamil Oratory and the Dravidian Aesthetic: Democratic Practice in South India*. New York: Columbia University Press, 2009.

Bates, Crispin, and Andrea Major. "Abstract: Becoming Coolies: Rethinking the Origins of the Indian Labour Diaspora, 1772–1920." UK Research and Innovation. http://gtr.ukri.org/project/0877EBC3-A567-4A13-9B19 -14ABE7A2A21D. Accessed May 21, 2017.

———. "Becoming 'Coolies': Rethinking the Origins of the Indian Ocean Labour Diaspora, 1772–1920." Arts and Humanities Research Council and the University of Edinburgh. www.coolitude.shca.ed.ac.uk. Accessed October 1, 2015.

Bear, Laura, Karen Ho, Anna Tsing, and Sylvia Yanagisako. "Gens: A Feminist Manifesto for the Study of Capitalism." *Cultural Anthropology*, March 30, 2015. http://culanth.org/fieldsights/652-gens-a-feminist-manifesto-for -the-study-of-capitalism.

Behrends, Andrea, Sung-Joon Park, and Richard Rottenburg. *Travelling Models in African Conflict Management: Translating Technologies of Social Ordering*. Leiden: Brill, 2014.

Berlant, Lauren. *Cruel Optimism*. Durham, NC: Duke University Press, 2011.

———. *Desire/Love*. Brooklyn: Punctum Books, 2012.

Besky, Sarah. *The Darjeeling Distinction: Labor and Justice on Fair-Trade Tea Plantations in India*. Berkeley: University of California Press, 2014.

———. "Fixity: On Inheritance and Maintenance of Tea Plantation Houses in Darjeeling, India." *American Ethnologist* 44, no. 4 (2017): 617–31.

Bhambra, Gurminder K. "Postcolonial and Decolonial Dialogues." *Postcolonial Studies* 17, no. 2 (2014): 115–21.

Biyanwila, S. Janaka. *The Labour Movement in the Global South: Trade Unions in Sri Lanka*. New York: Routledge, 2011.

Board of Governors of the Federal Reserve System. "Sri Lanka / U.S. Foreign Exchange Rate." Federal Reserve Bank of St. Louis. Accessed June 1, 2015. http://fred.stlouisfed.org/series/AEXSLUS.

Breman, Jan. *Taming the Coolie Beast: Plantation Society and the Colonial Order in Southeast Asia*. Delhi: Oxford University Press, 1989.

Breman, Jan, and Valentine Daniel. "The Making of a Coolie." *Journal of Peasant Studies* 19, nos. 3–4 (1992): 268–95.

Brown, Bernardo. "From *Guru Gama* to *Punchi Italia*: Changing Dreams of Sri Lankan Transnational Youth." *Contemporary South Asia* 22, no. 4 (2014): 335–49.

Butler, Judith, and Athena Athanasiou. *Dispossession: The Performative in the Political*. Cambridge, UK: Polity Press, 2013.

Campaign for Fair and Free Elections. "February 2009 Parliamentary Elections Report." www.caffesrilanka.org/No_NICs__Nuwara_Eliya_district _voters_lament5-248.html. Accessed February 28, 2009.

Campbell, Gwyn, ed. *Abolition and Its Aftermath in the Indian Ocean, Africa, and Asia*. London: Routledge, 2005.

Caron, Cynthia, and Shelby Margolin. "Rescuing Girls, Investing in Girls: A Critique of Development Fantasies." *Journal of International Development* 27 (2015): 881–97.

Carter, Marina, and Khal Torabully. *Coolitude: An Anthology of the Indian Labour Diaspora*. London: Anthem Press, 2002.

Caspersz, P., H. K. Wanninayake, S. Vijesandiran, Satyodaya, and Coordinating Secretariat for Plantation Areas. *The Privatization of the Plantations*. Kandy: Satyodaya Centre for the Coordinating Secretariat for Plantation Areas, 1995.

Cave, Henry W. *Golden Tips: A Description of Ceylon and Its Great Tea Industry*. London: Sampson, Low, Marston and Company, 1900.

Centre for Policy Alternatives. "This House Is Not a Home: The Struggle for Addresses and Land in the Estate Sector." August 17, 2017. www.cpalanka .org/this-house-is-not-a-home-the-struggle-for-addresses-and-land-in -the-estate-sector.

Chandrabose, A. S. *The Implementation of Outgrowing System in Selected Tea Plantation Sector in Sri Lanka*. Kandy: Institute of Social Development, 2017.

Chapin, Bambi. *Childhood in a Sri Lankan Village: Shaping Hierarchy and Desire*. New Brunswick, NJ: Rutgers University Press, 2014.

Chatterjee, Indrani. "Abolition by Denial: The South Asian Example." In *Abolition and Its Aftermath in the Indian Ocean, Africa, and Asia*, edited by Gwyn Campbell, 150–68. London: Routledge, 2005.

Chatterjee, Piya. *A Time for Tea: Women, Labor, and Post-Colonial Politics on an Indian Plantation*. Durham, NC: Duke University Press, 2001.

Choi, Vivian Y. "Anticipatory States: Tsunami, War, and Insecurity in Sri Lanka." *Cultural Anthropology* 30, no. 2 (2015): 286–309.

Clark, Rev. William. *Hand-Book of Tamil for the Use of Coffee Planters*. Madras: Gantz Brothers, 1876.

Clark-Decès, Isabelle. *The Right Spouse: Preferential Marriages in Tamil Nadu*. Stanford, CA: Stanford University Press, 2014.

Constable, Nicole. *Born out of Place: Migrant Mothers and the Politics of International Labor*. Berkeley: University of California Press, 2014.

———. *Maid to Order in Hong Kong: Stories of Migrant Workers*. 2nd ed. Ithaca, NY: Cornell University Press, 2007.

Cox, Aimee M. *Shapeshifters: Black Girls and the Choreography of Citizenship*. Durham, NC: Duke University Press, 2015.

Croll, Elisabeth J. "From the Girl Child to Girls' Rights." *Third World Quarterly* 27, no. 7 (2006): 1285–97.

Curtis, Debra. *Pleasures and Perils: Girls' Sexuality in a Caribbean Consumer Culture*. New Brunswick, NJ: Rutgers University Press, 2009.

Daniel, E. Valentine. "The Coolie." *Cultural Anthropology* 23 (2008): 254–78.

———. *Charred Lullabies: Chapters in an Anthropography of Violence*. Princeton, NJ: Princeton University Press, 1996.

———. *Fluid Signs: Being a Person the Tamil Way*. Berkeley: University of California Press, 1984.

———. "Lost Ūr." In *Village Matters*, edited by Diane P. Mines and Nicolas Yazgi, 317–39. London: Oxford University Press, 2010.

Davis, E. D. *Foreign Exchange Tables*. Minneapolis: E. D. Davis, 1912.

de Fontgalland, Guy. *The Impact of Globalization on the Plantation Sector in Sri Lanka*. Sri Lanka: Plantation Social Sector Forum, 2004.

Department of Census and Statistics and Ministry of Healthcare and Nutrition. *Sri Lanka Demographic and Health Survey 2006–7*. Colombo: Department of Census and Statistics and Ministry of Healthcare and Nutrition, 2009.

Dhillon, Jaskiran. *Prairie Rising: Indigenous Youth, Decolonization, and the Politics of Intervention*. Toronto: University of Toronto Press, 2017.

Dumont, Louis. *A South Indian Subcaste: Social Organization and Religion of the Pramalai Kallar*. Translated by Michael Moffatt, Lewis Morton, and Alice Morton. Delhi: Oxford University Press, 1986.

Duncan, Alfred. *The Private Life of a Ceylon Coffee Planter, by Himself*. Colombo: H. W. & A. W. Cave, 1881.

Dunn, Elizabeth. *No Path Home: Humanitarian Camps and the Grief of Displacement*. Ithaca, NY: Cornell University Press, 2017.

Ellingson, Laura. *Embodiment in Qualitative Research*. New York: Routledge, 2017.

Elyachar, Julia. "Before (and after) Neoliberalism: Tacit Knowledge, Secrets of the Trade, and the Public Sector in Egypt." *Cultural Anthropology* 27, no. 1 (2012): 76–96.

Emerson, Robert M., Rachel I. Fretz, and Linda L. Shaw. *Writing Ethnographic Fieldnotes*. 2nd ed. Chicago: University of Chicago Press, 2011.

Ferguson, Alastair Mackenzie. *"Iṅgē Vā!"; or, The Sinna Durai's Pocket Tamil Guide*. 4th ed. Colombo: A. M. & J. Ferguson, 1902.

Fernando, S. U. H. (Udan). "Uneasy Encounters: Relationships between Dutch Donors and Sri Lankan NGOs." PhD diss., University of Amsterdam, 2007.

Fernando, Udan. "Uneasy Encounters: Relationships Between Dutch Donors and Sri Lankan NGOs." PhD diss., Amsterdam Institute for Metropolitan and International Development Studies, 2007.

Fischer, Edward. *The Good Life: Aspiration, Dignity, and the Anthropology of Wellbeing*. Stanford, CA: Stanford University Press, 2014.

Footnotes Editor. "Guest Post: Citation Is a Gift: 'Punking' Accounting in #hautalk." *Footnotes*, July 7, 2018. http://footnotesblog.com/2018/07/07/guest-post-citation-is-a-gift-punking-accounting-in-hautalk.

Freeman, Scott. "'Cutting Earth': Haiti, Soil Conservation, and the Tyranny of Projects." PhD diss., Columbia University, 2014.

Frings, Manfred S. *Lifetime: Max Scheler's Philosophy of Time*. Dordrecht: Springer, 2003.

Forrest, D. M. *A Hundred Years of Ceylon Tea, 1867–1967*. London: Chatto & Windus, 1967.

Gamburd, Michele. *The Kitchen Spoon's Handle: Transnationalism and Sri Lanka's Migrant Housemaids*. Ithaca, NY: Cornell University Press, 2000.

————. "Milk Teeth and Jet Planes: Kin Relations in Families of Sri Lanka's Transnational Domestic Servants." *Anthropology Faculty Publications and Presentations* 42 (2008). http://pdxscholar.library.pdx.edu/anth_fac/42.

Gamburd, Michele R., and Dennis B. McGilvray. "Introduction." In *Tsunami Recovery in Sri Lanka: Ethnic and Regional Dimensions*, edited by Dennis B. McGilvray and Michele R. Gamburd, 1–16. New York: Routledge, 2010.

Ganesan, Mano. "Kathai Muththusamy: 68-Year-Old Badulla Woman Who Died after 19 Years in Welikada Prison." *Sri Lanka Brief*, September 1, 2013. http://srilankabrief.org/2013/01/kathai-muththusamy-68-year-old-badulla-woman-who-died-after-19-years-in-welikada-prison.

Garcia, Angela. *Pastoral Clinic: Addiction and Dispossession along the Rio Grande*. Berkeley: University of California Press, 2010.

Geetha, V. "The History of Tamil Nationalism and Secularism: From Madras Secular Society to Self-Respect Movement." Lecture presented at Centering Mobility in Tamil Worlds: Research Agendas for the Twenty-first Century, National University of Singapore, October 15–16, 2015.

Gidwani, Vinay. *Capital, Interrupted: Agrarian Development and the Politics of Work in India*. Minneapolis: University of Minnesota Press, 2008.

Gnanamuttu, George. *Education and the Indian Plantation Worker in Sri Lanka*. Colombo: Self-published, 1979.

Goffman, Erving. *Asylums: Essays on the Social Situation of Mental Patients and Other Inmates*. Chicago: Aldine, 1961.

Gramsci, Antonio. *Selections from the Prison Notebooks*. Edited and translated by Quintin Hoare and Geoffrey Nowell Smith. New York: International Publishers, 1971.

Griffith, David, Kerry Preibisch, and Ricardo Contreras. "The Value of Reproductive Labor." *American Anthropologist* 120, no. 2 (2018): 224–36.

Gunawardena, Samanthi, and Janaka Biyanwila. 2008. "Trade Unions in Sri
Lanka: Beyond Party Politics." In *Trade Unions in Asia: Balancing Economics
Competitiveness and Social Responsibility*, edited by John Benson and Ying
Zhu, 177–97. London: Routledge.

Gunetilleke, Neranjana, Sanjana Kuruppu, and Susrutha Goonasekera. *The
Estate Workers' Dilemma: Tensions and Changes in the Tea and Rubber
Plantations in Sri Lanka*. Study Series No. 4. Colombo: Centre for Poverty
Analysis, 2008.

Hancock, Mary. *Womanhood in the Making: Domestic Ritual and Public Culture in
Urban South India*. Boulder, CO: Westview Press, 1999.

Handbook of the Ceylon National Congress, 1919–1928. Edited by S. W. R. D.
Bandaranaike. Colombo: H. W. Cave & Co., 1928.

Hauser, Mark. "Land, Labor and Things: Surplus in a New West Indian Colony
(1763–1807)." *Economic Anthropology* 1, no. 1 (2014): 49–65.

Heidegger, Martin. "The Question Concerning Technology." In *The Question
Concerning Technology and Other Essays*, translated by William Lovitt, 3–35.
New York: Garland, 1977.

Hewamanne, Sandya. "Negotiating Sexual Meanings: Global Discourses, Local
Practices and Free Trade Zone Workers on City Streets." *Ethnography* 13,
no. 3 (2012): 352–74.

———. *Stitching Identities in a Free Trade Zone: Gender and Politics in Sri Lanka*.
Philadelphia: University of Pennsylvania Press, 2008.

———. "Suicide Narratives and In-Between Identities among Sri Lanka's
Global Factory Workers." *Ethnology* 49, no.1 (Winter 2010): 1–22.

Hodgson, Dorothy L. *Gender, Justice, and the Problem of Culture: From Customary
Law to Human Rights in Tanzania*. Bloomington: Indiana University Press, 2017.

Hollup, Oddvar. *Bonded Labour: Caste and Cultural Identity among Tamil
Plantation Workers in Sri Lanka*. New Delhi: Sterling, 1994.

———. "The Impact of Land Reforms, Rural Images, and Nationalist Ideology
on Plantation Tamils." In *Buddhist Fundamentalism and Minority Identities
in Sri Lanka*, edited by Tessa Bartholomeusz and Chandra de Silva, 74–88.
Albany: State University of New York Press, 1998.

Household Income and Expenditure Survey, 2009/10. Colombo: Department of
Census and Statistics, 2011.

Household Income and Expenditure Survey, 2016. Colombo: Department of
Census and Statistics, 2016.

Human Rights Watch. "Sri Lanka: Anti-Terror Bill Revives Concerns of Abuse."
May 18, 2017. www.hrw.org/news/2017/05/18/sri-lanka-anti-terror-bill
-revives-concerns-abuse. Accessed August 1, 2017.

Institute of Social Development. *Background Note: Proposed Amendment to the
Pradeshiya Sabhas Act No. 15 of 1987*. Kandy: Institute for Social Development, 2014.

———. *Inclusion of Hill Country Tamil Community Residing in the Kilinochchi District into the Ongoing Transitional Justice Process*. Kandy: Institute for Social Development, 2016.

———. "Quarterly Report, 2013." Girl Ambassadors for Human Rights Program Archive, Kandy, 2013.

———. *Report of the Experts Committee on Constitutional Reforms*. Kandy: Institute of Social Development, 2016.

———. "Story of Rosa" Girl Ambassadors for Human Rights Program Archive, Kandy, 2013.

———. "Student Participant Profiles." Girl Ambassadors for Human Rights Program Archive, Kandy, 2012.

International Coalition of Sites of Conscience. "About Us." www .sitesofconscience.org/en/who-we-are/about-us. Accessed June 1, 2017.

International Federation of Red Cross and Red Crescent Societies. "Coping with Loss after Sri Lanka's Aranayake Landslide Disaster." June 8, 2016. www.ifrc .org/en/news-and-media/news-stories/asia-pacific/sri-lanka/a-story-of-loss -and-survival-from-sri-lankas-aranayake-landslide-tragedy-72294/.

International Labour Organization. "ILO Ratification Index for Sri Lanka." www.ilo.org/dyn/normlex/en/f?p=1000:11200:0::NO:11200:P11200 _COUNTRY_ID:103172. Accessed October 5, 2018.

———. "Right to Organise and Collective Bargaining Convention, C98." July 1, 1949. www.refworld.org/docid/425bc23f4.html.

Jabbar, Zacki. "Cost of Living Has Risen 200 Percent in Eight Months." *The Island*, January 26, 2011. www.island.lk/index.php?page_cat=article -details&page=article-details&code_title=16857.

Jayaraman, R. *Caste Continuities in Ceylon: A Study of the Social Structure of Three Tea Plantations*. Bombay: Popular Prakashan, 1975.

Jayawardena, Kumari. *Feminism and Nationalism in the Third World*. London: Verso, 2016.

Jayawardena, Kumari, and Rachel Kurian. *Class, Patriarchy, and Ethnicity on Sri Lankan Plantations: Two Centuries of Power and Protest*. Hyderabad: Orient BlackSwan, 2015.

Jegathesan, Mythri. "Deficient Realities: Expertise and Uncertainty among Tea Plantation Workers in Sri Lanka." *Dialectical Anthropology* 39 (April 2015): 255–72.

Joseph, Abraham. *The Planters' Colloquial Tamil Guide in Roman and Tamil Characters; or, The Art of Speaking, Reading, and Writing Tamil without a Teacher*. Madras: Scottish Press, 1872.

Kadirgamar, Ahilan. "The Failure of Post-War Reconstruction in Jaffna, Sri Lanka: Indebtedness, Caste Exclusion and the Search for Alternatives." PhD diss., City University of New York, 2017.

———. "Myth of Self-Employment." *Daily Mirror*, June 18, 2018.

Kanapathipillai, Valli. *Citizenship and Statelessness in Sri Lanka: The Case of the Tamil Estate Workers*. London: Anthem Press, 2009.

Kandasamy, Menaha. *The Struggles Continues: Women's Leadership in Plantation Trade Unions in Sri Lanka*. Kandy: Institute for Social Development, 2002.

Karim, Lamia. *Microfinance and Its Discontents: Women in Debt in Bangladesh*. Minneapolis: University of Minnesota Press, 2011.

Kelegama, Saman. "Introduction." In *Migration, Remittances, and Development in South Asia*, edited by Saman Kelegama, 1–30. New Delhi: Sage, 2011.

Kelly, John D. "Coolie as a Labour Commodity: Race, Sex, and European Dignity in Colonial Fiji." *Journal of Peasant Studies* 19, nos. 3–4 (1992): 246–67.

Kockelman, Paul. "Agent, Person, Subject, Self." *Semiotica* 162, no. 1 (2006): 1–18.

———. *The Chicken and the Quetzal: Incommensurate Ontologies and Portable Values in Guatemala's Cloud Forest*. Durham, NC: Duke University Press, 2016.

———. "Enclosure and Disclosure." *Public Culture* 19, no. 2 (2007): 303–5.

Kriyāviṉ tarkālat tamiḻ akarāti (tamil-tamil-āṅkilam): Cre-Ā Dictionary of Contemporary Tamil (Tamil-Tamil-English). 2nd ed. Edited by S. Ramakrishnan. Chennai: Cre-A Publishers, 2008.

Kurian, Rachel. *Women Workers in the Sri Lanka Plantation Sector*. Geneva: International Labour Office, 1982.

Le Guin, Ursula K. "The Carrier Bag Theory of Fiction." In *The Ecocriticism Reader: Landmarks in Literary Ecology*, edited by Cheryll Glotfelty and Harold Fromm, 149–54. Athens: University of Georgia Press, 1995.

Li, Tania Murray. *Land's End: Capitalist Relations on an Indigenous Frontier*. Durham, NC: Duke University Press, 2014.

Little, Angela. *Labouring to Learn: Towards a Political Economy of Plantations, People, and Education in Sri Lanka*. New York: St. Martin's Press, 1999.

Lynch, Caitrin. *Juki Girls, Good Girls: Gender and Cultural Politics in Sri Lanka's Global Garment Industry*. Ithaca, NY: Cornell University Press, 2007.

Maliyagoda, Jayaratne. "Plantation Workers' Collective Agreements: Historical Background and Analysis, Parts One and Two." *Voice of the Voiceless Bulletin* 73–74, nos. 9–10 (2000): 6–13.

Manesca, Jean. *An Oral System of Teaching Living Languages*. 8th ed. New York: Roe Lockwood & Sons, 1847.

Manikam, P. P. *Tea Plantations in Crisis*. Colombo: Social Scientists' Association, 1995.

Meyer, Eric. "'Enclave' Plantations, 'Hemmed-In' Villages and Dualistic Representations in Colonial Ceylon." *Journal of Peasant Studies* 19, nos. 3–4 (1992): 199–228.

Mignolo, Walter. *The Darker Side of Western Modernity: Global Futures, Decolonial Options*. Durham, NC: Duke University Press, 2011.

Mines, Diane. *Fierce Gods: Inequality, Ritual, and the Politics of Dignity in a South Indian Village*. Bloomington: Indiana University Press, 2005.

———. "Waiting for Vellalakanthan: Narrative, Movement, and Making Place in a Tamil Village." In *Tamil Geographies: Cultural Constructions of Space and*

Place in South India, edited by Martha Anna Selby and Indira Viswanathan Peterson, 199–220. London: Oxford University Press, 2008.

Ministry of Health. "Family Health Bureau." www.familyhealth.gov.lk. Accessed July 28, 2011.

Ministry of Nation Building and Estate Infrastructure Development. *National Plan of Action for the Social Development of the Plantation Community, 2006–2015*. Edited by W. K. K. Kumarasiri. Colombo: Government of Sri Lanka, 2006.

Ministry of Plantation Industries. "Land Titling and Ownership of Housing." 2015. www.mpid.gov.lk/en/images/NPA_UNDP/10_Land_Titling_and_Ownership_of_Housing.pdf. Accessed October 1, 2015.

Mintz, Sidney. *Caribbean Transformations*. Chicago: Aldine, 1974.

Moeller, Kathryn. "Proving 'The Girl Effect': Corporate Knowledge Production and Educational Intervention." *International Journal of Educational Development* 33 (2013): 612–21.

Moffatt, Michael. *An Untouchable Community in South India: Structure and Consensus*. Princeton, NJ: Princeton University Press, 1979.

Moldrich, Donovan. *Bitter Berry Bondage: The Nineteenth-Century Coffee Workers of Sri Lanka*. Kandy: Coordinating Secretariat for Plantation Areas, 1989.

Muṇḍā and Dravidian Languages. Vol. 4 of *Linguistic Survey of India*. Edited by George Abraham Grierson. Calcutta: Office of the Superintendent of Government Printing, India, 1906.

Muthulingam, Periyasamy. "The Hill Country Tamils in the North-East and Their Political Aspirations." In *The International Conference on Remembering the Tea Plantation Workers' Contribution towards 150 Years of Ceylon Tea*, 70–101. Kandy: Institute of Social Development: 2017.

———. *Ilangai D.M.K. Varalāru* [The history of the Ceylon DMK]. Chennai: Nalantha Pathipagam, 2011.

Nabokov, Isabelle. *Religion against the Self: An Ethnography of Tamil Rituals*. New York: Oxford University Press, 2000.

Nadesan, S. "Plantation Workers: Their Wages and Conditions." *Voice of the Voiceless* 23 (December 1985): 6–11.

Nagaraj, Vijay. "Plantation Labour Buried by the Neoliberal Company-State." *Economic and Political Weekly* 49, no. 45 (2014). www.epw.in/journal/2014/45/web-exclusives/plantation-labour-buried-neoliberal-company-state.html.

National Building Research Organisation. *Impact Evaluation of Landslide Induced Displacement and Relocation: Case Study on Relocation of Meeriyabadda Landslide Victims in Makaldeniya Estate*. Colombo: National Building Research Organisation, 2017.

Neubert, Christopher. "Power, Everyday Control, and Emerging Resistance in Sri Lanka's Plantations." *Contemporary South Asia* 24 (2016): 360–73.

Nithiyanandan, M. *Cooly Thamizh: A Collection of Essays in Tamil by M. Nithiyanandan*. Chennai: Cre-Ā, 2014.

Pallister, David, and Gethin Chamberlain. "Sri Lanka War Toll near 6,500, UN Report Says." *Guardian*, April 24, 2009.

Peebles, Patrick. *The Plantation Tamils of Ceylon*. London: Leicester University Press, 2001.

Perera, Darshana. *Sri Lanka Export Development Board Industrial Capability Report*. Export Agriculture Division. Kandy: Department of Export Agriculture, 2014.

Periyasamy, Nithershini. "History, Health Care, and Challenges of Health of Estate Community in Sri Lanka." Ministry of Health and Indigenous Medicine, SLMA Annual Medical Congress, 2015. www.mpid.gov.lk/en/images/NPA_UNDP/hEALTH.pdf.

Phillips, Amali. "The Kinship, Marriage, and Gender Experiences of Tamil Women in Sri Lanka's Tea Plantations." *Contributions to Indian Sociology* 39, no. 1 (2005): 107–42.

———. "Rethinking Culture and Development: Marriage and Gender among the Tea Plantation Workers in Sri Lanka." *Gender and Development* 11, no. 2 (2003): 20–29.

Plantation Human Development Trust. "Welcome." www.phdt.org/phdt. Accessed August 12, 2011.

Planters' Association of Ceylon. "Planters' Association Chairman Says Productivity Increase Imperative for Industry's Survival." March 2015. www.paofceylon.org/sPA/MannPA.asp?action=8886&id=68.

"PM Modi Inaugurates Dickoya Hospital, Addresses Tamil Community in Sri Lanka." *Narendra Modi*, May 12, 2017. www.narendramodi.in/pm-modi-addresses-indian-origin-tamil-community-at-norwood-ground-in-norwood-sri-lanka-535399.

Povinelli, Elizabeth. "The Rhetorics of Recognition in Geontopower." *Philosophy and Rhetoric* 48, no. 4 (2015): 428–42.

Powis, Dick, "That's Enough about Tim Ingold! A Millennial's Reponses." *Footnotes*, June 29, 2018. http://footnotesblog.com/2018/06/29/thats-enough-about-tim-ingold-a-millennials-response.

Rahman, Smita. *Time, Memory, and the Politics of Contingency*. London: Routledge, 2014.

Rajadurai, Roshan. *Productivity-Based Revenue Sharing Wage Model*. Colombo: Planters' Association of Ceylon, 2016.

Rajapaksa, Mahinda. *Mahinda Chinthana: Towards a New Sri Lanka, Presidential Election, 2005*. Colombo: Government of Sri Lanka, 2005.

———. "President's Speech to Parliament on the Defeat of LTTE." Institute for Conflict Management. www.satp.org/satporgtp/countries/srilanka/document/papers/president_speech_parliament_defeatofLTTE.htm. Accessed October 10, 2013.

Ralph, Laurence. *Renegade Dreams: Living through Injury in Gangland Chicago*. Chicago: University of Chicago Press, 2014.

Rappaport, Joanne. "Anthropological Collaborations in Colombia." In *Anthropology Put to Work*, edited by Les Field and Richard Fox, 21–44. New York: Berg, 2007.

Red Flag Women's Movement. *Women's Leadership: Poverty, Violence against Women and Women's Leadership in Tea Plantation Trade Unions in Sri Lanka.* Kandy: Balasundaram, Chandrabose, and Sivapragasam, "Caste Discrimination among Indian Tamil Plantation Workers in Sri Lanka,", 2012.

"Report on an Enquiry into the Wages and the Cost of Living of Estate Labourers, April–May 1923." Sessional Paper 31, Government of Ceylon, Colombo, 1923.

Rizvi, Sumaiya. "How Did Jeevarani and Sumathi Die?" *Daily Mirror*, August 28, 2009.

Roberts, Nathaniel. *To Be Cared For: The Power of Conversation and Foreignness of Belonging in an Indian Slum*. Berkeley: University of California Press, 2016.

Rubinov, Igor. "Migrant Assemblages: Building Postsocialist Households with Kyrgyz Remittances." *Anthropological Quarterly* 87, no. 1 (2014): 183–215.

SAARC Secretariat. *Gender Initiatives in SAARC: A Primer*. Kathmandu: Lumbini Printing, 2007.

Sahlins, Marshal. *Stone Age Economics*. Chicago: Aldine, 1972.

Samarasinghe, Vidyamali. "Puppets on a String: Women's Wage Work and Empowerment among Female Tea Plantation Workers of Sri Lanka." *Journal of Developing Areas* 27, no. 3 (1993): 329–40.

Scott, James C. *Weapons of the Weak: Everyday Forms of Peasant Resistance*. New Haven, CT: Yale University Press, 1985.

Sen, Debarati. *Everyday Sustainability: Gender Justice and Fair Trade Tea in Darjeeling*. Albany: State University of New York Press, 2017.

Shanmugaratnam, N. *Privatisation of Tea Plantations: The Challenge of Reforming Production Relations in Sri Lanka—an Institutional Historical Perspective*. Colombo: Social Scientists' Association, 1997.

Smith, Linda Tuhiwai. *Decolonizing Methodologies: Research and Indigenous Peoples*. 2nd ed. London: Zed Books, 2013.

Solomon, Andrew. "Sri Lanka Is Ready for Its Close-Up." *Condé Nast Traveler*, December 6, 2016.

Somarathna, Rasika. "Estate Workers Get Wage Hike." *Daily News*, September 14, 2009. http://archives.dailynews.lk/2009/09/14/news01.asp.

Sri Lanka Bureau of Foreign Employment. *Annual Statistical Report of Foreign Employment, 2009–2010*. Battaramulla: Research Division, Sri Lanka Bureau of Foreign Employment, 2011.

———. *Annual Statistical Report of Foreign Employment, 2014*. Battaramulla: Research Division, Sri Lanka Bureau of Foreign Employment, 2015.

Sri Lanka Tea Board. "Why 'Ceylon' Tea?" www.pureceylontea.com/index.php/features/why-ceylon-tea. Accessed December 10, 2016.

Srinivasan, Meera. "The Long Journey of a Forgotten People." *The Hindu*,
    May 17, 2017. www.thehindu.com/opinion/op-ed/the-long-journey-of-a
    -forgotten-people/article18475181.ece.
Sriramachandran, Ravindran. "Life Is Where We Are Not: Making and
    Managing the Plantation Tamil." PhD diss., Columbia University, 2010.
Steuart, Mary E. *Every Day Life on a Ceylon Cocoa Estate*. London: H. J. Drane,
    1905.
Stoler, Ann Laura. *Duress: Imperial Durabilities in Our Times*. Durham, NC:
    Duke University Press, 2016.
———. "'The Rot Remains': From Ruins to Ruination." In *Imperial Debris: On
    Ruin and Ruination*, edited by Ann Laura Stoler, 1–35. Durham, NC: Duke
    University Press, 2013.
Sumathy, Sivamohan. "Gendered Fictions: Media and the Making of Malai-
    yaha Identity in Sri Lanka." *Sri Lanka Journal of the Humanities* 38, nos. 1–2
    (2014): 43–62.
Tadiar, N. X. M. "The Noranian Imaginary." In *Geopolitics of the Visible: Essays
    on Philippine Film Cultures*, edited by R. B. Tolentino, 61–76. Manila: Ateneo
    de Manila University Press, 2001.
TallBear, Kim. "Standing with and Speaking as Faith: A Feminist and Indig-
    enous Approach to Inquiry." *Journal of Research Practice* 10, no. 2 (2014).
    http://jrp.icaap.org/index.php/jrp/article/view/405/371.
Thambiah, Mirudhula. "Hill Country Tamils Face the Butt of Discrimination."
    Ceylon Today, June 13, 2017.
Thiranagama, Sharika. *In My Mother's House: Civil War in Sri Lanka*. Philadel-
    phia: University of Pennsylvania Press, 2011.
Tinker, Hugh. *A New System of Slavery: The Export of Indian Labour Overseas,
    1830–1920*. London: Oxford University Press, 1974.
Trawick, Margaret. *Notes on Love in a Tamil Family*. Berkeley: University of
    California Press, 1990.
UN General Assembly. Convention on the Rights of the Child, A/RES/44/25,
    November 20, 1989. www.refworld.org/docid/3ae6b38f0.html. Accessed
    September 21, 2015.
———. The Girl Child, A/RES/70/138, February 29, 2016. www.refworld.org
    /docid/56d7ebaa4.html. Accessed: September 21, 2015].
UN-Habitat. "Construction of Permanent Houses for Estate Workers Under-
    way in Nuwara Eliya District with Support from the Government of India
    and UN-Habitat." http://unhabitat.lk/news/construction-of-permanent
    -houses-for-estate-workers-underway-in-nuwara-eliya-district-with
    -support-from-the-government-of-india-and-un-habitat. Accessed
    June 23, 2017.
UN-OCHA Regional Office for Asia and the Pacific. *Sri Lanka: Floods and
    Landslides, Situation Report No. 2 (as of 26 May 2016)*. New York: United
    Nations Office for the Coordination of Humanitarian Affairs, 2016.

Vamadevan, M. "Sri Lankan Estate Sector Deprived of Full Budgetary Allocations." *Sunday Times*, February 20, 2011.

Viswanath, Rupa. *The Pariah Problem: Caste, Religion, and the Social in Modern India*. New York: Columbia University Press, 2014.

Visweswaran, Kamala. *Fictions of Feminist Ethnography*. Minneapolis: University of Minnesota Press, 1994.

Vora, Neha. *Impossible Citizens: Dubai's Indian Diaspora*. Durham, NC: Duke University Press, 2013.

Wallace, Tina, and Fenella Porter. "Aid, NGOs, and the Shrinking Space for Women: A Perfect Storm." In *Aid, NGOs, and the Realities of Women's Lives: A Perfect Storm*, edited by Tina Wallace and Fenella Porter, with Mark Ralph-Bowman, 1–30. Rugby, UK: Practical Action Publishing, 2013.

Warner, Michael. "Publics and Counterpublics (Abbreviated Version)." *Quarterly Journal of Speech* 88, no. 4, (2002): 413–25.

Webb, James L. A., Jr. *Tropical Pioneers: Human Agency and Ecological Change in the Highlands of Sri Lanka, 1800–1900*. Athens: Ohio University Press, 2002.

Wesumperuma, Dharmapala. *Indian Immigrant Plantations Workers in Sri Lanka: A Historical Perspective, 1880–1910*. Kelaniya: Vidyalankara Press, 1986.

"What Is Girl Rising?" http://girlrising.com/about-us/index.html#what-is-girl-rising. Accessed September 15, 2015.

Wickramasinghe, Nira. *Metallic Modern: Everyday Machines in Colonial Sri Lanka*. New York: Berghahn Books, 2014.

Wijesiriwardena, Panini. "Sri Lankan Plantation Workers Speak to the WSWS." *World Socialist Web Site*, May 13, 2011. www.wsws.org/en/articles/2011/05/slpl-m13.html.

Willford, Andrew. *Tamils and the Haunting of Justice: History and Recognition in Malaysia's Plantations*. Honolulu: University of Hawaii Press, 2014.

Williams, Bianca C. *The Pursuit of Happiness: Black Women, Diasporic Dreams, and the Politics of Emotional Transnationalism*. Durham, NC: Duke University Press, 2018.

Working Women's Front. "Vision and Missions Statement." Unpublished manuscript, n.d..

World Health Organization. "Meeriyabedda Landslide: Three Months Later." *World Health Organization Newsletters and Reports*, 2015. www.searo.who.int/srilanka/documents/meeriyabedda_landslide/en.

Index

Pages in italics refer to illustrations.

debt, 91–98; causes for, 97; to lenders, 93, 97, 169; in microfinance schemes, 93, 97, 195; in North and East, 97, 98; relational, 64; structural, 21; women's, 91–93. *See also* loans

Democratic Peoples' Congress, 21

Democratic Peoples' Front, 21

Democratic Socialist Republic of Sri Lanka, 65. *See also* Sri Lanka

Democratic Workers' Congress, 86, 215n38

Democratic Workers' Front, 191

desire: for dignity, 10–11, 23, 99, 154, 172–73; Hill Country Tamil, 47, 57; intended ends of, 38–39; iterative process of, 34–35; misrecognition of, 63; movement toward excess in, 39; *poēisis* of, 23, 37–41; rights-based, 103; risk in, 174; self-articulation of, 73; for self-employment, 70, 70, 72; women's, 11, 34, 37–41, 136, 156, 195, 201; world-making, 38; of youth, 22–24, 66–73, 204. See also *poēisis*

development: in decolonized countries, 181–82; gender-based, 182–83; international, 29, 183, 200; market-based, 182; rights-based, 181, 189–90; socioeconomic restraints constraints on, 189; on tea plantations, 186; traveling model of, 197, 199. *See also* human rights

Dickoya, 5, 42, 104, 122, 159, 165

Digambaram, Palani, 118, 204, 205

disaster management: in Hill Country, 121, 156–57

displacement, 121–23, 207–8

dispossession: civic, 125; economies of, 97; home within, 124; labor, 102; land, 18; through line rooms, 100–101; and minority women's rights, 209; plantation labor and, 102. *See also* land

domestic workers: abroad, 159, 161, 170–72, 186, 188, 196–97; following accidents, 140; in Colombo, 3–4, 7–9, 173; colonial, 158–59; National Identity Cards of, 9; non-contractual, 159–60; non-Hill Country Tamils' employment of, 157; among Paraiyar castes, 159; within plantation areas, 161; rural-urban migration of, 3–4, 135–36, 158; sexual harassment of, 196; social capital of, 25; surveillance of, 161; wages of, 8, 112. *See also* labor; migrant workers

Dravida Munnetra Kazhagam, 215n38

Duncan, Alfred: "My Beef Coolie," 60–62

Dunn, Elizabeth: on "places of being," 102

durai: in Colombo, 159; definition of, 4; on the estates, 50, 143. See also *sinna durai*; tea plantations

E

education: Advanced-Levels (A/Ls), 67–71, 158, 184, 187; and migrant labor, 158; Ordinary-Levels (O/Ls), 67–71, 158, 164; on plantations, 69, 126, 139; in Sri Lanka, 22, 97; unions' interest in, 67–70

Eelam People's Revolutionary Liberation Front, 215n39

Eelam Revolutionary Organisation of Students, 215n39

Ellington, Laura, 48

Elyachar, Julia, 112

Employees' Trust Fund, 140–41, 221n19

Employers' Federation of Ceylon, 85–86

Employers Planters' Association of Ceylon, 85

Employers' Provident Fund (EPF), 140–41

enclosures, 34, 38, 61, 102, 112, 125, 217n27

Estate Worker Housing Cooperative Society, 117–18; land and home ownership, 224n34–35

ethnographic research: as iterative, 40; methodologies in, 43–49; under surveillance, 44–46. *See also* ethnography; methodology

ethnography: constructing narratives in, 39–40; disciplinary demands of, 40; excisions in, 150; generative practices of, 36; "killer stories" in, 35; South Asian feminist forms of, 41. *See also* ethnographic research; methodology

F

family: aspirations of, 24; capital within, 166; colonial, 84; communication of love in, 167; economic security of, 79; effect of migrant labor on, 168–73, 176; generative futures of, 94; intermarriage among, 78

Family Background Report (FBR), 154–56, 161, 174

feminism, ix; in labor organizing, 178–79; methodologies in, 40–41; studies of Hill Country Tamils, 14, 23, 28–29, 201; transnational forms of, 199–201

Ferguson, Alastair Mackenzie: *"Iṅgē Vā!"*, 51–58

Forrest, D. M., 57; *A Hundred Years of Ceylon Tea*, 54–55

Freeman, Scott, 197

G

Gamburd, Michele, 157

Ganesan, Mano, 88; on child labor, 153–54

Garcia, Angela: on melancholy, 147

garment industry: labor in, 95, 157–58, 164, 184, 192, 203

Geetha, V., 198

gender: age attainment, 94–96; development, 179–90; discrimination, 21; dynamics in unions, 89–90; in ethnographic storytelling, 33–36; justice, 190, 200, 211; and kinship relations, 78–79; migrant work, 155–60, 163; relations on tea plantations, 17, 84–85, 207; reproduction and, 129–31; in Tamil language, 58; and wage valuation, 80–85. *See also* development: gender-based; Hill Country Tamils: women; labor: of Hill Country Tamils; violence: gendered

Gidwani, Vinay, 130–31

"girl-child": in gender development, 181–84

Girl Rising, 183–84

girls: development of, 183; as future workers, 190; gendered expectations for, 183; gendered violence against, 183; of Global South, 183; human rights of, 181–84, 197; longitudinal plans for, 200; rights-based development of, 181; safety of, 187; self-honor (*suya gowram*), 185; and suicide, 151–52; transnational relationships among, 181–84; unmarried, 8, 146, 226n25. See also *komari piḷḷai*; *vayacu catanku*

Goffman, Erving, 56, 219nn14–15

Grant of Citizenship to Persons of Indian Origin Act No. 35 (Sri Lanka, 2003), 20

H

Hatton: in Cyclone Mahasen, 122; International Children's Day in, 153; Māriamman festival, 226n22; in research, 42–44

Hauser, Mark, 116
health care: and accidents, 140, 147–49; government provided, 132; incentives and quotas in, 133; labor force and, 138; legal responsibility for, 133; and midwives, 133–34, 138; on the plantations, 48, 127–28, 130–34; privacy in, 134; Sri Lankan survey on, 130, 225n5. *See also* reproductive life
Hewamanne, Sandya, 157
Hill Country: ethnic diversity of, 31; nostalgia for, 29–30, 53, 208; tourism in, 54–55. *See also* Hill Country Tamils
Hill Country Tamils: activists, 10; agency of, 23; agro-industrial relations and, 38; ancestry of, 11; attention to change, 48; bodily experiences of, 24–25; burial practices of, 101, 105, 128, 149; challenges to injustice, 125; citizenship rights, 20, 74, 97, 124, 139, 207; constitutional recognition of, 16; coolie heritage of, 18, 175, 201, 209; culture of, 38, 79; desires, 47, 57, 63; desires for dignity, 10, 11, 23, 99, 154, 172–73; desires for future, 49; disempowerment of, 131; disenfranchisement of, 18, 89, 198; displaced persons (IDPs), 207–8; dispossession of, 100–102, 124; economic resources of, 201; ethical recognition of, 30; family photographs, 127–28; feminist perspective on, 23, 28, 201; foreign remittances to, 161–62, 166; forms of knowledge concerning, 28; future generations of, 190; gendered commitments of, 78; gendered mobility of, 97; geopolitical knowledge concerning, 28; grievances of, 20; health concerns of, 48; household income generation, 78; humanistic perspective on, 28; as Indian diaspora, 216n50; as Indian-Origin Malaiyaka Thamilars (IOMTs), 16; intergenerational reciprocity among, 78–79; kinship investments of, 78, 79, 84; labor aspirations of, 26; landless, 18, 115, 123, 125, 205; land rights of, 24, 118–20, 123; life expectations of, 78; love relationships of, 95–96; marginalization of, 11–12, 15, 20–21, 28, 31, 201; microeconomic data concerning, 80; modes of response, 57; music of, 168; mutuality among, 174; naming of, 16–17, 214n30; and other Tamil communities, 18; perceptions of research, 28; personhood of, 116; poetry of, 38; political events affecting, 206, 229n2; political participation by, 206; production of knowledge concerning, 23, 36; in public spaces, 32, 61; rights-based praxis of, 124–25; rules of commensality for, 32; scholarship on, 23; self-determination for, 19, 216n7; self-entrepreneurship among, 97; self-identification by, 16–17, 32; sense of self, 156, 175; sense of time, 110; social transformation for, 33, 48; socioeconomic challenges of, 23; Sri Lankan identity of, 22; statelessness of, 19, 89, 97, 215n36; structural debt of, 21; on tea plantations, 3; transitional justice for, 197, 205–9; union representation, 85, 89–90, 178; upper/middle class, 159; value of labor, 11, 24–25, 59, 102, 195; victimhood of, 23; violence

against, 19, 23, 151–52, 168, 174; work choices of, 22–23. *See also* caste; labor; plantation workers

Hill Country Tamils, women: as agents of change, 193; caste discrimination against, 203; casual worker status among, 8; childcare by, 140; civil status of, 155; as collective force, 177; coming of age rituals of, 77–78; communities' recognition of, 25; debts of, 91–92, 93; decolonial study of, 201; desires, 37–41, 136, 201; desires for dignity, 11, 195, 201; desires for movement, 37; empowerment of, 177; end of civil war and, xi; ethical endeavors supporting, 200; financial worth of, 96; gender-based programs for, 178–79; gendered labor of, 24, 33, 40, 119, 136; gestures of concern among, 6; hegemony of, 131; husbands' abandonment of, 192–93; illnesses of, 147–49; informal labor by, 25; "killer stories" of, 33–37, 188; labor shaming for, 25; leadership qualities of, 190–91; legal peripheries for, xi; life stories of, 37; marginalization of, 201; marriage age of, 78; melancholy among, 143–44, 147, 148; mobility of, 155; patriarchal domination of, 20, 149; political recognition for, 11; restrictions on movement, 44; search for husbands, 3–4, 95; sense of home, 11; social peripheries for, xi; solidarity with, 197; state discrimination against, 155; state restrictions on, 156–57; sterilization of, 33–34, 127, *127*, 130, 133, 135–39; structural constraints on, 11, 201; subordination of, 29, 193, 198; in

unions, 89–90, 178; urban migration among, 3–4, 135–36; value-making experiences of, 201; value of labor, 11, 195, 211; widows, 141–44, 226n21. *See also* domestic workers; labor: of Hill Country Tamils; plantation workers; reproductive life

Hill Country Tamils' People Forum, 208

Hindu festivals, 32; *Civarāttiri*, 226n23; *Māriamman*, 146, 226n22

Hollup, Oddvar, 31, 218n14

home: advocacy for, 224n39; anthropological debates on, 102; investments in, 119; loans for, 116–17; and natural disasters, 121–22; ownership, 116–20, 124; renting of, 121; on RPC-owned estates, 132; on tea plantations, 117; territoriality in, 115. *See also* housing; line rooms; *ūr*

housing: estate programs for, 116–20, 124, 21n44; EWHCS assistance for, 224nn34–35; in-kind grants for, 116–17; prefab, 224n39; rights, 119, 121, 123–24; structural types, 117. *See also* home; land: rights

human rights: and girls, 182, 197; instrumentalist narratives of, 36; in international law, 182; and intersectionality, 189; on tea plantations, 136, 197. *See also* development: rights-based

I

Ilanchezhian, A., 215n38, 216n7; anti-caste movement of, 206

indentured labor, 13–14

India: indentured laborers from, 13–14; remittances from, 84. *See also* Tamil Nadu

Indian and Pakistani Residents Act No. 3 (1949), 18
Indian Housing Project in the Central and Uva Provinces, 119
Indian National Congress, 84
Indian Ocean tsunami, 121, 225n52
Indian Slavery Act (1843), 13
Indian Workers' Federation, 85
inequality: in Hill Country communities, 94; in migrant labor, 162; in plantation labor, 79, 157, 173; socially embedded, 98
Ingiruthu, 14. *See also* Sivamohan, Sumathy
Institute of Social Development, 191
instrumentality, 53, 58–59, 208
International Coalition of Sites of Conscience, 74
International Conference on Population and Development, 182
International Labour Organization (ILO): on Convention, No. 98, 86–87; on Convention No. 138, 227n11; on Convention No. 189, 160
intersectionality: anthropological attention to, 35; of gender violence, 184, 187; in rights-based development, 174, 189, 199

J

Janatha Vimukthi Peramuna, 1970–71 insurrection, 216n7
jāthi. See caste
Jayawardena, Kumari, 29, 177
Joint Plantation Trade Union Centre (JPTUC), 85
Joseph, Abraham. 52, 218n3

K

Kanapathipillai, Valli, 29
kankānis, 4, 6; and education, 69; female, 176; prestige of, 143–44

Karim, Lamia, 97
Kilinochchi, 207–8
kinship, Tamil: in castes, 95; in communities, 24, 56, 69, 78; investment in, 162, 207; through marriage, 142; in migrant labor, 158, 168–72, 173; of plantation workers, 78, 79, 84; on tea plantations, 56; wages and, 79; widowhood in, 142; women's labor and, 156. *See also* family
kirāmam, in relation to *ūr*, 120
knowledge: embodied, 48; geopolitical, 28; about human needs, 133; kin-based, 134; production of, 23, 36; situated, 78, 188, 208; tacit, 112; visual, 47; by working women, 200
Kockelman, Paul, 101, 217n27
komari piḷḷai, 8, 146, 226n25. *See also* girls
kūli, 12, 59. *See also* wages
Kumaravel, Sivapākkiam, 89–90, 222n31
Kurian, Rachel, 29

L

labor: anthropology of, 157; capitalist extraction of, 154; decolonial perspective on, 29; feminist forms of solidarity and, 199–200; gendered, 22, 24, 29, 33, 40, 119, 136, 198; informal, 25, 154; on Malaysian plantations, 115; negative reciprocity in, 156; production of life, 123; regenerative, 150; Sinhala women's, 157; smallholding, 92, 114, 147, 166; versus work, 123. *See also* plantation workers; unions; wages
labor, of Hill Country Tamils: in art, 202, 202–4; challenges to, 179;

child, 25, 67, 136, 153–54; in Colombo, 4, 7–9, 161–63, 168; conditions of, 197; dignity of, 174; generative future of, 175, 178; interventions for, 200; kinship and, 156; negotiation with stakeholders in, 199–200; organizing, 190–93; productive, 156, 198; reorientation of, 190–93; reproductive, 156, 198; rights-based discourse of, 174, 175, 178; shaming of, 25, 156–58, 174–75; solidarity movements for, 174; state surveillance of, 174; value of, 11, 24–25, 59, 102, 195, 211. *See also* Collective Agreement; domestic workers; migrant labor; plantation workers

labor, plantation: affordances of, 55, 76; aspirations in, 23, 26, 39, 64–65, 175; colonial data on, 82; deconstruction of, 115; dispossession and, 102; disrespect for, 107; disrupted narratives of, 40; exploitative, 66, 124; fluidity in, 162; gendered, 22, 29, 40, 119, 136; history of, 74; inseparability from plantation life, 64; livability of, 96; versus migrant labor, 165; negligibility of, 96, 97; personhood and, 102; productive, 97, 131–34; reproduction of, 64, 97, 101; reserve force for, 72; social inequalities in, 173; structural inequalities in, 157; surveillance of, 45, 133–34, 161; unenclosed spaces of, 61; *ūr* and, 101, 111–12; value of, 11, 24–25, 59, 102; viability of, 96. *See also* plantation workers

labor, Sri Lankan: colonial relations, 21; complacency concerning, 211; embodied realities of, 192; hegemony in, 178; informal, 193–97; politicization of, 178; relations on tea plantations, 17, 40; reimaginings of, 199

labor rights: discourse of, 174–75, 178; instrumentalist ethics of, 174; for migrants, 158; plantation workers', 88; unions on, 88; women's, 178. *See also* development: rights-based; labor

land, 24; displacement from and resettlement on, 207–8; dispossession and landlessness, 102–3, 108; industrial, 106–8; natural disasters on, 121–23, 225n52; rights, 115–20, 123–24, 216n44; state ownership of, 224n35,37. *See also* landscape

landscape: community mapping, 73, 73; individuals and, 102; language and, 23; livability of, 73; terraforming of, 115; workers on, 53–60, 63, 76. *See also* land

landslides, 121–23; casualties in, 121, 225n47; displacement and resettlement after, 121–22. *See also* land

language: illocutionary force in, 219n22; learning of, 52; perlocutionary acts of, 219n22. *See also* Tamil language

Lanka Jathika Estate Workers' Union, 85

Le Guin, Ursula: "The Carrier Bag Theory of Fiction," 34–35; on "killer stories," 33–35, 187; on life stories, 35–36

Liberation Tigers of Tamil Eelam: in civil war x–xii; eviction of Muslims, 102; murdering of Rajani Thiranagama, 228n23; violence against Tamil militant groups, 215n39. *See also* civil war, Sri Lankan line rooms, 5–6, 7, 24; altars in, 112, 145, 226n24; in art, 202; colonial, 103; in Cyclone Mahasen, 122–23; dispossession through, 100–101; fluid structures of, 116; historic preservation of, 74; as *layam*, 5, 103; living conditions in, 100, 103; maintenance of, 55; occupancy of, 218n14; under privatization, 120; as punitive spaces, 60; renovation of, 112–15, *113*, 134, 170; sense of home in, 120–23; sense of ownership for, 115–17; state policing of, 120; subjectivity in, 103; *ūr* in, 112–16. See also *ūr*

Little, Angela, 29, 67, 69

loans: for home ownership, 116–17; to plantation workers, 91–93; predatory, 72, 195. *See also* debt

Lynch, Caitrin, 157

M

Malaiyaka. See Hill Country Tamils

Manesca, Jean: methodology of, 58, 64; *An Oral System of Teaching Living Languages,* 52

mapping: of aspirations, 70, *70, 71*; body, 45, 47, 135–36; community, 73, *73*

Māriamman, 107, 213n6; festivals of, 146, 226n22; temples to, 4–5, 7, 109, 205

marriage: age for, 78; *catanku* as, 94–96; among migrants, 164–65; and widowhood, 142–43. *See also* kinship, Tamil

methodology: decolonizing approaches in, 28–30; and ethnographic research, 45–48; of language learning, 58, 64, 218n3. *See also* ethnographic research; ethnography

Meyer, Eric, 219n15

microfinance, 72, 93, 97, 195. *See also* loans

migrant labor: abroad (*veliyūr vēlai*), 158, 160–61, 163, 170–72, 186, 188, 196–97; caste consciousness and, 163; education and, 158; effect on families, 168–73, 176; effect on value systems, 170; illegal, 154–55; inequalities in, 162; informal, 159–60, 163–64, 173; kinship networks in, 158; pride in, 174; remittances from, 161–62, 166; reproductive life and, 166–67; rhetoric of shame for, 173; rights-based discourse on, 158; risks of, 160; service-based, 160–61; standards for, 160; status in, 162, 167; types of, 158–59. *See also* Hill Country Tamils; labor: of Hill Country Tamils; migrant workers

migrant workers: abroad, 158–61, 163, 170–72, 186–88, 196–97; caste discrimination against, 159, 161; "Colombo boys," 162–63, 167–72; education of, 158; employer-employee relationships among, 160; kinship relations of, 158, 168–73; marriage among, 164–65; remittances, 77, 158–60; return visits by, 168–72; rural-urban, 3–4, 135–36, 158; split subjectivities of, 162; state policies concerning, 154–56; statistics of, 160–61; stigmatization of, 161, 163, 173; wages of, 164–65; work leave for, 164. *See also* Family Background Report; migrant labor

militancy, x–xi, 19, 215n39. *See also* civil war; Liberation Tigers of Tamil Eelam

Mines, Diane, 101–2; on motile discourse, 111–12

Minimum Wages (Indian Labour) Ordinance No. 27 (1927), 84

moi, 77–78

Muṇḍā and Dravidian Languages (1906), 51–52

Muniandi, 107

Muthulingam, Periyasamy, 74, 215n38, 216n7

Muthusamy, Kāthai: x–xi, 19

N

narratives: of desire, 41; disrupted, 40; of mutuality, 174; of shame, 25; of Sri Lanka, xiii–xiv

National Building Research Organization (NBRO), 121

National Identity Cards (NICs), 9, 139, 174

nationalism: exclusion of Hill Country Tamils, 56, 215n39; Sinhala forms, x–xi, 19–20; Tamil forms, 19–20, 215n39. *See also* civil war; militancy

National Labour Migration Policy, 155

National Plan of Action, 118–19

National Union of Workers, 20–21, 86

negative reciprocity, 156, 227n9

NGOs, 19; access to tea estates, 41–42; instrumentalist narratives of, 36; international connections of, 180, 228n1; training programs of, 42

Nike Girl Effect, 182, 184

Nithiyanandan, M., 15

O

Ollendorf method, 52, 218n3

Ordinance to Make Provision in Rural and Planting Districts for the Education of Children in the Vernacular Languages No. 8 (1907), 82

Ordinary Level Certificates of Education (O/Ls), 67–70; migrant workers', 158, 164. *See also* education, Ordinary-Levels (O/Ls)

P

paramilitaries: violence by, xii–xiii

parava kāvaṭi, 144

Peebles, Patrick, 13, 29, 214n30

People's Liberation Organisation of Tamil Eelam, 215n39

pey, 105

Phillips, Amali, 29

Plantation Housing and Social Welfare Trust, 132

Plantation Human Development Trust, 132–33, 216n44

plantations: researchers' access to, 27–28; as site of inquiry, 27–28; as total institutions, 219n15. *See also* rubber plantations; tea plantations, Sri Lankan

Plantation Social Sector Forum (PSSF), 176–78, 228n1

plantation workers: anti-casteist strategies for, 208; candidates' appeal to, 5; childbirth of, 126, 134–35, 138; colonial, 53–54; colonial legislation concerning, 82; death benefits for, 126; desire for dignity, 10, 172; desires, 23, 39, 64–65, 175; desire to migrate, 156; divorce rates among, 176, 193; embodied experiences of, 131; equality for, 15–16; family responsibilities of, 93, 190–91, 205; full-time, 3, 22, 92; gender relations of, 17, 84–85, 91, 207; health care for, 48, 127–28, 130–34, 138; idealized images of, 54; impact on tea industry, 12; "killer stories" and, 33–37, 130; knowledge production about, 23, 36; labor

riots, 19, 140, 142, 207, 215n41, 229n2

rituals, 77–79, 94, 128, 226n22; contribution to families through, 146–47; diversity of, 147; *pūcai*, 144–45; spiritual, 144–49. See also *pūcai*; *vayacu catanku*

Rōtamuni, 107

Rottenburg, Richard, 189

rubber plantations, 18, 19

Rubinov, Igor: on migrant assemblages, 116

Rural Schools Ordinance (1907), 69

S

Sahlins, Marshall, 156, 227n9

Samarasinghe, Vidyamali, 29, 214n30

sampalataya, 217n29

santōcam, 221n9

santōsums, 82–83

Scheler, Max, 217n22; on becoming, 37

self-employment (*suyaththozhil, suya vēlai*): organizing of, 195; pitfalls of, 195; among women, 194–95; as a youth aspiration, 67, 70, 70, 72

Sen, Debarati, 97

shrines on tea plantations, 107, 223n16

Sigiriya, 209

Sinhala: in Ceylon National Congress, 80; as employers of Hill Country Tamils, 3, 140, 143, 159, 168; in garment industry, 157; language and concepts, 120, 143, 226n20; nationalists, x, 19, 20; on tea plantations, 21, 31, 42–43, 106–7

Sinhala Only Act (1956), 18

sinna durai (assistant superintendent), 21, 218n1

Sirimavo-Shastri Pact (India-Sri Lanka, 1964), 18

Sirisena, Maithripala, 16, 21; housing programs on estates, 117, 122; TPA alliance with, 206

Sivamohan, Sumathy, 14–15, 36. See also *Ingiruthu*

slavery, 13, 181, 214n19

Smith, Linda Tuhiwai, 48

solidarity: and contingency, 178–79; and debt, 98; through marriage, 79; political, 206; as praxis, xi, 11, 23, 33, 174, 190, 197, 208; in rights-based and transnational, 174, 177, 182, 186, 190; among workers, 60, 173. *See also* contingent solidarities

Solomon, Andrew, 55

Somasundersam, Hanusha, 201–3; *Stain II*, 202, 202–4; *Untitled II*, 209–11, 210

South Asian Association for Regional Cooperation, 182, 228n8

Sri Lanka: abductions in, xii; Bureau of Foreign Employment (SLBFE), 159–60, 193, 196; Cabinet of Ministers, 119; caste hierarchy in, 32, 153, 161; civic belonging in, 115; class hierarchy in, 161; collective bargaining in, 85–91; Constitution, 155; cost of living in, 88; daily life of, 29–30; decolonization in, 181; Department of Census and Statistics, 222nn36, 38; development sectors of, 178; diaspora from, 15; economic development of, 10–11; Export Development Board, 65; foreign employment within, 160; gender justice in, 190; geontological crises in, 122; health survey of, 130, 225n5; housing programs of, 116–20; imperial nostalgia in, 23, 49, 53, 76; internal migration in, 61; international development of, 189–90; labor stakeholders in, 198; labor standards in, 160; land dispossession in, 18; land reform

Sri Lanka (*continued*)
in, 19, 118; middle/upper classes of, 156; Ministry for Foreign Employment, 154–55; Ministry of Estate Infrastructure and Development, 132; Ministry of Health, 138; Ministry of Hill Country New Villages, Infrastructure, and Community Development, 118–19, 224n36; Ministry of Nation Building and Estate Infrastructure Development, 117; Ministry of Up-Country New Villages, Estate Infrastructure, and Community Development, 224n36; multilingualism of, 17; national conscience of, 76; national language register of, 18; National Plans of Action (NPAs), 117–18, 132; national poverty line in, 93; natural disasters in, 225n52; pluralism of, 16; postcolonial past of, 15, 21, 175; postwar political imaginary of, xi; privatization in, 56, 85, 118; ratification of International Labour Organization's Convention on Domestic Workers, 160; sense of belonging in, 57, 109, 111; Tea Board, 65; Ten-Year National Action Plan, 176–77; transitional justice in, 16, 197, 205–9; transnational gender labor movements in, 200. *See also* Ceylon
Sri Lankan Tamils: caste discrimination of Hill Country Tamils by, 30–31, 41; in Ceylon Tamil Congress, 80; demands for a separatist state for, x; distinction from Hill Country Tamils, 18; as employers of Hill Country Tamils, 159; nationalist agendas of, 20; in postwar North and East, 207

Srinivasan, Meera, 119
Steuart, Mary E.: *Every Day Life on a Ceylon Cocoa Estate,* 62–63
suicide: following domestic violence, 176; protests concerning, 153; suspected, 151–53
Sundaram, Peri, 90

T

Tadiar, Neferti: on *sampalataya,* 217n29
taiyattai (protective pendant), 164–66
Tallbear, Kim, 45, 150, 217n29
Tamil Eelam Liberation Organization, 215n39
Tamil language, 23, 30, 46; -a suffix in, 226n18; commands in, 58–60, 219n22; coolie, 51–54, 57–60, 76; guides to, 51–52, 76; motile discourse in, 111; planters' strategy for, 53, 57–60; resistance through, 53; transliteration of, 51; written, 53
Tamil Nadu: migration of Tamil to Ceylon from, 11, 104, 139; repatriation to, 105
Tamil Progressive Alliance, 21, 204; land ownership initiative, 119; parliamentary seats of, 205; *Report of the Experts Committee on Constitutional Reforms,* 16; in Sirisena government, 206
Tamils, South Indian: British recruitment of, 17, 30; caste-based oppression of, 13; migration to Ceylon, 11, 12–13, 17–18, 63; repatriation of, 18, 30
Tampoe, Bala, 216n7
tea, "Ceylon tea": consumption of, 23, 29–30, 211; CTC method for, 66; in international market, 65; nostalgia for, 30, 59; plucking (*koluntu velai*) of, 50–51, 93, 107,

112, 140; social importance of, 30; in Tamil language, 51

tea industry, Sri Lankan: capital accumulation in, 57, 75, 76, 162; caste in, 33; destruction of narratives, 39; economic crisis of, 38, 123; economic importance of, 15; exports, 65; formation of, 17, 18; global communication in, 56; labor shortages in, 107; movement in, 59, 73; patriarchy in, 189–90; production process of, 65–66; profit motive of, xi; quality standards of, 108; smallholding work in, 92; social crisis in, 57; socio-ecological structure of, 190–91; sustainability of, 66, 123; Tamil language in, 51–54; violence of accumulation in, 209; women's impact on, 11. *See also* plantation workers; regional plantation companies; tea plantations, Sri Lankan

tea plantations, Sri Lankan: anthropological perspectives on, 28–29; bureaucratization of, 124; caste on, 30–33; class on, 30–33; coercive power of, 129; colonial aesthetics of, 55; colonial economy of, 81–85; colonial returns from, 83; coolie culture of, 15; decolonial perspective on, 29; economic phases of, 131–32; education on, 126, 129; enclave myth of, 219n15; ethnicity on, 30–33; ethnography of, xiv; food rations on, 82; gender development on, 186; gendered labor on, 22, 29, 40, 119, 136; gender relations on, 17, 84–85, 207; governmental issues in, 72; health care on, 127–28, 130–32; hierarchy of, 55; Hindu shrines on, 107, 223n16; home ownership on, 117; housing policies of, 24; human

rights on, 136, 197; imperial imaginary of, 54; industrial care on, 131; inequality in, 79; infrastructural issues on, 72–73; kinship on, 56; labor relations on, 17, 40; language of control in, 57–60, 76; line schools of, 69; modes of production, 55; nationalization of, 132; patriarchal subordination on, 29; population of, 221n14; poverty at, 93, 187; power structure of, 28, 56; privatization of, 85, 118, 132–33, 172; recording of life on, 43–45; researchers' access to, 41–42; reserve labor forces of, 192; residential spaces of, 102; resident/non-resident differences in, 108–9, 168–72; resilience of, 209; restructuring of, 19; rights-based engagements on, 189, 197; sense of belonging on, 57, 109; Sinhala on, 42–43, 106–7; as sites of conscience, 26; as sites of hegemony, 129–30, 150; social relations of, 55; state subsidies for, 157; structural change on, 208; success of, 29; technology of, 56; tourists to, 54–55, 74, 126; transitional justice on, 197; in travel literature, 55; *ūr* on, 115–16, 125; worker footpaths on, 109–11, 110; youths' escape from, 67–68. *See also* Hill Country Tamils; labor, plantation; plantation workers; regional plantation companies

Tea Plantation Workers' Museum and Archive, 74, 76

terraforming, 112–16

territoriality, 55, 115

thēkuti, 144

Thiranagama, Rajani, 228n23

Thiranagama, Sharika: on Colombo, 163; on cultural life, 79; on *ūr*, 102

Thondman, S., 90

tiru vizhā (estate festival), 144

Torabully, Khal: on "Coolitude" movement, 13–14

tōttam, 17, 50, 104; Colombo as a, 173. *See also* tea plantations, Sri Lankan

Trade Unions Ordinance No. 14 (1935), 85

U

unions, Sri Lankan: Collective Agreements with, 10, 85–91; connections with workingwomen, 196; educational meetings of, 67, 69–70; female leadership of, 25–26; "go slow" campaigns of, 86, 87, 221n22; Hill Country Tamil representation in, 85; on labor rights, 88; lack of trust in, 87, 192; minority representation in, 89; organizational structure of, 192; patriarchal practices of, 26, 89, 178, 199; patronage in, 90, 97, 198–99; politicization of, 97, 192; in PSSF, 176; talaivars, 87; unconventional forms of, 199; women in, 89–90, 178. *See also* Collective Agreement; collective bargaining; Working Women's Front

United National Front for Good Governance, 204; TPA in, 206

United Nations: CEDAW Convention, 176; Convention on the Elimination of All Forms of Discrimination Against Women, 182; Convention on the Rights of the Child, 152, 182; Development Programme (UNDP), 117, 132; Millennium Development Goals, 117, 132, 176, 182; principles of sustainability, 200; Resolution 51/76 ("The Girl Child"), 182; Sustainable Development Goals, 182

United People's Freedom Alliance, 21

Up-Country Peoples' Front, 21

Up-Country Workers Front, 86

ūr: attachment to, 102; belonging in, 106; boundaries of, 111; cognitive investments in, 103; in colonial era, 104; connections with soil, 101, 104–5, 108, 124, 223n15; connectivity in, 121; connotations of, 101; *conta*, 106, 223n15; disclosing, 101–2; within dispossession, 124; enclosing, 101, 102; human interactions with, 111; in India, 105–6; industrial, 106–8; knowledge of, 101; labor and, 101, 111–12; and landslide of 2014, 121–23; in line rooms, 112, 116; location of, 104–6; loss of, 120; motile, 101–2, 108–12, 121, 124; *piranta*, 104, 105; on plantations, 104, 106, 115–16, 125; pricelessness of, 120, 121; production/consumption of, 103; protection by, 111; reconfirmation of, 106; reconstructive projects and, 121; sense of knowing, 111; sense of time in, 109; spatiotemporal fluidity of, 104; in transition, 116–21; visibility of, 125; in *vita activa*, 123–25; world making in, 121. *See also* home; line rooms

ūrmakkal, 101. *See also* Mines, Diane; *ūr*

V

vayacu catanku: cost of, 77–78, 91–92; as marriage, 94, 96; memories of, 94–95; monetary gifts at, 77–78; representational force of, 95; saris for, 95; social implications of, 95 violence: of counting, 79; gendered, 136, 187–88, 211; against Hill Country Tamils, 19, 23, 151–52, 168, 174; intersectionality of, 187; paramilitary, xii–xiii; shaming, 196

Viswanath, Rupa, 13

Visweswaran, Kamala, 41

W

wages: cumulative, 222n27; domestic workers', 8, 112; *kai kācu*, 140; language of, 59; migrant, 164–65; for smallholding work, 92, 114, 166; valuation of, 78

wages, plantation, 10, 21, 172; anxiety over, 88; in Collective Agreements, 85–91; colonial, 80–85; conditioning to, 99; as condition of life, 98; coolie, 24, 98, 221n8; cost-of-living raises, 85; daily (*adipadai sampalam*), 10, 20–21, 24, 57, 78, 85–89, 92–93, 96, 141; daily attendance allowance, 92; kinship and, 79; lack of dignity in, 155; politics of, 79; quantitative data on, 79–80; reproductive, 166; socioeconomic constraints on, 80; structuring aspects of, 98; women's, 91–93. *See also* Collective Agreement; collective bargaining; wages

Wants and Diseases Ordinance No. 9 (1912), 82

Wickramasinghe, Nira, 223n16

widowhood, 141; caste-based behavior in, 142; economic uncertainty in,

144, 226n21; kinship-driven behavior in, 142; melancholia in, 143–44; status in, 143

Willford, Andrew, 115

women: desires of, 34, 41; health care, 131–34; labor organizing among, 190–95; rights-enabling venues for, 180; Sinhala, 157; Third World, 183. *See also* domestic workers; plantation workers; Hill Country Tamils, women

Working Women's Front (WWF), 178; challenges to labor organizing, 198; labor cases of, 192–93; mobilization on plantations, 194; organizing of informal labor, 193–94; organizing of self-employment, 195; promotion of rights, 191; support of nuclear family, 192; transnational strategies of, 196–97

Y

Yogeshwari, K., 191–92

youth: career aspirations of, 22, 23, 24, 66–73, 204; conscription of, 207; economic resources of, 69; education levels of, 68; education of, 22, 67, 69, 70; mapping exercises, 70, 70, 71; national expectations for, 181; obstacles facing, 72; opportunities for, 72; rejection of plantations, 67–68; self-employment for, 70, 70, 72; teaching jobs for, 69, 71; vocational training for, 42. *See also* children